Give
the Lady
What
She Wants!

Give the Lady

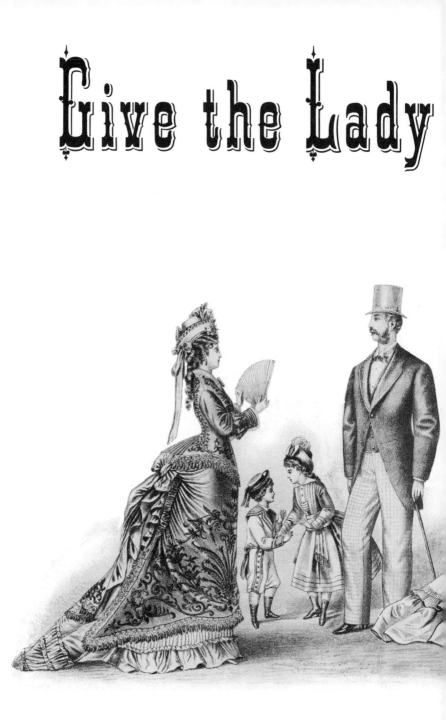

What She Wants!

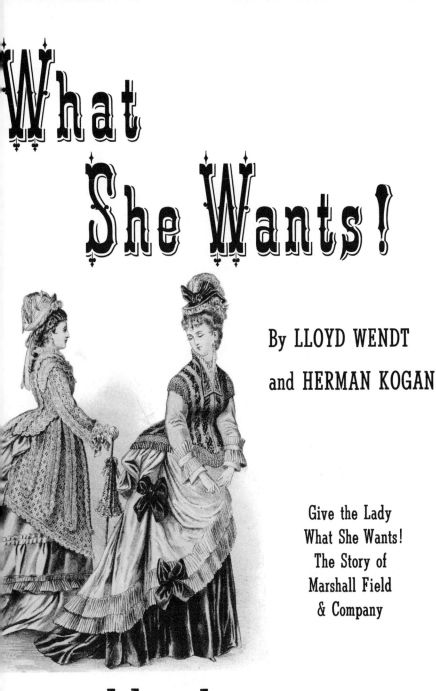

By LLOYD WENDT
and HERMAN KOGAN

Give the Lady
What She Wants!
The Story of
Marshall Field
& Company

and books • South Bend

GIVE THE LADY WHAT SHE WANTS!

By Lloyd Wendt and Herman Kogan

Copyright © 1952 by Marshall Field & Company

Library of Congress Catalog Number
52-7501

International Standard Book Number
ISBN 0-89708-020-3

Published through special arrangement with Marshall Field & Company

Manufactured in the United States of America

First Printing, May, 1952; Second Printing,
May, 1952; Third Printing, June, 1952; Fourth
Printing, January, 1953; Fifth Printing, October,
1966; Sixth Printing, September, 1979; Seventh
Printing, July, 1981; Eighth Printing, January,
1984; Ninth Printing, October, 1985; Tenth
Printing, September, 1987.

Additional copies available
and books/the distributors
702 South Michhigan
South Bend, Indiana 46618 U.S.A.

CONTENTS

Since its first publication in 1952, GIVE THE LADY WHAT SHE WANTS! has provided a sprightly account of an almost legendary retailing phenomenon. The book enjoyed wide critical acclaim and attracted a large and diverse readership. Once out of print, it continued to be the subject of many requests to the publisher from libraries whose copies had worn out, from schools teaching various aspects of merchandising, and from readers throughout the country, whether motivated by history or nostalgia.

This reprint edition preserves the contents of the original intact. No attempt has been made to bring the reader up-to-date with the development of Marshall Field & Company which, of course, has continued to grow. The story as told by the authors in 1952 distills the essence of a Chicago institution, and its unique place has not been substantially altered by time.

Lloyd Wendt and Herman Kogan have written of the Chicago scene with an intimacy born of long and devoted association. In their preparation of this book, they had access to valuable documentary material in the Field archives, including official reports, records, company publications, advertisements, photographs, confidential papers, unpublished letters, and, most notably, manuscripts of interviews with officials and employees by the late Lloyd Lewis, historian and newspaper editor. The authors interviewed company officials and workers employed at the time of writing, and they sought out and talked to many who had long since retired. They combed the collections in several libraries, principally the Chicago Public Library, Newberry Library, and the Chicago Historical Society Library. They also went outside of Chicago, to historians Clarence O. Lewis and Robert Wycliffe Twyman, to obtain information of inestimable value. With this edition, GIVE THE LADY WHAT SHE WANTS! makes the lively result once more available.

The Publishers

LIST OF ILLUSTRATIONS

Credits for the illustrations are given in parentheses following the listing.

Give
the Lady
What
She Wants!

COURTHOUSE, CHICAGO, ILLINOIS

WOOD-BURNING LOCOMOTIVE

YOUNG MAN,
YOUNG CITY

It is June, hot and muggy.

Each morning brings new yokels from the Yankee farms; gamblers and adventurers from New Orleans and Memphis with their keen eyes out for fast money; agents of the staid New York banking houses; clerks and dock workers, failures and men of roaring ambition, restless ones and hungry ones and brave ones— all here to see for themselves what the local boosters and even the nation's sages have been telling the country about Chicago and the West.

On such a day in this boom year of 1852 a bright young Quaker named Potter Palmer comes to town.

He is twenty-six, lank yet sturdy, blue-eyed and clean-shaven. Back in sleepy Lockport, New York, he owns a little dry-goods store but it has not prospered as he had hoped, despite his eight years' experience as a clerk and country merchant. Like many other young men in the slow-moving villages of the East, he has been tempted to head for the city in the midst of a vast prairie land where farms are sprouting, opportunities grow by the day, and money is to be made.

For a week Palmer walks through muddy Chicago, talks to dealers and storekeepers, reads the high flown words in the newspapers, listens to the loud braggarts in the hotel lobbies, counts the schooners in the harbor. Now he stands stiffly at the foot of ill-smelling Lake Street, called "the street of merchants."

Along sagging wooden walks lined with buildings three and four stories high, burly men unload bales and barrels of merchandise. Near these islands of commerce carpenters and bricklayers labor at a frenzied pace, raising more store fronts, hauling timbers into place, driving piles, seeking bottom under the muddy morass to hold limestone bases for corner posts. Mud-splattered farm carts wheel up, overburdened with baskets of eggs, boxes of green produce, crocks of butter, broods of squalling children. An enormous prairie freighter stands with brakes locked, horses stomping, while drivers and stevedores cram it with loads of merchandise outward bound for the new farms and villages. In the throng are peddlers, astride ponies or on foot with racks on their backs, newly arrived in Chicago to replenish their stocks; trappers, bringing in for trade the last of their winter's catch; paunchy traveling salesmen lugging carpetbags bulging with samples; mechanics rushing about with armloads of tools; barkeepers in white aprons watching incoming stocks of whisky.

And always, everywhere, the women shoppers. Wagons and buggies and creaking omnibuses discharge them onto the walks and into the mud—women in calico and here and there one in silk, daintily lifting her skirts; women hurrying, women chattering; women striding with stern purpose into the dry-goods stores and the millinery shops, searching out goods or, unable to wait any longer, stopping to bargain and buy from freshly opened crates on the wide walks.

To the north, against the row of red and yellow elevators, stretch the masts and spars of a hundred freight boats, which bring these needed goods to Chicago and carry back its grain and pigs. Among them are the low-lying barges, come up the new Illinois and Michigan Canal all the way from New Orleans with their cargoes of sugar, molasses, cotton, and tobacco. Small

For years before the Great Fire, Lake Street was Chicago's "street of merchants." This was its east end at Wabash Avenue, teeming with trade.

wonder boosters cry that Chicago will soon outdistance her fiercest rivals, St. Louis, Cincinnati, Detroit, and Toledo. Already they are howling happily that the commercial axis of the nation has been reversed, with Chicago at one end and New Orleans at the other. Already Chicago is the ninth port of the land!

In his brief week Palmer has heard again and again of the vast trade also coming into the city over the plank roads. "Poor men's railroads," the local folk call them, huge slabs of wood spiked to lengths of heavy timber and reaching out toward dozens of tiny towns springing up on the prairies. There are real railroads, too, as Palmer has seen and heard: the Galena and Chicago Union, tapping the West; the Michigan Central and Michigan Southern;

the new Illinois Central, which would bypass St. Louis—and others are stringing their iron-strap and steel lines to the city.

Palmer walks on, crowding past stacks of merchandise until he is stopped just west of Clark Street by the sight of workmen busy with stone and piling as they fence in an enormous mud-hole. He crosses the street, picking his way among the carts, stepping clear of a dashing dray. He seizes a sweating foreman by the arm, asks questions. He is told there are four men involved in this project of building a big four-story, stone-fronted business block. All will be ready in October.

Palmer pauses for another look, then hurries to the offices of John High and William Magie, leaders of this venture. A lease is soon signed calling for a rental of $1,500 a year for a dry-goods store, a tiny space only 20 feet wide and 160 feet deep. The rent seems high but prices, after all, are soaring in this growing town.

Palmer shakes hands with Magie, blurts his thanks, and hustles back to the Sherman House to arrange for his permanent residence there in October. Soon he packs his belongings in his carpetbag and climbs aboard the rattling Sherman House omnibus, bound for the Michigan Central train. He will return East to end his affairs in Lockport, say last farewells to his father and brothers, and buy stock for his store; then he will be ready to start supplying the wants and needs of these busy women shoppers who crowd into Lake Street.

II

In making his decision to start fresh in Chicago, Potter Palmer was cutting his ties with a tranquil way of life he had known since he was born on May 26, 1826, in the Quaker village of Potter's Hollow in Albany County, New York.

He was the fourth of seven children born to Benjamin and Rebecca Palmer, his mother a descendant of the Potters who had founded the town. By the time he had finished two years at the

Friends Academy in nearby Rensselaerville, Potter was finding life dull in the quiet, green hamlet with its population of little more than one hundred, its Friends church, post office, and two tiny stores. Nor did he have any fondness for working on any of the four dairy farms his father owned. He wanted a job elsewhere, so he persuaded his father to let him go.

An uncle, Samuel P. Potter, who manufactured door trimmings, coffee mills, and corn shellers in Durham, a dozen miles south, got young Palmer a position as clerk for Colonel Platt Adams, who owned Durham's biggest general store. Colonel Adams was no ordinary storekeeper, content to gossip with customers or barter with farmers from the nearby grasslands or set up drinks for buyers from the inevitable whisky barrel behind the

From the courthouse windows the Chicagoan of the 1850's looked down on the Sherman House, where Potter Palmer and Levi Z. Leiter first lived.

back counter. He was a man of considerable ambition, trained as a lawyer and serving also as Durham's banker, postmaster, real-estate dealer, and justice of the peace. When he saw that the rangy Quaker boy was learning the business quickly, he devoted more time to his outside activities and soon was elected Greene County sheriff and finally a member of the New York House of Representatives. Palmer was left in charge of the store, Colonel Adams' bank, and the post office. He had no time for anything but work, no time for excursions into the Catskills. He had few friends and no fun, but he was pleasant and diligent in his tasks and especially affable to the rich women from the summer hotels on Mount Pisgah and High Peak, who sometimes came to the store to buy "imports" from New York and Albany.

By 1848, after Palmer had worked for three years, Colonel Adams, planning to run for the state senate, offered to make him a partner. But Palmer thanked him and informed him he was ready to go into business for himself, elsewhere. He borrowed money from his father and opened a small country-road store in Oneida County, New York, a Quaker community.

Heeding the injunctions of George Fox, the Quaker leader, who had urged his followers to eschew sharp bargaining some two centuries earlier, Palmer established a one-price, cash policy. The well-ordered Friends gave Palmer what business they could, but the store-bought requirements of these hardy, self-sufficient farmers and their wives were slight. After two years Palmer boarded up the windows and set out on the Erie Canal for Lockport, a boom town in the years when the canal was being dug.

But Lockport's heyday was over. Its fame then derived largely from the manufacture there of Dr. George W. Merchant's Gargling Oil, a concoction for horses that sold well among the Erie barge teamsters and farmers. This business, though lucrative for Dr. Merchant, provided little employment for the townspeople.

Palmer advertised in the *Journal* that his dry-goods store on Main Street was "The Cheapest Place in Town." He sold for cash and he set a single price on his wares. But this meant little to the customers who wanted to haggle over prices, to drive a neater bargain. Business was laggard and slow moving. Palmer had just about decided to close his shop and try his luck in New York when there came to Lockport's deep quarries an order for limestone to build Chicago's new courthouse. It was the largest single order Lockport had received since the building of the Erie Canal. Palmer, determined to see what Chicago had to offer, hustled to the Midwest and forgot about New York.

Now Palmer was back, long enough to sell his Lockport store for the best price he could get. His sale completed and the proceeds put into a bank, he went on to Potter's Hollow to tell his father and brothers of the many inducements Chicago offered, of the startling things he had learned in his week's stay. He spoke of Chicago's property values shooting from $240,000 in 1839 to $9,000,000 in this year of 1852; of the reports that Buffalo now shipped to the port of Chicago more goods than it sent to the three states of Michigan, Indiana, and Wisconsin combined; of the hustlers and the business and the excitement.

He quoted the predictions of the much-respected *Hunt's Merchant's Magazine:* "Chicago's great future destiny is too plainly written on the map to need any array of facts or reasons to show that she will be among the greatest of our American cities!"

There were those who sniffed that Chicago was an ugly town, a mudhole with neither past nor future, "a universal grog shop." But Potter could point to the statistics in Hunt's magazine —a New York magazine at that—to show that Chicago was no ordinary frontier place. In its nineteen short years of official existence it already had a theater, 54 churches, 3 colleges, 7 public halls, 3 hospitals, 380 factories, and 1,184 stores—one merchant for every 92 persons. When Benjamin Palmer marveled that so many dry-goods merchants could survive, Potter excitedly told of the burgeoning Northwest, with its new towns, forests, mines, wheatlands, plank roads, and railroads. There he would find his trade.

The aging father agreed to advance Potter $3,000 in gold, to be added to the $2,000 his son had salvaged from earlier ventures and the sale of his Lockport store. But he balked at helping Potter obtain bank credit, for, as befitted a good Quaker, he was against debt and interest. Then he urged his son to return frequently; promises were made, farewells said, and Potter set out for New York to buy goods.

III

In New York Potter rushed from house to house on Wholesalers' Row on William Street and into the jobbing establish-

To wear the crinoline, wryly commented *Godey's Lady's Book* in the 1850's, "women must buy a considerable amount of dry goods."

ments on John and Pearl streets. He spent his money carefully, arranging for credit with those few who would trust him and his plan for adding yet another dry-goods store to Chicago's well-filled ranks. He pondered whether Chicago's women would want what New York's women seemed to want: silks and fineries in the latest Paris mode, gloves and fancy bonnets, point lace and rustling brocade.

And what of those small-town storekeepers who would come to Chicago in their wagons and take back goods to the rough-skinned farm wives? For them no silks for fancy gowns, but gingham and calico, cotton stockings, and perhaps some straw bonnets and knitted caps for winter—or should it be yarn, so they might knit their own? Palmer hurried to auctions of bankrupt firms, buying at bottom prices, driving good bargains; and he found choice specialties among the importers to give him a well-assorted stock.

Like all other storekeepers who came to New York, he could not leave without another visit to the fabulous "Marble Palace" of Alexander Turney Stewart on Broadway. This blue-eyed, chin-whiskered Irishman was the king of merchants in the dry-goods business. He catered exclusively to the ladies and kept them in a perpetual tizzy with his imports of new laces and fabrics from Europe, his fashion exhibitions, and special sales. Stewart's was the big store, the exciting store, the women's store that often took in as much as $10,000 a day.

There was much a young storekeeper about to invade Chicago could learn here. Stewart was famed for the devoted personal attention he gave to his customers. He employed well-mannered young men, expert in the arts of pleasing ladies. Stewart himself could be seen strutting about the store, hurrying to greet an important customer at the door before turning her over to a dandified usher whom some called a "floorwalker." Sometimes he did shoddy things, as when he bought up distressed and damaged goods for his "fire sales" or required clerks to cut bolts of cheap cloth into "remnants" for the remnant sales he invented. But he always insisted that his salespeople be honest and courteous.

"You must never cheat a customer, even if you can," Stewart advised. "If she pays the full figure, present her with a hank of dress braid, a card of buttons, a pair of shoestrings. You must make her happy and satisfied so she will come back." His "Ladies Parlor" on the second floor was the talk of all the women's magazines. There feminine customers could see themselves in full-length mirrors from Paris—the first, it was said, in America.

Palmer absorbed it all. On his trip back to Chicago he planned how he could apply Stewart's ways to his humble enterprise on mucky Lake Street. He had the skeleton of a scheme in his mind, combining the lessons he had learned the hard, unprofitable way in Oneida and Lockport and what he had seen in New York. He would sell for cash whenever possible. If necessary, he would barter and bargain and extend credit, but only under most rigorous terms. He would always be on hand to see that customers received courteous treatment. He would hire reliable, self-assured clerks. He would seek out customers wherever he could find them, on the streets of Chicago and in the country towns. And the ladies—he would certainly try to please the ladies.

IV

Before Palmer opened for business there were preliminaries. He ordered a sign painted and, since the painter charged by each letter, Palmer was content with only the initial of his first name— "P. Palmer & Co." With part of his fast-vanishing funds he paid carpenters to build rough counters and shelves, then he bought a stove and desk and a big map of the United States.

One expense he avoided, for he had determined that his store would have no whisky barrel around which men from the dusty

Chicago in 1852: The boosters called it "Gem of the Prairie"; the critics, "a universal grog shop." But the town already was the nation's ninth port.

roads could gather as they did at country stores and even in many of the emporiums along Lake Street. This was to be a store to attract ladies, vowed Palmer, not a gathering place for fellow-merchants or clerks' friends or country-town storekeepers.

Soon Palmer's stock arrived by lake boat. But after he and his clerks—Angus McDowell, an unsmiling Scot, and John M. Phelps, a youth of twenty—worked day and night setting up the goods, fully a quarter of the shelves and display racks were still bare, and there were only empty barrels and crates to put in the basement stockroom. Palmer acted quickly. He arranged with his landlords to sublease the basement—an advertisement duly appeared offering "a dry cellar 20 by 160 feet"—and set out to make a fancier, shrewder display of his wares.

He spread out wide mantillas and gay new shawls, draped fabrics from their bolts, scattered ribbons and laces to provide an aspect of profusion. At the front of the store, on tables opposite the counters, he placed items most certain to delight a

23

woman's eye: more shawls, French lawns and prints, hosiery and gloves, bonnet ribbons, tarlatan silks, embroidered collars and cuffs, laces and edging, beads, rings, and tassels. On shelves behind the counters lay bolt goods and articles of intimate apparel to which a lady might only point, blush, and nod.

Toward the center of the store was the millinery department, a few hats and bonnets, more ribbons, and artificial flowers. And, in the rear, flanking the airtight Revere stove and Palmer's desk, stood the inevitable mourning-goods department, where the bereaved could purchase black sleeves and veils, stiff bombazines, and even black bed sheets. Across from this dolorous section was a contrasting array of pillow linens, white sheets, fluffy blankets, and toweling.

So pleased was Palmer with the way he had arranged the inside display of his skimpy lot of goods that he extended it to the small store window. Most of the other merchants neglected their windows entirely or put into them an indiscriminate clutter of goods. But not Palmer. He picked gloves and black silk hosiery for his first display. Into the window went kid, Lisle thread, and silk gloves, long ones and short ones, and merino, silk, and cotton hosiery—all against a background of white crepe shawls. New-style phosgene lamps gave the store a glare that shone brilliantly on the important window display at night, and into the street beyond.

It was November 13, 1852, before any Chicago newspaper took notice of the newcomer, and then only to include him in a story about the seven establishments in the building. The weekly *Gem of the Prairie*, noting that the structure had been planned "with no useless, gaudy show," cited P. Palmer at 137 Lake Street along with H. H. Husted, clothing manufacturer; H. E. Barbour, boot- and shoemaker and dealer in trunks and carpet-bags; William Wheeler, alderman and hardware merchant; D. B. Cooke, publisher and dealer in books; Ray and Baldwin, druggists; and Ross, Bamber and Company, another dry-goods firm.

A week later Deacon Bross's *Daily Democratic Press* commented that Palmer's goods "are fresh from Eastern markets and appear very well." Bross had some words of advice for the new businessmen: "Have good articles to sell, deal honestly and honorably, be courteous to all; and what is, if possible, more important than all these, study the right use of *printer's ink.*"

V

Deacon Bross's injunction to advertise frequently had long since been taken to heart by those who had things to sell to Chicagoans. T. B. Carter, the city's richest and most popular merchant and founder of the local Bible Society, was one of the largest buyers of newspaper space. H. W. Bigelow used two columns to announce his "ANNUAL BENEFIT CLEAR-THE-TRACK SALE!" running the same advertisement for eight months.

L. D. Olmsted, another Lake Street merchant, spread the news about "Party Dresses and Evening Dress Goods," with woodcuts and grotesque type arrangements over three columns. Murray's, across the street from Palmer, blared about its "Real Paris Cloaks." The People's Cheap Store chanted, "Cheap! Cheap! Cheap!" Chicago's only female merchant, Mrs. Georgia Carberry, occasionally inserted a one-column notice: "Ladies Trimmings and Fancy Store."

But Palmer was in no position to follow Deacon Bross's advice. He had no money to pay for advertisements, nor had he been able yet to establish extensive credit. As he stood at the door of his store, watching busy shoppers streak into Carter's big store or into the smaller, long-established shops, he realized that along with his window displays and tempting wares he would need even greater inducements to lure the ladies to his counters.

I. M. SINGER & CO.,
140 LAKE ST., CHICAGO.

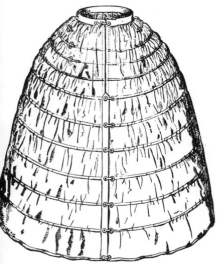

PATENT SKIRT.

WILKINS' MODEL STOVE

GO OUT
AND BUY!

The women whose patronage Potter Palmer sought were ready for new ideas.

By the winter of 1852 the movement called Feminism, begun four years earlier as a mild insurrection against the dominance of men, reached proportions of a national revolution. It had its dedicated leaders, its high priestesses, and its fanatics and followers—all uniting against the concept that women had to be shielded from the evils and hardships of life. Feminists opposed the rituals of the times which required of women inordinate modesty, discreet ignorance, physical frailty, utter submission.

Some of the women wanted political independence. Some cried for equal rights in love, employment, and dress. Most of them wanted simply the privilege of doing their own choosing and buying in stores, without husband or father deciding what must go on their backs and into their homes. All these ideas intermingled so that Feminists preaching political freedom taught independence and self-reliance to women seeking merely the right to a share of the family purse; and those who clamored to love freely passed a measure of defiance to ladies who wanted only to wear more comfortable clothes.

Feminism almost was laughed out of existence before it was well started when, in 1851, Mrs. Amelia Bloomer, editor of *The*

Lily, a temperance newspaper, urged that all women adopt a costume of loose-fitting pantaloons bound at the ankles and a three-quarter-length coat. She affixed her name to this Turkish-style garb and even wore the ensemble at a public reception in Washington, where her father was a congressman. Feminists adopted the bloomers as a symbol of their revolt; they lectured in them, did their housework in them, and held bloomer parades in New York, Boston, and Philadelphia.

The men of the nation, slightly incredulous at first, swept to the counterattack. Gibes and insults were thrown at the Bloomer Girls. In some cities mobs of rowdies raided Feminist meetings; newspapers and magazines printed satirical cartoons; ministers inveighed against the scandalous costumes. Small boys followed the bloomer-clad ladies, chanting:

> "Gibbery, gibbery gab,
> The women had a confab,
> And demanded the rights
> To wear the tights,
> Gibbery, gibbery gab!"

Others jeered:

> "Heigh! Ho! In rain or snow
> The Bloomer now is all the go.
> Twenty tailors take the stitches,
> Twenty women wear the breeches.
> Heigh! Ho! In rain and snow
> The Bloomer now is all the go!"

Elizabeth Cady Stanton, that rugged, firm-minded female who had started the insurrection, appeared on lecture platforms in the costume, shouting, "I feel like a captive set free from his ball and chain!" Her insistence on the right of women to wear pantaloons if they wished was, however, less strident than her espousal of the other aims of the Feminist movement—the right of women to hold property or take a job, the right to moral equality, the right to independence in the home. Shrewdly she concentrated on still another aspect of the fight, demanding for women the right to buy for themselves, their children, and their households.

To dramatize her appeal that women were partners in the family and should have the privilege of sharing the family purse, Mrs. Stanton invariably told her audiences her tremulous tale of "The Congressman's Wife." This unfortunate lady, she related, had an ill-equipped kitchen, with a faulty stove. Whenever her husband returned from Washington, he chided her about her poor cooking and miserable meals. The woman had been hysterical when she asked Mrs. Stanton for advice.

"Of course you can't cook here!" Mrs. Stanton shrilled as she replayed the scene before avid crowds. "Go out and buy a new stove! Buy what you need! Buy while he's in Washington!"

The housewife was horrified, Mrs. Stanton declared. It would never do! Her husband would be enraged! He bought everything, even her clothes! He might beat her!

At this point Mrs. Stanton always paused to pierce the nearest male in her audience with an angry stare. Then she cried, "I told her—and I tell this to you women—'Go out and buy! When he returns and flies into a rage, you sit in a corner and weep. That will soften him! Then, when he tastes his food from the new stove, he will know you did the wise thing. When he sees you so much fresher, happier in your new kitchen, he will be delighted and the bills will be paid.' I repeat—*GO OUT AND BUY!*"

Such excellent advice was heard and heeded not only by the congressman's wife, but by hundreds of women in scores of towns and cities. Laws governing the legal status of females would be slow to change, and the bloomers would never really become popular for regular wear, but the impact of women on the cash boxes of stores was more immediate. An offshoot of the Feminist movement was a vast buying spree in the early 1850's, led not only by the radicals but by the more numerous conservatives who wore crinoline hoop skirts.

To the delight of dry-goods merchants and textile industrialists, the day of the crinoline flowered. Now these costumes billowed to unprecedented proportions, requiring as many as forty yards of goods for a single outfit. In addition to a muslin shift or knitted underwear and corset, the proper housewife was expected to don a flannel petticoat, a muslin petticoat, a padded petticoat reaching to the knees, a white starched petticoat, two additional muslin petticoats each three or four yards wide, and then her gown.

Since pads and starch failed to distend such mounds of cloth properly, steel hoops, covered with cotton cloth and laced together with tapes, were used. When it was found that a tilting hoop skirt could be quite revealing, the ladies sheathed their limbs in pantalets, trimmed with lace or flounces.

Women in crinoline crowded men out of omnibuses, and some men found it almost impossible to reach the counters in stores because of the hoop-skirt barricades. Since drawing rooms could not accommodate a large number of crinoline-clad women, parties became smaller. In Chicago sponsors of various cotillions had to drop the number of invited couples from 200 to 150.

The men turned to ridicule to offset this latest fashion trend, using newspaper jokes, nasty cartoons, ribald saloon ditties. Editors played up the story of Lady Dorothy Neville, who almost lost her life at a London party when her hoop skirt caught fire, and others were unable to get near enough to help her. Men chortled over the story of the Chicago woman who fell from a footbridge into a pool of mud and was, someone avowed, moving away under full sail when she was rescued. They chuckled

Most Chicago women shunned the Bloomer costume, preferring to battle muddy streets in voluminous skirts. Small girls fared better, however.

at the lady in San Francisco who thwarted the dog catcher by hiding her unlicensed spaniel under her skirts.

To the scoffers, the indomitable Mrs. Stanton, having discarded bloomers for crinoline, shouted, "Men say we are frail! I'd like to see a man who can bear what we do, laced up in steel-ribbed corsets, with hoops, heavy skirts, trains, high heels, panniers, chignons, and dozens of hairpins sticking in our scalps, cooped up in the house year after year. How would men like that?"

There was no answer except jeers and more taunts and general masculine agreement with the strong statements about the Feminists and their followers made by the *Albany Register*. "These unsexed women," raved the editorial, widely republished in other papers, "would step out of their true sphere of mother, wife and daughter to take upon themselves the duties and business of men. By stalking into public gaze, engaging in politics, the rough controversies and trafficking of the world, they will unheave existing conditions and overturn all social relations of life! How long must the doings of these creatures be tolerated?"

II

In Chicago, on the edge of the new frontier, the outcry was less harsh than elsewhere. It was not unusual for a woman here to take on a man's responsibilities, and the women who battled Chicago's dust and mud and epidemics were valued for qualities other than their feminine frailty.

Chicago was realistic, changing, and sensitive to change. If its women were not fully prepared to march in the ranks with Mrs. Stanton's Feminists, they did feel the effects of the national urge toward independence, and they marched to the dry-goods stores, which became their havens and their gathering places. The dry-goods store was more than a place to buy. Here an unescorted woman was received with deference, catered to, waited upon.

Few other such retreats existed, even in Chicago. No lady would dare venture without an escort into a downtown restaurant, for she would not be served. There were no beauty shops, tearooms, clubrooms. The hairdressers, such as those in the fashionable salon of the Tremont House, cut the hair of men.

Women of the best families did not go to the grocer's or the farmer's markets. The drugstores, cold and marble-tiered, were forbidding places at best, to be visited in acute emergencies. Ladies were welcome at the new soda fountains where they could purchase ice cream or "a cooling draft of pure soda and a little Boston neck oil," but they were not expected to linger. But in the dry-goods store they could linger as long as they wished, shopping, comparing bargains, checking quality, chatting until household duties or hunger drove them home.

To guide them in their purchases, they had the most popular woman's magazine, *Godey's Lady's Book*. Its editor, Sarah Josepha Hale, was the arbiter of feminine customs and fashions; hers was a firm voice in all matters pertaining to woman's place in the world. In her publication she dealt with everything of possible feminine interest—from home furnishings and dress styles to "the effect of tears on a dry piece of paper stained with the juice of violets." She was righteous, orthodox, and enterprising. She hated French novels, but she was the first to send artists to Paris to sketch the new styles, and she staged the first fashion show in America.

Mrs. Hale fought for the right of women to work at any job and to enter any school. Spurred by her, Harvard University Medical School agreed to admit "a female person." But its invitation was quickly withdrawn after enraged students passed a quaint resolution protesting any woman's appearance "in places where her presence is calculated to destroy our respect for the modesty and delicacy of her sex."

She also assigned Mrs. Alice B. Neal to write a series of articles on the feminine job situation, and Mrs. Neal reported there appeared to be only two fields of employment for women —"teaching and the needle." But in cities where Mrs. Hale's magazine had the greatest influence, said Mrs. Neal, there were lady clerks in stores, especially dry-goods stores. "The amount of dry goods a woman wears is considerable," she noted. "A woman would rather buy certain articles of apparel from another woman."

III

Potter Palmer was not yet ready to do anything so drastic as hire a woman clerk, but he was coming to know how he could best please the ladies who were invading Lake Street and discovering the delights of dry-goods shopping.

Already he had made a notable advance by his refusal to keep a whisky barrel. He also studied *Godey's Lady's Book* to learn the kind of goods its stylish readers wanted to buy. He freshened his window displays with new colorful goods—gay umbrellas, shawls, and Parisian cloaks. Mindful of Mrs. Hale's persistent demands that women be treated as equals, but with polite courtesy, he stood primly in a frock coat, like the great A. T. Stewart, ready to greet them with a smile and a bow.

And he did more.

While competitors roared with glee at such a stupid scheme, he permitted some favored customers actually to take home goods on approval. "If your husband doesn't like it," he told them, "you bring it back, and I'll refund your money. If you decide it doesn't look good, come back and you can have another or your money back." In these early months this was not a general policy of Palmer's, but a private arrangement accorded to certain ladies. It was daring and risky. But it honored a basic and precious right that even the Feminists had missed—the right of a lady to change her mind.

Palmer also slanted a canny appeal toward the women's pocketbooks by citing specific prices for his wares and underselling his rivals on certain items. This practice irritated the other merchants. Few cared if he wished to court ruin by offering customers the unheard-of privilege of exchanging goods or refunding the purchase price. But price-quoting and price-cutting were another matter.

When Palmer offered dress lawns for 6 cents a yard and declared they usually sold for a shilling—worth 12.5 cents—he called public attention to the extreme profits most merchants were enjoying. And when he stated he would sell delaine for a shilling while goods of similar quality sold elsewhere for 20 cents a yard, he invited a comparison that his competitors found odious. They murmured indignantly.

The Tremont House, Chicago's finest hotel, later raised on 5,000 jackscrews by George Pullman, the man who finally solved the problem of Chicago's mud.

His proud assertion that he could sell embroideries and needlework for "20 per cent less" because he bought them directly from importers drew brays of indignation. Anyone, sneered his foes, could buy directly from importers. Palmer was willfully upsetting a solid system of nice profits.

Palmer cared little that the only other Chicago store venturesome enough to state prices—Stanley and Hutchins' One-Price Store—had found the practice unprofitable. Nor did he mind that he was overlooked in the spring of 1853 when the other merchants formed the Early Closing Association, intended to induce housewives to buy early so that clerks could be home at eight o'clock in summer and seven o'clock in winter. Palmer preferred to go it alone; besides, he wanted to keep his clerks until nine and ten o'clock.

He continued to sell for less. And, to accommodate the wealthier ladies who set the shopping modes, he announced he no longer would try to stock all lines of goods as his competitors did. In an obvious move to lure the carriage trade from the larger stores, he placed more emphasis on quality goods of special interest to women—from crinolines to fine carpets. And in that season's issue of John Gager's *Mercantile Record*, circulating in the wholesale markets, he bluntly called himself a specialist in this field. The tactic won immediate response; and with *Godey's Lady's Book* loud in its praise of new Paris fashions, Palmer's claim that his goods were imported directly from abroad had a sparkling appeal, undimmed by the efforts of his imitators along Lake Street.

Within a year after he started, Palmer's store was a tiny, splendid world of laces and silks, Parisian cloaks, hosiery, and gloves for women who found excitement in buying or just looking. The coaches, broughams, landaus, and little pony phaetons which always had stopped in front of Carter's or Olmsted's started to come to P. Palmer's, lining up in the soggy street while grooms waited impassively and the ladies shopped.

Newcomers to the growing town, such as Lucy Drummond, daughter of Federal Judge Thomas Drummond, were soon writing to their friends that of all the stores in the business district the two most favored were Carter's and Palmer's. Mrs. William Blair, who had come out of the Pittsfield mill region of Massachusetts to marry the city's leading hardware merchant, was so taken with Palmer's establishment that years later she would recall, "Mr. Palmer was always about the store himself. He would stop to chat while you tried on your new coat, and he would perhaps cheapen the price."

IV

Palmer was alert to business changes and methods, new styles and new ideas, but in his personal life he was the staid Quaker. While the *Chicago Times* was complaining, "Most of our young merchants, living on borrowed capital, are spending $2,000 and $3,000 a year in riotous living," Palmer stuck to his store. At night, when the place closed, he often stayed late, preparing orders for new merchandise or working on his books. In many respects he personified the kind of man praised by George W. Light of Boston in his much-read book, *Advice to a Young Merchant*. Any young merchant, wrote Light, "must possess sentiments of honesty and candor, firmness, prudence and truth, economy and temperance, politeness, good temper, and perseverance. These cardinal virtues, so essential to respectability and success are to be observed."

Neither Chicago's saloons nor concert halls—where girls danced or sang tearful ballads on a button-sized stage—held any attraction for Palmer, nor was he among the Lake Street bachelors who sponsored the cotillions and the assembly balls. He stayed clear of the gambling halls; he rarely attended the popular lectures sponsored by the Chicago Mutual Improvement Association or the meetings of the Chicago Mechanics' Institute, an organization of young men interested in "natural, mechanical and chemical philosophy."

Later Palmer would have more time to be gay and sociable, but now he remained aloof from such pleasant recreations as the soirees, promenades, and kitchen junkets and the dance mania sweeping Chicago. He was glad that there was such a craze for dancing, however, for it brought hundreds of women, young and old, scurrying to the dry-goods stores to buy endless yards of goods for dresses. He was happy, too, that the female population of the city increased as young women from the East and South came looking for husbands, not because he was ready for marriage but because more women meant more business.

These female visitors did much to enliven the social seasons and to stimulate the dry-goods trade, but they brought down editorial wrath.

"In dancing Waltzes and Polkas now most in favor," stormed that forthright Whig organ, the *Daily Journal*, "such liberties were taken with the persons of young ladies as no one with

37

correct sentiments can witness without disgust and indignation. Young ladies who have not overcome their delicacy sufficiently to suit the times are excluded from the dance altogether to make way for such as can see no impropriety in having their waists encircled by the arms of a fellow whose collar and hair are out of proportion to his brains, and in rushing from one end of the room to the other through all the exciting mazes of the most indefensible Polkas, with their faces buried in the whiskers of their partners, and their persons drawn as closely as the movements of the dance will allow."

Not all Chicago women led such a madcap life. Half the population was foreign born, many of the immigrants clustering in hovels and tenements. The immigrant women needed no Feminist movement to spur them into working, for their husbands made only $7.00 to $10.00 a week. They got jobs as washerwomen, seamstresses, and servants; or, in the business district, they cleaned stores and offices, prepared greengroceries and fish for market, served as chambermaids, housekeepers, and cooks in hotels and boardinghouses.

Those with a few precious dollars to spend found their way to the dry-goods stores on Lake Street, but clerks in the better stores treated them rudely. Cried the *Daily Democratic Press:* "How long will merchants continue to keep behind their counters such apes who insult the daughters of toil, who are far more worthy of respect and more noble in position than he who is willing to confine his intellect and shape his capacities to the length and breadth of a piece of tape?"

Such women who wandered into Palmer's small crowded store could hardly afford his wares, for in these first five years he concentrated on drawing the "quality trade" and the large middle class that could pay cash. But even these women were given courteous treatment and permitted to look at the fine silks and other goods without buying, for had not George Light, whose book was the young merchant's bible, called for "politeness" and "good temper"?

V

By the beginning of 1857 the rumblings of financial panic were heard in the city. The nation had gone too far and too fast on the stimulus of California gold and westward expansion. Banks tottered and "wildcat money" blanketed the country.

Potter Palmer was calm. Unable, because of the feverish activity in the city, to find larger quarters for his business, he had built a good cash reserve. He was wary of extending credit. He knew at a glance the true value of a bank note without referring to the *National Bank Note Detector*, kept at hand by his competitors. Nor did he need the bottle of nitric acid used by others to test spurious coins. His wholesale business was small but solid; he shipped orders from river-front warehouses by rail and on plank roads to carefully chosen customers in country towns who paid cash or exchanged furs.

Prices started to fall. Other Lake Street merchants ordered signs painted for "Panic Sales," "Distress Sales," "Going-out-of-Business Sales." But Palmer was watching for a chance to move into larger quarters. As the year darkened, the *Book of Commercial Ratings*, predecessor to Dun and Bradstreet's reports, had sad things to report about many merchants who had inflated their stocks and bought too much on credit. Of Palmer it stated, "Making money, economical, business not too much extended, attends closely to business, does not pay large interest, good moral character, credits prudently, not sued, pays promptly. Credit good. Capital $25,000."

CHILDREN'S FASHIONS.

BASQUINE.

MEN WITH
MERCHANT INSTINCT

Potter Palmer, bowing to his lady customers and paying strict attention to business, was not alone in heeding the admonitions of George Light. A block away in the city's main wholesale dry-goods house a young clerk and merchant-to-be was observing every maxim and setting up new ones of his own.

A clear-eyed fellow with thinly pressed lips and a slight Yankee twang in his quiet voice, he often slept in the store at the end of a twelve-hour working day. He always arrived long before the store opened so that he could help load wagons heading for the railroad stations and docks. Taciturn and shy, except when expounding the virtues of the latest shipments of muslin or Irish poplins to a customer, he seemed to some to lack confidence. He spoke little but listened hard and long. His name was Marshall Field, but the brasher clerks, snickering at his soft ways, labeled him "Silent Marsh."

On a chugging Michigan Central train Field had come to Chicago from the tradition-bound "blessed old Commonwealth of Massachusetts" four years after Potter Palmer. He was twenty-one then, having been born on September 18, 1834, in a one-and-a-half-story farmhouse on Field's Hill, a mile from the center of Conway. His father, John, whom the townsfolk called Jack, glumly plowed and tended his rocky 200-acre tract of land, but only twenty-five acres regularly yielded crops. His mother, Fidelia, for whom Marshall was the fourth of eight children, was a prim, sensible woman given to uttering pious aphorisms and advising, "Avoid the appearance of evil."

In a community where labor was all-honorable and the slightest show of indolence degrading, Marshall went to work on his father's farm even before he was old enough to attend school two miles away in Pumpkin Hollow, a slight valley where pumpkins from the vines on an adjacent hillside farm rolled down against the frame schoolhouse.

At school he was one of the quieter pupils, fond only of mathematics. He was agile in games that sometimes degenerated into free-for-all fights in which the boy more than held his own, either with his fists or tart words. When a rough lad in one such tussle shouted, "You go to hell, Marsh!" the youngster retorted, "That doesn't scare me. I'll kick the fires all out."

By the time he was turning sixteen, neither life at school nor the morning-till-sunset drudgery on the farm satisfied Marshall. Conway, a rural community of placid meadows and little homesteads, showed only the most meager signs of the encroaching industrialization that would change the whole pattern of life in New England. Near the old gristmills and tanneries were such new neighbors as a woolen-goods factory and a cotton mill.

The village was too tame for anyone with even the mildest ambitions to be something other than a farmer, especially if his parents were not rich enough to send him—should he have chosen such a career—to Harvard College to study medicine or law. Feeling that his bent for figures might be useful in store-keeping, Marshall plagued his father—with proper humility, as was required in the household—to permit him to get a job in one of the stores in Deerfield or even in Pittsfield, some twenty-five miles away on the road toward Boston.

At twenty-four Marshall Field was an ace salesman for Cooley, Farwell and Company; a prudent and ambitious young man, "he had the merchant's instinct."

A family conclave was held. Backing Marshall was his brother, Joseph, three years older, who also longed to abandon farming for other more lucrative endeavor. The parents finally agreed to let Marshall go to work for a fellow-Congregationalist, Henry G. Davis, chin-tufted church deacon and owner of a "Dry Goods and Crockery" store in Pittsfield.

II

The storekeepers of Pittsfield were a proud and thriving lot. They had their traditions and their own heroes. Back in the Revolutionary War, when the town was fifteen years old, James Easton, who kept "store goods" in his tavern, had been a colonel with the Continental Volunteers, under the daring Ethan Allen. Not only had he and another merchant, David Noble, turned over all their stocks of cloth and grain to the Yankee rebels, but

43

Easton had sat down in that very tavern on May 1, 1775, with two other men to help plan the capture of Fort Ticonderoga.

After the Revolution and for years to come, many of the Pittsfield merchants still took barter for their goods. They exchanged bonnets and ribbons and other luxuries from Boston and New York for the products of farm looms, anvils, and tanneries in surrounding Berkshire County. But when Marshall Field went to work as errand boy and clerk for Deacon Davis, Pittsfield's slow-paced life had already felt the tremors of the man-made industrial revolution.

Along the shores of the Housatonic River, running the length of the town, stood mills and factories. Their spinning jennies and carding machines turned out cotton goods, satinet, and broadcloth. Other mills on a second river, the Pousatonic— Indians had once called the town by this name, meaning "run for deer"—produced piles of woolen blankets. Two railroads stretched south to Bridgeport, Connecticut, from whose landings the mill products were shipped to New York.

The transformation from an agricultural to a manufacturing city was under way fast, although few in the prospering community were aware that a few years before a young New England scholar and poet named Ralph Waldo Emerson had written, "This invasion of Nature by Trade with its Money, its Credit, its Steam, its Railroads, threatens to upset the Balance of Man and establish a new universal Monarchy, more tyrannical than Babylon or Rome."

To Deacon Davis' smaller establishment farmers and farmers' wives came to barter, and they gave his young clerk plenty of chance to overcome his shy ways. They were expert bargainers, these Berkshire farm folk. More often than not they went away from the store cackling over how they had outwitted the befuddled youngster as they traded eggs and butter for calico and yarn. Yet Marshall was learning fast and working

44

almost as hard as on the Conway farm. For this, too, was a job with long hours.

He often rose at dawn in his room above the store, ate a meager breakfast, then went downstairs to take the shutters from the store windows. He swept the floors, brushed dust from the tables, arranged the goods on counters and shelves. Deacon Davis always opened the day with a quick prayer asking for God's blessing on the store and its fortunes. Then, clearing his throat, he would direct the order of the day's activities.

Although he remained more a good listener than a talker, Marshall grew less shy. He was most popular with the women who came to the country-style store. In a little book he made notes of their names, their families, their special preferences for certain merchandise. He studied *Godey's Lady's Book* and, like Potter Palmer and scores of other clerks and storekeepers, learned about merchandising and about opportunities in Chicago, that growing metropolis in Illinois, from *Hunt's Merchant's Magazine*.

Marshall's work day lasted ten hours, six days a week. Other young men attended "kettle drum" and "small and early" dinners or enjoyed candy pulls and oyster roasts in the Berkshire farmhouses. But he lived a quiet life, shunning even these innocent pleasures. He attended services in Deacon Davis' South Congregationalist Church without missing a Sunday, but when others went swimming in the Housatonic or rowing on Silver Lake, Marshall was memorizing the list prices of dry goods.

III

For nearly five years Field worked in Davis' store. He developed a sound, but not brilliant, reputation as a man with a sharp memory for faces and names, a great sense of curiosity, a smooth sales technique, and an air of quiet intensity. He was courteous, painstaking, eager to please.

He also heard there about the West and Chicago. Some of Davis' customers knew of that town personally. Not far from the store was Pittsfield's pride, the Maplewood Young Ladies' Institute, set up in 1841 by the Reverend Wellington Hart Tyler after he lost his voice from preaching too loudly. Its 100 students received an "extensive and liberal" course of studies which, in the words of the Reverend Mr. Tyler, "cannot fail, in all cases where it is diligently and systematically prosecuted, to exert a decided influence over the female mind and, through that powerful and pervading agency, secure most happy results in our rising Republic."

In the years Marshall Field worked in the store, half a dozen students and teachers with "powerful and pervading" minds had departed to travel to Illinois' growing metropolis. Mary Eveline Smith, one of the teachers, had met and married Charles B. Farwell, a rising young official in Chicago's municipal government. She wrote to other Maplewood girls about her life in the lively town. Two students who followed her to Chicago had also married well. Mary Brewster was now the wife of George H. Laflin, the grain merchant, and Sarah Seymour wed William H. Blair, a rich hardware dealer. Both were delighted with Chicago, they wrote. It was a town with a future.

On her trips to visit her family and friends the new Mrs. Farwell stopped in at Deacon Davis' store to tell of her experiences in the West. She found the grave young clerk, Marshall Field, an eager listener. He asked many questions, especially when Mrs. Farwell spoke of Chicago's business. She described the dry-goods stores along Lake Street—T. B. Carter's, P. Palmer's, William Ross's. She assured Field of the opportunities in Chicago. Years later she would remember his quiet, intent manner as he waited on her and listened, "a handsome young man with regular features and cheeks as red as a rose."

Late, in 1855, Field was ready to leave Pittsfield. For him, as

46

for those other scores of young men ready to burst from the confines of static New England towns, there was only one direction to go—west. He talked over his plans with Joseph, who had worked briefly for another Pittsfield merchant and for a time shared Marshall's room. He had saved some money, Marshall said, and he thought he could borrow $1,000 or so from their father or from their brother, Chandler, when he should need it. Joseph encouraged him. Chicago would be the place, they decided. Joseph was proud of his brother, knew he would succeed. Even in Pittsfield he had sensed, as he often said later, that Marshall had "a real merchant's instinct."

When Marshall Field told Davis of his intentions, the storekeeper, trying to dissuade him, offered him a partnership. Quietly but firmly, Field thanked Deacon Davis and declined the offer. Davis shook his head, but by the following January when Field was ready to go, the gruff storekeeper wrote a warm letter, addressed "To Whom It May Concern":

"The bearer, Mr. Field, has been in my employ for nearly the past five years and now leaves me for the West. I can without qualification commend him as a young man of unusual business talent worthy of the confidence of any who would employ him. His character and principles as well as his business qualifications are such I cannot doubt he will meet that success in life which usually accompanies industry, perseverance, and integrity when combined with strict energy of character.

"He has my warmest wishes for his success in whatever situation he may fall or business he shall engage."

IV

A cautious young man of twenty-one was this Marshall Field as he picked his way through Chicago's streets in the spring of 1856. His brother, Joseph, had preceded him by a few weeks and already had made friends in the wholesale houses of the town. But Joseph planned to move on. He was less certain now that Chicago held the promise he had once foreseen. Marshall was almost as disappointed in the first few weeks.

Undisciplined Chicago gave a shock to his orderly mind. The noise, the confusion, the mud, the stench, the loud heartiness of the people made him yearn for Pittsfield's quiet. But as he made the rounds systematically of the dry-goods stores along Lake Street and the big wholesale establishments on the banks of the evil-smelling Chicago River, he began to absorb some of the underlying excitement of the town.

He met other Yankee clerks who had left their country stores to find jobs in Chicago, to make money here. They were Chicago boosters now. They talked of the ten railroad lines, with thirty-eight freight trains and fifty-eight passenger trains coming and going in a single day; of the "Maderia Pet," which had sailed all the way from Liverpool to the port of Chicago with a cargo of hardware and crockery; of that fellow named Potter Palmer and his crazy ideas—letting women take goods home "on approval," advertising his prices, selling "at cost." They talked of fortunes being made in dry goods, meat, furniture, grain.

Field met a commercial traveler, Thomas Brenan, who told him how he traveled to the far end of the Mississippi Valley for Cooley, Wadsworth and Company, the town's big wholesalers, sometimes staying away on a single trip for six months.

"And do you find the country opening up?" asked Field.

"Ha!" cried Brenan. "Why, every inch of the land is rich and the class of people settling there are of good character. On my last trip my trade increased 200 per cent over the one before!"

In Potter Palmer's store one day, while Palmer was away, Brenan pulled Field toward a big map on the wall near Palmer's high-top desk. He pointed out the expanse of prairies, the new rail lines Palmer had inked in, the towns, the trails over which

The Rush Street bridge linked the residential and business districts of early Chicago. It crossed the Chicago River, "an evil-smelling artery of commerce."

a northwestern salesman would have to plod when the trains carried him to the end of their lines.

"But it won't be like that always, boy!" Brenan told him. "In ten years Chicago will lead St. Louis. Galena'll go down and down. Up there"—and he stretched a long finger—"places like St. Paul and Minneapolis are growing fast." He pointed to a new town. "Superior!" He chuckled. "Superior to what?" he demanded. "Not superior to us. Wait'll these railroads hit the Missouri and still go west! There'll be no stopping Chicago then, just no stopping her."

Brenan was sure Marshall Field could get a job with Cooley and Wadsworth. His letter from Deacon Davis tucked into his waistcoat pocket, Field went to see the senior partner, Francis B. Cooley. Joseph Field, too, knew Cooley, and he went along to supplement Brenan's words in behalf of his brother. Cooley, who prided himself on hiring only top prospects, stared hard at the thin-lipped youth, muttered while he read Davis' letter, and allowed as how he was unimpressed. Joseph pleaded that Marshall should be given a chance. Finally Cooley agreed. Young Marshall would have a trial. If he did all right, snapped Cooley, he'd get an annual wage of $400.

Marshall Field was determined to make good. He set a furious pace for the other clerks, hard-working, fast-talking young fellows, wise in the ways of the city. No pleasures for "Silent Marsh," only long hours of toil. When he was not busy selling, he helped unload bales of merchandise or served on the crew that worked the cumbersome rope elevator which lifted goods to the upper three floors of the creaky building.

In his off-duty hours Field studied invoices and order blanks, memorizing, as he had when he worked for Davis, the inventories of stock, the prices of goods, and their quality. He lived in a cheap rooming house, paying $2.50 a week for room and board, but in the busy weeks he slept in the store night after night. Unusually frugal, he managed that first year to save half of his $400 salary. All he bought for himself was a pair of overalls. He appeared, said his fellow clerks to have no bad habits. His word was deemed good, he was quiet, sharp, and eager to make money.

Field showed interest in the tiniest details of the wholesale business, but he especially liked the small section devoted to retail sales. He developed a habit of asking many questions of the traveling salesmen and buyers who came in on the Illinois Central, or by train or stagecoach from the west and north. These details—the price of muslin in St. Paul, the hats ladies liked in Milwaukee, crop conditions in Indiana, news of new factories, new stores, new jobbing houses, how many reapers Cyrus McCormick had sold in Iowa—he jotted down in notebooks. Often he passed the information on to Cooley or his partners or to other salesmen and buyers.

The firm's junior partner, John Villiers Farwell, noted quickly that when Field worked in the retail section he showed a knack for dealing with the women customers, but with none of the old-timers' tricks, the little compliments, the slick niceties, the fawning and exaggerated graciousness. Instead, Farwell saw, Field had an earnest manner and a vast store of interesting information about the goods he had to sell the ladies. He showed genuine interest in what they might have to tell him, even the most inconsequential matters. "He seemed to have a wonderful comprehension of feminine nature," Farwell remembered years later. "He had the merchant's instinct. He lived for it, and it only. He never lost it."

Farwell, the moving spirit of the wholesale house, was a sophisticated and careful judge of men. At nineteen he had worked his way into the raw Chicago of 1844 from a squatter's homestead in southern Illinois with $3.50 in one pocket and his mother's Bible in the other. Adept at bookkeeping, he got a job in the office of his older brother, Charles B. Farwell, whom Mary Eveline Smith, the Pittsfield schoolteacher, married.

Later he went into the dry-goods business as a clerk for Elisha Wadsworth. When Wadsworth joined Cooley to form the wholesale house, Farwell was taken in as a junior partner. Now, prospering, married to Cooley's sister, devoting much of his energy to such uplift projects as preaching to the rum-soaked prisoners in the Bridewell and backing the young evangelist, Dwight L. Moody, Farwell had time to keep an eye on a likely clerk. Especially a clerk as diligent, smart, and well behaved as Marshall Field.

So it was Farwell who first proposed that Field should be given new duties. He would prove himself to be an extraordinary salesman, Farwell predicted. Cooley agreed to a further trial. Field was told to have some cards printed designating him as a traveling salesman for the company. He would start along those country trails Brenan had described from Potter Palmer's map, carrying his samples and little black notebooks.

MARSHALL FIELD'S BUSINESS CARD

NEW STYLE BODY

THE MAMMA CHEMISE.

FIELD, PALMER, AND LEITER

This was opportunity, and Field was one to seize it. He traveled to those towns and mercantile establishments he had so meticulously described in his stack of black books. The information was useful. Field knew all about the merchants and the jobbers he met, and their problems. He was still a good listener and the questions he asked made sense. His advice, charily given, was solid and sensible.

Young Field was not a friendly man in the tradition of that day's commercial traveler, but he made friends on the road. He tried neither to unload slow-moving goods on the unwary nor to build a man's inventory beyond its proper proportions. He could be trusted and relied upon. When blizzards swept over the Iowa prairies and stopped trains, Field still arrived close to schedule by sleigh or on horseback, wrapped in a fur-lined greatcoat. In the spring, mud and floods bogged down much of the countryside, but Field managed doggedly to make his rounds, winning new customers for Cooley, Wadsworth and Company.

But although he was making more money and had a chance to learn more about selling in this western market, Field cared little for the life of a commercial traveler. An orderly, fastidious man, he detested the slow, smelly trains. A trip in a lumbering stagecoach was painful for him. Most of the small-town hotels were an ordeal. Sometimes he lived for days on cheese and crackers because he could not eat the food served in taverns. And he was also racked by the suspicion that things might be going on in Chicago, that chances might be slipping by. He had not been on the road long before he was planning how he could get back to the big city.

Things *were* happening in Chicago. Despite the Panic of 1857, Cooley, Wadsworth and Company built a new store and warehouse on Wabash Avenue, south of Lake Street. It was Farwell who had suggested quitting the old wholesale district after a horrified customer wrote that the Chicago River nearby was "the source of all the most detestable, filthy smells that the breezes of Heaven can possibly float to the olfactories." But, more important than the new store, so far as the fortunes of Field were concerned, Wadsworth and Cooley had quarreled, and Cooley demanded a reorganization of the firm. Farwell came in as senior partner. The name was changed to Cooley, Farwell and Company.

Wadsworth, weary of business but still eager to share in the profits, agreed to provide 40 per cent of the capital and to continue as a silent partner. But the panic frightened Wadsworth, and he failed to come up with his promised share. Cooley and Farwell struggled to keep their company from falling in the debacle that destroyed 267 other wholesale houses and retail stores about the country. They tightened their credit to customers, borrowed where they could, reduced inventories. When wildcat banks crashed by the score and most bank notes became worthless, Cooley and Farwell took bushels of wheat in payment for goods. "Right as wheat!" became a slogan of the day.

On the road Marshall Field had news of some of these events. He heard reports, too, of the activities of one P. Palmer, who had gone against the times to open a grand new store on Lake

Potter Palmer at thirty-five. He finally found in Chicago the success and wealth that had eluded him elsewhere. "You've got to think big!" he said.

Street. While the Chicago newspapers continued to report failures in dry goods and to publish columns of distress sale notices, this fellow Palmer, it was said, underpriced everyone and still made profits. One thing was fortunate. P. Palmer had dropped his wholesale activities, and Field acquired some of his customers. But others he failed to get because he could not send goods "on approval" as Palmer had done. Field made a note of that in his black book.

Neither panic nor the depression which followed in 1858 could keep Field from doing well as a commercial traveler. Even Cooley was appreciative when his young drummer returned from a long, hard, but successful trip. And things were looking up for Cooley and Farwell despite a continuing wrangle with Wadsworth. The firm had survived the worst with some losses, but now Levi Z. Leiter, their bookkeeper, was using black ink again. They had been fortunate in moving from the river-front wholesale district in advance of a disastrous October fire which leveled several competitors. They had been lucky to escape the competition of Palmer during the worst of the depression. This advantage, however, went glimmering. In the summer of 1858 it was rumored that Palmer intended to expand again. And he was going all out for wholesale trade.

II

It was true. Potter Palmer was doing well, incredibly well. A year before, in the midst of panic, he had dropped his wholesale efforts to conquer his retail rivals along Lake Street. He opened his campaign from his new four-story store at No. 139. On October 5, 1857, five years after his arrival in Chicago, he bought columns of space in the newspapers to announce his "Great Removal Sale." His entire stock from 137 Lake Street had to go at less than cost, he said, "in consequence of the tightness of the money market and other startling causes combined, and to enable me to stand from under in the present crash!"

His advance while others retreated won the attention of the newspapers and a eulogy from the *Chicago Times:*

"Our business columns today announce the removal of Mr. P. Palmer from 137 to the more commodious store, 139 Lake street. But we feel inclined to say a word in regard to this establishment. No tradesman better deserves the commendation of an impartial press. He clipped the wings of extortion by introducing moderate prices into the fashionable dry goods business, and with perhaps the most splendid stock in his line in Chicago, he adheres to the policy he has practiced so successfully for the past five years."

The panic raged. While other stores about him continued to crash, or staged frantic sales, Potter Palmer shipped in more goods. Banks went down. Leading wholesale houses closed their doors. Michigan Southern railroad stocks fell from 88 to 9, pacing a general decline. Dry-goods prices collapsed. But Palmer, buying his merchandise from wholesalers and importers at panic lows, could undersell competitors and still make profits. Unlike them, he had not been caught with heavy inventories of goods bought at inflated prices.

And, like Cooley, Farwell and Company, he missed the ravages of a second calamity that befell Chicago. On October 19, 1857, fire, starting in a nearby brothel, swept the dry-goods district. Twenty-one persons died in the flames, and 10,000 attended their mass funeral in City Hall Square two days later. Damage was estimated at $675,000. Subsequent investigation disclosed that the fire department lacked hose and pumping equipment, that water supplies were inadequate, and that vicious resorts like the one where the blaze originated were common and tolerated by the police.

"What we have just witnessed is but a slight breaking out of the volcanic fires that are burning under our feet," said the Rev. W. W. King, of St. Paul's Church, with prophetic gloom. "It is shameful to witness that complicity between authority and vice and crime by which our city is cursed and degraded."

But neither fire nor panic could stop Chicago. Grain prices dropped from $2.00 to $1.00 a bushel; wheat, hog, beef, and lumber receipts fell; railroad earnings declined 25 to 33 per cent; and soup kitchens were opened for the city's 10,000 unemployed. But Chicago and the West swiftly recovered. Early in 1858, $4,000,000 of new buildings were planned. There was talk of spending $600,000 to improve the Illinois and Michigan Canal. The City Council proposed deepening the Chicago River, and a street-raising project moved ahead at an eventual cost of $10,000,000.

Nor did the ladies let panic discourage them. New low prices touched off a buying frenzy. "The panic has brought business upon us!" happily exclaimed *Hunt's Merchant's Magazine.* "It has brought us the lady buyer!"

In New York a writer for *Harper's Magazine* went to A. T. Stewart's to see what went on at those endless "bargain sales" Stewart staged throughout the panic. "I had to storm *cheveaux de frise* of hoops to reach the counter," he wrote. "Observe your wife at dry goods if you would know her. She may be sweet in the parlor, but she is like a ghoul at the counter, as if she might steal a dress or tear out the eyes of a clerk who refused to abate the price. . . . The shopping mania is a disease peculiar to women. It is a species of insanity."

In Chicago the ladies flocked to Potter Palmer's new store, already known to them for quality goods at low prices. As the depression ended, other merchants found that bargain sales had enabled them to survive. Despite earlier closing announcements, both T. B. Carter and W. M. Ross continued in business, the latter reorganizing as Ross & Gossage. But Potter Palmer had leaped ahead of them. While they sustained losses, he made profits. His gross sales in the new store were running $120,000 ahead of 1857. Within a few short months Palmer was again ready to expand, and to restore his wholesale division.

Walter and Edward Wright, Chicago lawyers, were building a splendid marble-fronted business block, five stories high, at 112-116 Lake Street on the site of buildings destroyed in the October fire. It was initially intended that three firms would occupy the block, but Potter Palmer leased it all, arranging with the owners to cut archways through the first-floor side walls to give him the most extensive display space for dry goods of any store in the West.

Palmer's grand opening in his new marble palace was on September 23, 1858. Newspapers dispatched their reporters, who came away goggle-eyed at the vast assortment of fine goods, fetchingly displayed. They hailed Palmer as "the A. T.

Stewart of the West." The building, effused the *Chicago Tribune*, was "one of the finest and most costly business blocks in the United States. It is opened as a first class dry goods house by P. Palmer, one of our best established and most widely known merchants. He carries with him to his new quarters (a block east of his former location) a business reputation and standing in itself a fortune to any house, and he is prepared to expand to complete the occupation."

"P. Palmer, Dry Goods and Carpets" dominated Lake Street in the early 1860's.

The west portion of the first floor, the *Tribune* noted, was a "magnificent sales room fitted up tastefully and well, and after the manner of first class stores and with perfect system." A carpet hall filled the other half of the floor, at its rear "a gem of an apartment which the fair shopper will readily appreciate as a shawl and mantilla room."

In this new store Potter Palmer dominated Lake Street. He was the town's big advertiser. Almost daily he announced the arrival of new goods: real English carpets, velvet Brussels, fine silks and embroideries, Balmoral mantle shawls. Always he reminded the public that Palmer's offered the best bargains. "Possessing facilities not enjoyed by any other firm in the trade," his inevitable postscript read, "I am prepared to offer DRY GOODS at less prices than any other house in this city." He advertised, too, to the wholesale trade, promising to undersell any competitor. He sent out more commercial travelers.

His fame grew and spread. Among the visitors to his new store was one from New York, representing Rowland H. Macy, who had just opened his own dry-goods establishment after failing in business in Superior, Wisconsin. Palmer himself did the honors, pointing out the efficient organization of his various departments, the attractive displays, the cash boys, errand boys, and wrappers who saved the time of the clerks. Later, when Macy became famous, Potter Palmer loved to boast that the New York merchant got his best ideas from him.

III

By 1860, the nation moved toward the War between the States. Palmer had no interest in politics. But he was quick to see that a showdown between the North and the South might cut off sources of cotton and boost prices of cotton textiles. While others, jittery from war scares, began to sell and prices dropped, Palmer started to buy. It was said northern markets would collapse should the South withdraw its trade, yet Palmer was unworried. He was looking west. On April 12, 1861, the Charleston batteries opened fire on Fort Sumter, and three months later troops clashed at Bull Run. The nation knew at last it had a war in its midst though there were few to foresee its duration or to predict its cost.

Potter Palmer continued to buy. He stuffed warehouses with cotton goods. Then supplies fell off and prices began to rise. In the first year of the war American spinning mills shut down one-third of the time. A year later they were operating one-quarter to one-half time. The British textile industry was demoralized. Eastern cities lost their southern market, as predicted. Over the country, 6,000 commercial houses failed, 2,000 more than in 1857. Cincinnati and St. Louis, on the perimeter of the war, were cut off from much of their trade territory.

But Chicago boomed. Central to the country's biggest railroad network, the city became a collecting point of foodstuffs not only for the army, but much of the East as well. Within two years, Chicago grain receipts jumped from 31,000,000 to 56,000,000 bushels, and the town had become the world's biggest pork-packing center. As farm boys went to war, the demand for farm machinery made in Chicago increased. Railroad profits tripled. New factories opened to make military equipment. Horse-railway lines were built from one end of town to the other to carry busy workers and buyers. Not even the failure of scores of Illinois state banks could halt Chicago's stride.

Potter Palmer, with his unlimited supplies of cheaply bought goods, was in the forefront of the war prosperity. Now he informed the public: "I have the largest stock of goods west of New York City, bought before the late advance in price and it will be sold invariably 10 per cent less than can be bought elsewhere in this city." At the same time he disclosed the arrival of fifty bales of cotton sheeting and 200,000 cotton bags.

Early in the war he announced for the first time in the newspapers his "on approval" policy for out-of-town customers: "Notice to country customers. I will send by express, to customers in any part of the country, promptly, patterns of different styles of DRESS GOODS, SILKS, SHAWLS, CLOAKS, EMBROIDERIES, Or any kind of DRY GOODS, from which the customer may select or not, at pleasure, ..."

Customers needed only to pay the express charges one way on goods they did not care to buy. Palmer again explained his ability to undersell competitors: "Buying my dress goods entirely by the package for cash, I can and will sell them 20 per cent less than can be bought elsewhere."

Then, on November 26, 1861, came Palmer's famous announcement of a money-back guarantee on all his goods, published that morning in the *Tribune* and the following day in the *Journal:* "Notice. Purchases made at my establishment that prove unsatisfactory either in price, quality or style, can be returned (to the Cashier's Desk) for which the purchase money will be with pleasure returned. P. Palmer."

IV

Though they had been less foresighted than Palmer, Cooley and Farwell also were profiting by Chicago's war boom. There had been a complete break with Wadsworth. The business was rapidly expanding, and the partners needed an additional trustworthy hand. One was available. In his serious but quiet way Marshall Field, their commercial traveler, had made it known he wanted in. He had been corresponding with his former employer, Deacon Davis, in Pittsfield. Now the good deacon offered to make Field a full partner in his enlarged store. Field hinted that the offer had its attractions.

He got action. Farwell long had regarded Marshall Field as a young man with an absolute passion for merchandising. He

Palmer's ads startled his rivals but pleased his customers. Both of the ads, appearing late in 1861, offered buyers the unheard-of privilege of returning any unsatisfactory wares. This idea has prevailed in the 100-year history of Marshall Field & Company.

At the right is the ad of Farwell, Field & Co., formed in 1864, the first firm in which Marshall Field's name appeared as a partner.

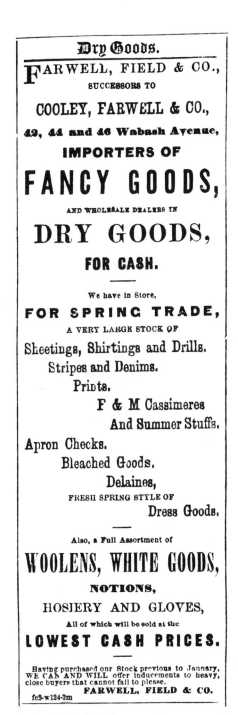

and Cooley agreed to accept Field as a junior partner and to give him $3,000 a year as his "share of the profits." Field was put in charge of sales and credit. Farwell was responsible for the company's financial affairs. Cooley made long buying trips to New York, finally moving there permanently. The problem now was not selling goods, but getting them.

Swiftly, Marshall Field proved he was exactly the man for his job. He managed the corps of salesmen with system and precision. He kept the company's clerks at work until ten or eleven o'clock at night. With Field setting the example, employees worked all day selling to customers, then returned at night to push trucks from one department to another, gathering the goods they had sold and preparing them for shipment. Then Field would stay on, helping the entry clerks with their records.

Within a year, Cooley and Farwell bought out Wadsworth and offered Field a full partnership for $15,000. Field had saved $4,000 since his arrival in Chicago and could borrow an additional $1,000 from his family. He got the rest from Cooley, who loaned it at 6 per cent, with the stipulation that the money should be paid back out of Field's share of the profits. Back to New York went Cooley, there to fret over his health and the strange buying antics of his chief rival, Potter Palmer.

Palmer, too, had opened a New York office, at 20 Reade Street, and spent much of his time in the East. His volume of business was enormous. He purchased the entire output of some factories, selling the goods to retail stores and other wholesalers without ever receiving them in his own warehouses. He dispatched his own buyers to Europe. In a single shipment, he sent to his Chicago store 1,000 packages of shirtings, sheetings, ticks, stripes, denims, and flannels.

Cooley wrote to Marshall Field from New York, "I took dinner today at the same table with Mr. Sheldon of Buckley, Sheldon & Co. He remarked that Palmer was a strange chap. He did not know what to make of him, etc. etc. & remarked that he [Palmer] had been buying goods at high prices . . . . the same thing I had noticed. . . . I stopped buying and he [Palmer] is in no better shape than we are. . . . I *may be* wrong."

Cooley was wrong. Prices continued to soar so that by 1864 they were almost double those of 1861. Field, selling everything he could get, was annoyed at Cooley's inaction. Palmer's methods were more to his liking. Farwell also was irked and wanted to quit; he wrote to Cooley, asking him to find a buyer. But Cooley, chronically ill, did nothing.

The opportunity was one that might not again be found. Desperately Field sought capital which would enable him to buy out Farwell. He even approached William McCormick for aid from his brother, Cyrus, the Reaper King. Before William could get a decision from Cyrus, Cooley insisted on leaving.

A new firm was hastily patched together, Farwell, Field and Company. As junior partner, Field and Farwell agreed on Levi Z. Leiter, who had served as head bookkeeper and accountant under Cooley at the unusually high salary of $2,500 a year. Leiter had been in Chicago since 1854, having come from his job as a dry-goods clerk in his home town of Leitersburg, Maryland, founded in 1760 by an ancestor, James Van Leiter, a Dutch Calvinist. Leiter's great aptitude was for figures. Burly, brusque, with a set of bushy whiskers, he showed great enthusiasm for any policies curbing credit. "Cash the rule, credit the exception," was his motto.

Despite personal coolness between Farwell and Field, the firm made money. Field went to New York to buy on the scale Palmer had been buying, while prices went higher. Trade was generally spurred everywhere by the new national bank law of 1863 which stabilized currency. Within three months after partnership contracts had been signed, the firm enlarged its quarters to care for the goods Field was shipping from New

York. Month by month the company's customers were informed that the market was "very firm—tendency upward."

Three months more, and the *Tribune* ranked Farwell and Field above Potter Palmer in the category of wholesale trade.

"Scarcely any department of the trade of the Northwest has displayed more progress than the dry goods trade of Chicago," the paper continued. "A few years back there was business scarcely sufficient to keep more than one or two establishments moderately busy and then the merchants from the interior of Illinois, Iowa, Wisconsin and Indiana bought from New York, St. Louis and Cincinnati. All this is changed now. Outside of New York, Chicago is the market of the West."

But the Field and Farwell personalities continued to clash. Field was determined to get out. He could command $200,000 of capital, derived in part from the dry-goods business and also from wartime investments in railroads, real estate, and the new national banks. Leiter, eager to join him, had $100,000.

Again Field talked to William McCormick, this time of his plan to start a new wholesale house. William liked the idea, writing Cyrus they should get rid of the grain gamblers they were then involved with to join "the quiet, gentlemanly capitalists" in wholesale dry goods. Marshall Field, wrote William, "is a close, calculating and safe business man who devotes himself to his business." Cyrus was slow to reply. Weeks went by. Then, William wrote again, informing him it was too late.

The crinoline fashion, which achieved this extreme in the 1860's, had proved a boon to dry-goods merchants who happily supplied the necessary quantities of yard goods.

Potter Palmer was the man who acted. The hard, driving years had taken his health, and late in 1864 his physician told him he would have to quit. Palmer was only thirty-eight, trim, somewhat grim-faced, with a trace of gray in beard and hair. He was rich, though, and could afford to quit. But who would carry on? His brother, Milton, who was one of his salesmen? Milton was not the man for it.

There had been talk in the clubs of Marshall Field's overtures to William McCormick. Leiter, some said, was in on it too. They seemed likely prospects. Palmer admired them both as solid men who had matched him in the wholesale trade and had $300,000 between them. So, just before Christmas, Palmer made an offer. He would sell them his business, wholesale and retail, at 20 per cent below the inventory value if they would take Milton as a junior partner. There was an added inducement. Palmer promised to leave $330,000 in the firm and remain as a silent "special partner." Milton would contribute $50,000 to a total capitalization of $750,000.

Palmer's price seemed high, but the opportunity was a rare one. The partnership with Farwell was drawing to an end. In January, 1865, as the end of the War between the States approached, with prices still at their wartime peak, Field and Leiter accepted Potter Palmer's offer. With the scratching of their signatures on a voluminous contract they became the nominal heads of Field, Palmer, and Leiter.

Palmer made ready for a European vacation which, he said, would last three years. Again the newspapers hailed him. "One of the most successful business men of the age," said the *Tribune*. "He has unquestionably done more than any other citizen of Chicago to build up the city's trade." With his retirement, said some of the editorials, a fabulous era in merchandising was ending. They were wrong. It was only beginning.

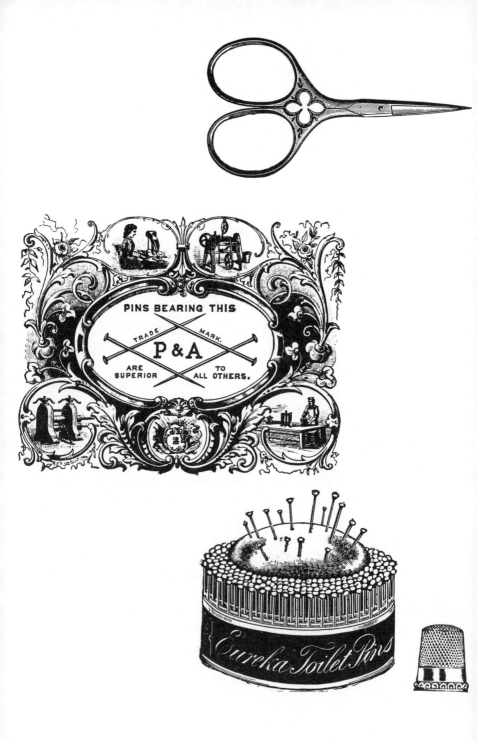

SILKS, SATINS,
AND YANKEE NOTIONS

The new partners hailed the occasion on January 17, 1865, with an advertisement that had little of John V. Farwell's conservatism and more of Potter Palmer's gusto. Their business cards made it clear that they were "Successors to P. Palmer." To Palmer's old customers they pledged themselves to continue his policies. And they looked forward to good days.

But in April the Confederacy collapsed. The War between the States was over. Prices plummeted. Merchants throughout the North went into bankruptcy. Others vainly pleaded with customers to take off their hands the merchandise they had purchased at inflated prices. Field, Palmer, and Leiter were caught with heavy inventories like the rest. "Low Prices!" cried their advertisements. "Low Prices!" And then: "Panic Prices! We are selling our Stock at Panic Prices!"

By underselling competitors, as Potter Palmer had done, the partners continued to attract a lively business, but their losses were heavy. They appealed to Palmer, who had hurried back from Europe, cutting his planned three years of vacation to three months. Glumly, Field and Leiter outlined the situation. Calamity was certain if they continued their sales at ruinous prices. Their own finances were insufficient to absorb the shock. But Potter Palmer . . . . perhaps he would buy back his store?

Palmer, freshened by his brief travels, optimistic when others despaired, had no such intention. The fate of his own $330,-000 did not worry him. He urged them to take heart, recalling his own experiences in the Panic of 1857.

"Why, boys," he shouted, "if I take it all back now, you'll lose 50 cents on every dollar. You listen to me and stay in business. This day of low prices won't last. Take my advice. Go into the market and buy all you can. Buy! You buy and think faster than the fellow down the street, and you'll come out all right."

To help the partners pay their most pressing bills, Palmer bought back $25,000 of Field's original investment. But more had to be done to steady the new firm. Conference after conference was held in Leiter's bachelor rooms at the Sherman House or late into the night in Field's little office on the second floor of the store. And out of these meetings came the moves that yielded millions in decades to come.

A corps of "bright young men" was added to the staff that had served Palmer. Each was given specific duties and assured that attention to work—plus results—would win a bonus of $200 a year. To Farwell's irritation, some of his most promising employees were easily lured to the new store. Harlow N. Higinbotham, a tall, raw-boned veteran of the city's Mercantile Battery in the war, was appointed bookkeeper and assistant to the canny Leiter in judging who would or would not be given credit. Henry J. Willing, once a star salesman for T. B. Carter, took command of the calico section, one of the store's largest and most popular. Lorenzo Woodhouse, a sedate fellow still in his middle twenties, was hired as a buyer. Two of Farwell's best salesmen also came: the McWilliams brothers—John, a war hero who showed up on his first workday still in uniform, and Lafayette, only twenty-two but a wizard at speedy sales.

Field's two brothers, Joseph and Henry, also joined the company. In the years since working with Marshall in Pittsfield,

Henry Field (*top*) joined his brothers Marshall and Joseph in the company.

Harlow N. Higinbotham (*bottom*), later a civic leader, helped keep the ledgers.

(*Right*) January 17, 1865, Field and Leiter announced themselves as P. Palmer's successors, indicating they, too, planned to please the ladies.

Joseph had gone on to Sioux City, Iowa, then to Omaha, where he had risen to the post of cashier of the Omaha National Bank. Henry, youngest and handsomest of the brothers, had clerked for Cooley, Farwell and Company in 1861 and stepped along with Marshall in each new venture. Now both were hired as general salesmen. Another salesman was Montgomery Ward, who remembered years later when he became head of his huge mail-order house, that his salary was $23.08 every two weeks.

To offset the competition of Farwell, Leiter was urged to relax his strict credit rules and his insistence on a thirty-day limit for payment. Leiter grumbled and growled. He was fiercely proud of the credit system he carried over to the new firm after setting it up at Farwell, Field and Company. Leiter was a strict believer in the short-time, prompt-paying theory, and it was a rare customer who could persuade him to allow more than sixty days to pay his debts.

Applicants for credit underwent a careful screening and scrutiny before Leiter would tug at his reddish whiskers, nod his grizzled head, and shove papers before them to sign. He knew from many sources a lot more about these credit-seekers than they realized. The store's traveling salesmen telegraphed tidbits of gossip they had heard about the financial condition of small-town customers. Friendly letters from bankers, lawyers, and railroad station agents came regularly to both Field and Leiter from dozens of towns in the Northwest, each containing pieces of information. Field studied carefully the growth of population and condition of crops in the areas from which the applicants came and passed on the data to Leiter.

Prominent on Leiter's stand-up desk were the volumes of credit commercial ratings issued by such companies as Hurst and Garlock, Bradstreet's, and Dun and Barlow. Even if credit had been granted, no goods left the store unless Leiter or Higinbotham signed the sales tags personally. Always a last-minute check was made for any developments that might prevent the merchant from paying on time; if such were found, the orders were held up.

Many prospective wholesale customers, indignant at such strictures, often stalked from Leiter's office in anger. But those who passed his tests not only were granted credit but knew they were getting the best wares available in the Middle West, reasonable prices, and special discounts when they paid promptly.

With Leiter's credit methods Field found little fault. "No man is good," he liked to say, "who does not pay his debts, no matter how wealthy he may be." He himself paid promptly in cash and insisted the store do likewise, even if this meant borrowing at high interest rates.

But now he realized that too strict an application of Leiter's credit regulations might be ruinous. Since so many small merchants were faced with the same falling prices and unsettled postwar conditions, the best-intentioned, he advised, might go bankrupt if pressed for prompt payment; or they might go over to those wholesalers who would grant them as long as a year to pay. Leiter was forced to agree, and during this panicky period he extended the previous ten- and thirty-day limits to ninety days and even four months.

The move proved wise. The grateful customers got the breathing spell they needed. By the time payment was due many had recovered from the momentary slump and were more eager to deal with those smart young successors to P. Palmer.

II

The big step that helped Field and Leiter survive this crisis was the intensification of their efforts to keep the ladies happy with what they could buy in the retail section. Low prices, of course, were a definite attraction, but a fleeting one. They alone, Field felt, could not make their store a favored shopping place.

There must be goods of the best quality, attractively presented. Customers must receive courteous and considerate treatment. Nothing should be done that seemed little or petty. A feeling must exist that the customer could trust the store. And Field and Leiter would be alert to what the ladies wanted—or ought to be made to want.

To speed the store's pace in keeping up with the latest styles, Field set out for New York to take charge of the firm's Broadway office. For two years he would serve there, except for occasional trips back to Chicago, watching the fashion trends, keeping his eyes on what the great A. T. Stewart did, ordering latest imports from Paris, sending on stocks in good condition to grubby Lake Street.

To entice the ladies further, the partners set up a spanking new department—notions.

Other dry-goods establishments featured such "Yankee Notions" as sewing needles, dressmakers' tapes, threads, hairpins, curlers, and similar small daily necessities. Some stores carried such dubious items as Hogan's Magnolia Balm—"Will Eliminate tan, freckles, ring marks and moth patches, or a Red, Rustic Face." Others praised the seductive effect of such scents as "Bloom of Youth," "Liquid Pearl," or "Kiss-Me-Quick," a perfume, its makers claimed, distilled from fragrant tulips.

But in their notions section Field, Palmer, and Leiter had better attractions. They specialized in wares not only to please the "shawl shoppers" who came with baskets on their arms, but also the fine ladies who drove up in their sparkling phaetons. Here a woman could find combs and brushes and spools of thread, but near these prosaic articles were gay sun umbrellas with handles of carved wood, ivory, or twisted metal. Here were buttons, elastics, and scissors, while on a rack hung a dozen Bon Ton Hova skirts, "the most elegant, useful, and serviceable skirt in America." Back in an inconspicuous corner

of this section was tucked a counter with such men's goods—
"Gents' Furnishings"—as suspenders, ties, and shirt fronts.

To make women more at ease in purchasing skirts or frocks
or lingerie, three female clerks were hired. For an added bit of
distinction to the entrance, two men were employed to sweep
the stretch of street in front of the store, and three times a day
the pair moved brushes up and down the wooden blocks with
which Lake Street had recently been paved.

Above all, their daring goods-on-approval policy remained
steadfast with Field, Palmer, and Leiter. For most women this
notice, appearing in the months following the momentary panic,
was the best reason of all for trading at the store: "IF, WHEN YOU
GET YOUR GOODS HOME, AND DO NOT FIND THEM ENTIRELY SATIS-
FACTORY, PLEASE RETURN THEM AND YOUR MONEY WILL BE RE-
FUNDED."

The "careful" merchants continued to shake their heads at
these practices just as they had done when Palmer printed his
startling offer to take back unsatisfactory goods. In New York,
A. T. Stewart himself, learning how Field and Leiter had enlarged on Palmer's ideas, bristled and predicted pompously that
such methods would lead them to certain disaster.

Stewart was wrong and so were the local skeptics. Some
women did try to take advantage of the partners, and for years
there would always be those who sought to cheat on their
return policy. But the firm's losses through such practices were
small when marked up against the profits and good will the unusual policy built. Even those who tried to cheat were overlooked—the first time. Clerks were advised that, except for the
chronic tricksters whom they could recognize, they should refund money even if they were certain that this sacque or that
plaited skirt had really been worn since being purchased.

So the ladies came, bought, and carried home their goods in
bags stamped "Field, Palmer and Leiter." The store had only

one horse and a two-wheeled dray, used chiefly to bear goods from the railroad stations or docks or to wholesale buyers in other parts of the city. As yet there was no delivery system for these retail customers. A cash boy, however, might tote the ladies' purchases to a waiting carriage, or even to their homes, for a 10-cent tip. Stock boys on the wholesale floors often added to their $3.00 weekly wage by carrying bundles to the railroad stations for the out-of-town merchants. These men usually tipped as much as 25 cents.

Sales climbed. So did prices. Field, buying in New York, as Potter Palmer had advised during the days of the postwar panic, piled up low-cost goods for the store. As Palmer had done in 1857 and 1858, the partners now offered quality merchandise at prices their competitors were unable to meet.

"Under *NEW YORK* prices!" they boasted to wholesale and retail customers. "We guarantee to make *LOWER PRICES* than any House in Chicago and as Low as any in New York!"

And when their first year ended, despite their fright in the spring panic, the ensuing national turmoil, and the skepticism with which their methods were received by more experienced merchants, Field, Palmer, and Leiter had reason to be happy. Their carefully kept ledgers showed a sales volume for the year of $8,000,000, of which some $300,000 was clear profit.

III

It was, of course, in the wholesale business where most of these profits had been made although Field realized the enormous prestige and popularity to be gained by maintaining the retail division.

The reason for the huge wholesale trade was obvious. The Northwest was blooming more than ever with new railroad lines and new towns. The business that Chicago had grabbed from St. Louis and her other rivals during the War between the

States continued to increase. "Chicago has kept her exchange accounts even," wrote that indomitable booster, John Stephen Wright. "The grain merchant gets a bill of exchange. This is transferred to the Chicago dry goods and grocery merchant. To every point from whence comes grain to the Chicago market, Chicago dry goods and grocery merchants send bills of goods. Every Northwestern town is visited by the Chicago merchants and orders are solicited."

There was considerable truth even in Wright's exaggerations. Not only the small towns but the bigger cities seemed to be overrun with Chicago's traveling salesmen. In Kansas they called the brash fellows "drummers." In embittered St. Louis the local gentry tagged them with a name that would remain as a symbol of excessive boasting—"blowhards."

With jests on their lips, they invaded cities, hamlets, farms, villages. They carried funny papers and joke books, but the text most widely used was John R. Walsh's popular *Chicago Jokes and Anecdotes for Railroad Travelers and Fun Lovers*, printed, its publisher noted, to bring a light touch to a "time when the mind of man is strained almost to the utmost tension in making money."

At a crossroads store or hotel lobby, a blowhard could prove himself a wit of sorts by dipping into Walsh's volume. If those in his territory frowned on newcomers still trekking from New England, he could quip, "Know how to revive a drowned Yankee? Jest search his pockets!" Or he might tell the latest he-she joke—He: "Sally, keep away from me or you will set me afire." She: "No danger of that, you are too green to burn!" And if his customer favored puns, the drummer was well supplied with these witticisms: "Why is a literary man like a pig in a sty? Because he's confined to a pen!" or "Why is a jailer in danger of becoming corrupted? Because he keeps bad company."

In a saloon a salesman always got a laugh, what with all this nonsense about women's rights and suffrage, with a Walsh inspired toast—"To woman! Now and forever, one and insufferable!" And, in parting, he could cry out, "Well, drop me a line if you wish to see me, as the fish said to the angler."

But the blowhard and the more reserved commercial traveler both brought huge volumes of business to Chicago. Marshall Field preferred to have his customers ride into town to see his wares and place their orders. Yet, when his rivals sent more salesmen on the road, he and Leiter did likewise.

IV

The wholesale business, plus the lively retail trade in Chicago, meant quick prosperity for Field and Leiter. New customers were added, few were lost. Competitors were pressed hard. So well was the new firm doing, that in July, 1866, no less a rival than John Villiers Farwell seemed ready to yield.

In a letter to Field marked "CONFIDENTIAL," Farwell wrote, "As you are aware I have given but little attention to business for some time, being anxious to retire entirely from active business and go abroad for a few years of rest. . . .

"Notwithstanding I have thought that you and Leiter had given me such treatment as at least I should not have expected, still I can forget the past and any injury I may have sustained & should you desire to rent my store and succeed to my business on first of Jany next, I will entertain a proposition from you favorably. Our business was never in better shape to run smoothly than it is at present."

But Field was in no mood or position to accept the offer. He and Leiter had enough business to handle without taking on more. Overexpansion was a thing to be avoided like the deadliest epidemic, Field perennially warned. His "bright young men" had been molded into a smooth-working organization. Willing, especially, had proved adept at more than managing the calico section and was now in wholesale to try out his ideas on cutting down waste motion in filling large orders. Higinbotham proved a real disciple of Leiter's, as careful as the older man in granting credit. The clerks were busy; orders from the traveling salesmen streamed in.

A second note from Farwell came in November. "I will say confidentially," he wrote, "that if you wish to buy our stock and rent our store, terms can be made satisfactory. I will talk with you on the subject." This offer also went unheeded. Field and Leiter had other plans. They brought to an end the two-year contract with the Palmers. Milton withdrew part of his capital and so did Potter, although the older brother, despite schemes for other ventures that would bring him great fame and more riches, was especially reluctant to leave the profitable dry-goods business. He suggested that he keep a financial hand in some of the firm's affairs, and the two partners agreed to let him retain part of his original investment.

Shortly the firm's name became "Field, Leiter and Company." On the new stationery, Leiter penned gleeful tidings to Field, who had hustled back to New York to bid for the latest shipments of the incredibly popular Alexandre kid gloves.

Potter Palmer, he wrote, had "pressed me very hard to keep more of his money, and when the matter of M. J. [Palmer] came up I agreed to take $25,000 of his to July 1 at 10% and then I took $25,000 more of PP on 10 days' call after 60 days at 7%. He wanted me to take more but I told him I did not want it. I thought it best to take their amounts as it would enable us to take advantage of all short time discounts without borrowing from anyone else. . . . . The retail rooms are looking splendidly."

1868

THE MARBLE PALACE

When Potter Palmer offered Field and Leiter "very handsome terms" in 1865 to take over his Lake Street store, some cynics in Chicago maintained Palmer, that sly one, had anticipated falling prices and shoved his inflated stocks on two innocents. Events of the months that followed almost proved them right. Others doubted Palmer was as ill as his doctors said he was, and they chuckled when he returned from his three months' trip to Europe—"That Potter'll be up to something soon. He's got something up his fancy sleeve."

Palmer did. Quietly he began to invest much of his available cash in real estate. Land values after the war had dropped, and many wealthy men were buying tracts on the limits of the city to build residential subdivisions. But Palmer scorned such districts. Week after week he went along, buying first this shack, then that building, a blacksmith shop here, a saloon there, and on, of all places, State Street.

State Street was narrow, grimy, and slovenly. Along its rickety walks ranged twine and cordage shops, tailor shops, cheap hotels, spice stores, coffee stores, groceries, butcher shops, and bookstalls—all in unsightly confusion. Although a proposal to improve this north-south thoroughfare had been a topic of lusty debate in the City Council for years, the street had been left to grow by itself. It did have a streetcar line, but the vehicles, "bobtailed" cars—drawn by horses and running on a single rail—often jumped the track into the mud.

Many Chicagoans scoffed at Palmer's new venture. He was lucky to have so much money of his own—$2,500,000 in cash and securities and an equal amount in government bonds—for few of the big bankers would have financed his wild scheme. People giggled when he hired builders to move back the properties he had purchased—those low boardinghouses, grogshops and tumbledown meat markets—and strode from store to store arguing with other owners to do likewise. A few yielded, but most shunned his plan. Soon State Street was more ragtag than ever, some stores set back twenty feet from the next.

Palmer's motives grew clearer. It was still true that property on Lake Street was the costliest in Chicago, the corner of Lake and Clark streets near his old store being adjudged just about the best business spot in town and selling for $2,000 a front foot. Yet Palmer, as always, looked ahead. Lake Street was doomed as the city grew bigger, if not this year, then the next, or in five years. On a hot day the women who came shopping on Lake Street still had to hold their lace handkerchiefs to their noses to ward off the smells of the filthy river. "The Street of Merchants," bursting with stores, warehouses, and shops, was approaching its limits, said Palmer, and the time had come to move.

To give dramatic reality to his idea, Palmer tore down a jungle of shacks and hovels at the south end of his stretch of new State Street properties. Here he would erect a hotel, he declared, and it would be called the Palmer House, stand eight stories high, have 225 rooms and cost $300,000. And near the north end, at State and Washington streets, a second corps of architects and contractors, avowed Palmer, would soon go to work on another huge building. It would cost $350,000 and stand six stories, built of limestone and Canaan marble and

In 1865 "bobtailed" cars passed a tombstone carver's at State and Washington. On this site Potter Palmer would build a marble palace for Field and Leiter.

fronted by Corinthian columns. It sounded, Palmer hinted, like an ideal location and site for a "dry-goods palace." The two projects, together with the purchase of other land on the street, cost Palmer some $2,000,000.

Palmer himself had no intention of actively leaping back into the dry-goods world. But he thought he knew the logical ones to occupy his marble palace. State Street, he declaimed to Field and Leiter, was the center of the city's future trade. He pictured to them the eminence of the building to be finished by the summer of 1868. Some day, he bellowed, State Street would be one of the world's great business thoroughfares.

Field and Leiter were easy to convince. An onrush of business had cramped their Lake Street quarters all through 1867. The women still came, of course, but mud still spurted from between the wooden blocks on wet days, and the street itself was crowded more than ever with stevedores, sidewalk peddlers, water-front loungers, and fishmongers.

Palmer was asking the lofty rental of $50,000 a year for his store. But it might well be worth it. By moving to State Street

83

Field and Leiter saw their chance to expand their retail business, to lead a march of other merchants to a new trade center, to grow as Chicago and the nation's heartland grew.

II

For the rest of the year and into the spring of 1868 the partners waited for the building to be completed. They continued to advertise "Quality Goods," and when imports lagged they opened their "Ladies' Cloak Department," with products from workrooms they established on the top floor of the store. Proudly they announced that these cloaks were of a "great variety of new and beautiful designs of our own manufacture."

As in the retail section they emphasized to their wholesale customers their "return policy." They were still the only ones in the city to follow such a method. Not even the second biggest house, that of John V. Farwell, would hold with such unbusinesslike nonsense. Farwell's men stamped on all bills the unmistakable warning: "POSITIVELY NO GOODS WILL BE TAKEN BACK UNLESS DAMAGED WHEN DELIVERED."

But Field and Leiter affirmed that they would take back any goods "if not entirely approved" and "at our expense." They did all they could to assure their hinterland customers they would be amply protected in case prices dropped. "Should there be any change," read a typical circular, "we guarantee to make you the very lowest prices upon every article. Our constant aim will be to make it to the interest of all merchants in the Northwest to make Chicago their market for dry goods."

Thousands of small merchants in the Middle West welcomed these pledges as eagerly as the ladies of Chicago took to the same promise in the retail department. Many dropped their accounts with wholesalers in other cities and began to order from the Chicago drummers, not only those employed by Field and Leiter but even those representing their competitors.

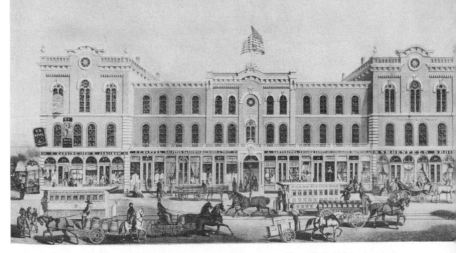
Chicago in the 1860's had no right-hand, left-hand traffic rules. Here in the Uhlich Block on Clark Street dray wagons and carriages travel at random.

When government figures showed that Chicago had at least fifty-nine firms whose annual sales exceeded one million dollars, while the city's trade foes, Cincinnati and St. Louis, each had only fifteen, the *Chicago Tribune* crowed, "Hereafter the pre-eminence of Chicago as the metropolitan city of the Northwest will be a matter of record. Figures sometimes lie, but the truth of these must be so indubitable that we suspect we shall hear no more from either of the rival wood stations on the Ohio and Mississippi about their aspirations to be reckoned as rivals of Chicago."

III

By October, 1868, "Palmer's Palace" was ready.

For ten days before the formal opening of the new store—"Largest and Finest in America," cried the newspapers—the stock was moved from Lake Street. Each night, half a dozen employees, led by John Devlin, a big-muscled Irish stock boy, stood guard over the towering piles of goods.

One midnight Devlin thought he caught a prowler on the fourth floor of the store. Startled by the man's footsteps, he drew his revolver and yelled, "Halt or I'll shoot!"

The man, stepping from behind a post, was Potter Palmer. "I just had to walk around and see this store," Palmer said happily. "It's a marvel, isn't it? Young man, you are an alert fellow. I hope you will always be so alert. I commend you highly for your vigilance."

On the Saturday night of October 10, the last of the retail goods came over in trucks and carts. Next morning the newspapers carried the announcement: "Our Entire Stock is now removed to State and Washington Streets and will be open for sale Monday. . . . . If the weather is favorable the entire building will be thrown open and we shall be happy to have the public look through it."

On the same day, F. N. Hamlin, the merchant whose trademark was "The Sign of the Golden Eagle," took two full columns in the newspapers to announce: "Sale! Sale! Great Inducements in Dry Goods!" At another grand opening down the street Charles Tobey festooned the front of his furniture and upholstery store with Chinese lanterns. But neither could match the brilliance of Field, Leiter and Company's gala opening.

Hundreds watched from the streets and sidewalks as barouches, landaus, and phaetons drove up and men and women— "a dazzling assemblage," commented the *Tribune*—marched into the store past doors held open by freshly scrubbed boys wearing blue uniforms with brass buttons. All the partners, senior and junior, stood by to greet the visitors. Each man received an expensive cigar, each woman a rose. "For once," remarked the *Chicago Times*, "the women came not so much to be seen as to see."

Those who rode the steam elevators to the top floor viewed a special section where men did nothing but pack and crate.

Chicago's pride in 1868: Potter Palmer's marble palace, built for Field and Leiter, which began the march of merchants from Lake Street to State Street.

These huskies hammered together boxes of merchandise, fastened bales of silk and shawls, used brush and ink to write the names and places where the boxes were to be sent. Then the goods were lowered to the ground floors in the elevators—"Strong enough to carry a three-ton safe," bragged one operator—and hauled in wagons, drays, and trucks to boat landings and railroad depots.

The upper floors were devoted to wholesale stocks, such "Fancy Goods" as woolen Balmoral petticoats, hoop skirts, perfumes, soaps, and hosiery; counter upon counter of gloves, white goods, linens, woolen clothes, cassimeres, flannels, blankets, cotton goods, dress goods, muslins.

But the big attraction was the main floor—the retail floor. The counters were of walnut, the walls frescoed, and the gas fixtures were designed to throw shafts of light on the dazzling display. In the cloak department there were satin and striped silks at $19 a yard and embroidered silk robes in rose and white at $125; rich velvet cloaks lined with sable and a striped plush Bedouin opera cape trimmed with cord and tassels; sealskin cloaks and black and white astrakhans. Nearby in the shawl department the ladies were enchanted by Persian cashmeres selling from $400 to $1,200 and Paisleys from $15 to $175 and point-lace shawls for as much as $300. Not far away was a new "Gents' Furnishings Goods" with cravats, scarves, Norwood Watch Guard neckties, cardigan jackets and Scotch tweeds in green and brown, French broadcloth.

A "Ladies' Suit Department" featured the latest styles from Paris: a green-and-black-silk striped ensemble; another with

PARIS IMPORTED DRESSES.
From Field, Leiter & Co.

Steel fashion plates advertise Field and Leiter's Parisian imports in the *Chicago Magazine of Fashion, Music and Home Reading.*

gold- and black-striped underskirt, trimmed with puffs, the upper garment of black silk and silk fringe. A third, the Panier Sorosis walking suit—for $160—had an underskirt of blue and black satin, and a top skirt of black velvet with five puffings of blue satin; the outside garment opened in the back to allow puffs with blue satin piping and heavy fringe to protrude.

"The formal opening by Field, Leiter and Company of Potter Palmer's new marble palace on the corner of Washington and State," reported the *Tribune*, "was the grandest affair of its kind which ever transpired even in Chicago, the city of grand affairs. . . . .

"The attendance of wealth, beauty and fashion which assembled last evening to take the benefit of the grand opening was something unparalleled in Chicago's history, and the event was one long to be remembered. One would have thought that the opening last night was an adjourned meeting of the Charity Ball, judging from the long line of carriages on the avenue. The attractions were unusual—a dry goods store in a marble palace, and in a new dress at that. Enough to turn almost any female head. . . . . From now on, if an inquiring lady should ask, 'Oh, Julia, where did you get that superb shawl?' the reply will be, 'At Field and Leiter's, my dear!' "

The *Tribune's* editorialist refused to let the occasion pass without a typical Chicago slap at its commercial rivals. "We congratulate the ladies upon their rare good fortune," he wrote. "They have good cause to thank God that they are not as other cities are, for instance, like the dear creatures of Cincinnati and St. Louis and other suburban villages. New York cannot boast such a gorgeous palace for the display of dry goods . . . . and even Lord and Taylor and A. T. Stewart, the great, himself must hide their diminished heads and acknowledge the supremacy of their peculiar lines, at all events, of the Garden City."

GRECIAN CURLS

PLEASING THE LADIES

Marshall Field paid close attention to the way in which Chicago's women swarmed over the first floor of the new State Street store. Although the wholesale dealings of the firm would continue for years to bring returns nearly ten times those of the retail section, Field began to devote as much thought to developing the retail phase of the business as to supplying the growing wants of thousands of small merchants in the Northwest.

Transferring Lorenzo Woodhouse to the New York office, Field moved back to Chicago for good. He rented for himself and his wife, Nannie Scott Field, whom he had wed five years before, a house on Michigan Avenue, furnished with Victorian rosewood furniture, white marble mantelpieces, and carpets with gay floral designs. Each morning he strode stiffly along the street to the store, arriving always half an hour before the doors swung open at eight o'clock. He spent much of his time greeting buyers who came to the wholesale floors, but a day never passed without his presence in the retail section.

He was still quiet mannered, not given to pleasantries, and seemingly cold and aloof. Clerks came to attention when he appeared and bowed slightly if he favored them with a nod. Sometimes he paused to inspect a display of silk or see that the new full-length mirrors in the cloak department were clean and bright. Sometimes he spoke crisply to a head salesman or, smiling slightly, chatted with a favored customer.

Word spread quickly about the delights of the store. That *Chicago Tribune* reporter with his quip about Julia and the new shawl had been a good prophet. From Michigan Avenue in their carriages or from the outlying neighborhoods by horsecars the women came, some to buy, some to do little more than walk around the marble palace and steal glances at themselves as they tried on one of the "Special Parisian Frocks."

In their new store Field and Leiter were determined to adhere to the ideas inherited from Palmer and, whenever possible, to enlarge on them. These methods had built prestige and profits for Palmer and for them in their brief years of partnership, and would continue to do so.

The retail stocks, agreed the partners, must attract the best people of Chicago and satisfy the best tastes. "Don't ever be small in anything you do," was Palmer's warning. For the wealthy customers whose desires ran to luxuries—$1,000 lace tablecloths and $750 shawls—the store must go to all reasonable lengths. "Such little things," Field soon wrote to Woodhouse, "are the life of our retail trade."

Over and over again in these letters he stated his own merchant's philosophy. There must be no misrepresentation of goods, no attempt to foist upon customers inferior wares for quick profit. No haggling over prices—one price and one price only. Quality would be maintained regardless of price, competition, or popular demand. "Never let a nickel loom so large that you fail to see the dollar behind it," Field counseled his salesmen. And, above all, the customer must always have the right to return anything that failed to satisfy; there would be no edict of "All Sales Final" at Field and Leiter's. "Always remember," Field told William Clarke, head of his upholstery department, "we are the servants of the public."

II

The public—and principally its feminine segment—yearned to be served.

All over America the cumbersome hoop skirts had been diminishing in circumference since 1865, and those merchants who followed the styles sought to anticipate the next new mode. The fashion now was the bustle, the "dress improver," a contraption worn so that one's dress might expand and flare out at the back. Some bustles were made of horsehair with a concentric series of ruffles, or of cambric stretched over wire supports. The big seller at Field and Leiter's in this important realm was the Tape Front Hoop Skirt, "with Pompadour Bustle," a specialty that combined old and new.

For ladies interested in corsets the store had a variety of styles, keeping in mind the advice on this important matter

The ladies favored the "Widow Machree" corset for the "feminine form divine," but the bustle dinner gown offered a problem—how to sit while dining.

Corsets—Continued.

A Plaster Paris Bust of the Widow, for showing the Corset, packed ready for shipping . . . . $2 50 net.

offered by *Godey's Lady's Book:* "Corsets should be accurately fitted and modified to suit the peculiarities of each wearer." Accordingly the corset-seeker could select either the "Widow Machree," which sported forty bones and kid-covered "Everlasting" clasps, or one of the others—the "Gold Elsie," "My Mary Ann," and "Good Enough."

A fanciful assortment of wares crammed the notions counters and display racks. The woman shopper could always find the favored Alexandre kid gloves, but there were also others of silk and taffeta "in plain and eccentric colors." She might want to buy silver-plated napkin holders or lace handkerchiefs, mirrors, drapes, or ostrich feather dusters. Field and Leiter no longer scorned sweet-smelling scents, but now sold "Jessie Oakley's Rose Geranium Toilet Soap." For their husbands, the ladies could choose here from stocks of Italian silk kerchiefs, razor straps, domestic suspenders or "Pratt's Combined Shoulder Braces," new-style "Shakespeare Collars," Prince Teck neckties, and "CANTBREAKEM" shoelaces.

Field and Leiter advertised regularly. They adopted Palmer's technique of listing specific prices: "Cloth suitable for pants and suits, $1 to $2 a yard" or "Fancy linen for boys' wear, 25 cents and upward." Their advertisements, appearing mostly on Mondays when the rates were less costly, were outshouted by those of their competitors, of which "The City of Paris" was a startling example. This establishment called itself "ONE DOLLAR STORE" and invariably insisted, "CHICAGO ELECTRIFIED!! THE MOST ATTRACTIVE GOODS FOR ONE DOLLAR EVER OFFERED IN THIS CITY! TRUTH IS STRANGER THAN FICTION!" But such blaring and crass methods were not to the taste of the men of the marble palace.

To guide the women in their selection of the latest styles, Field and Leiter became chief supporters and biggest advertisers

FASHIONS FOR JANUARY 1871.

FROM FIELD, LEITER & CO.

Lith by Chicago Lithographing Co. 152 & 154 S Clark Street

Field and Leiter advertised regularly in Martha Louise Rayne's *Chicago Magazine*, keeping Chicagoans abreast of women's and children's fashions.

in a new publication, the *Chicago Magazine of Fashion, Music and Home Reading*. The editor, Martha Louise Rayne, was a hustling young matron who had already written two guide books to Chicago. A real representative of the "New Woman" arising everywhere in the country, she was determined that her bustle-wearing readers be well informed, well read, independent and assertive, yet wise in feminine ways.

95

All the leading merchants advertised in Mrs. Rayne's magazine. The Gage brothers—John, Seth, and Albert—were proud of their imported French hats. J. B. Shay, in rebuilt Lake Street quarters, tempted the hopeful readers with "Ladies' Trousseaus to Order." But the biggest displays were Field and Leiter's.

In its very first issue of April, 1870, a two-page inside spread portrayed vividly the store's "Fashion Specials," featuring a French import of silk velour and a Pomponette, "a new wrap of silk and wool, woven especially for summer." In every issue thereafter during the five years the magazine flourished, similar illustrations—as large and often lavish with color—were printed, together with detailed descriptions of each garment.

III

Rivals were finding it increasingly difficult to compete with Field and Leiter in offering such unusual and startling imports to the ladies. Their system had various advantages. The retail section of the marble palace bought most of its wares from its own wholesale departments. The immense buying power of the wholesale division developed early. Palmer had maintained an ace buyer, George W. Vail, in Europe to spot fashion trends, buy what the European experts were favoring, and send on the purchases to Chicago. Field himself had made a few trips to Europe when he maintained the firm's New York office. "Our foreign goods," bragged a circular of that period, "are selected with much care by our Mr. Field . . . . with especial view to the wants of the trade." Now Vail and an expert in notions, George Stanton, spent most of the year in Europe, especially in France where the newest styles originated, and in England where mill products were to be obtained quickly.

But this was not enough for the aggressive Field. He wanted to maintain a permanent office in Europe so that his firm could have not only the first orders but advance fashion information.

Joseph Field, in a chilly British office, bought wisely and shipped promptly. But Englishmen thought him eccentric.

Field felt that his store had to stay far ahead of the Lake Street merchants. Soon there would be others on this new street to vie with him, but he intended to keep well in advance of all possible rivals. He believed that the company could afford a European office, which should be in the charge of a responsible man who could assure Field and Leiter of best quality goods at best possible discounts. Why not guarantee quality by checking the goods at their source—the mills? Why pay importers and New York wholesalers for such a service?

Once he had made up his mind and persuaded Leiter that the step would prove wise and profitable, Field picked Joseph, his older brother, to go to England. There, in Manchester, a city that teemed with mills and commerce, a permanent office was established. "Take an office in Manchester, good central location for our kind of business," read Marshall's memorandum. "For one or two years, former preferred. . . . . Want, say, three rooms in second story so that can pack any small lots of

97

goods. . . . . Open bank account in Manchester with some first class bank or private banker, for payment all English."

Joseph Field was now a partner under a new agreement drawn up at the end of 1869. He was a solemn, frugal man with little sympathy for people who frowned on hard work. He packed a few belongings, including a worn Bible, and sailed for Manchester, where he rented an unheated suite of rooms in the heart of the mill district.

Joseph knew merchandise, and he knew prices. He could drive bargains and call for the most favorable discounts. Some Englishmen regarded him as mildly eccentric, for he refused to ride in what he called their "filthy cabs," and he usually wore his topcoat in his office. But no better person could have been selected for the job. Joe was keen, alert, dependable. He bought wisely and carefully and sent his goods by fastest possible liner.

Now Field and Leiter could advertise their "unparalleled foreign imports." They had outdistanced their western competitors in both wholesale and retail trade, but they yearned for

Flower-trimmed sailors, shell bonnets, or burnoose-like affairs topped the smart Chicago coiffures in the spring of 1871.

a greater triumph. They wanted to outrank even the New York wholesalers in being first to offer new foreign goods.

This was difficult. Chicago was not a federal port of entry. Often the dresses and cloaks Joe Field had dispatched so speedily lay for weeks in government warehouses in New York while customs officials made their appraisals. Chicago importers were kept waiting while the goods of New York competitors were appraised and released.

Chicagoans bombarded Congress with requests that their town be officially made a port of entry. Finally a bill was passed to establish in Chicago a federal customhouse, warehouse, and a corps of appraisers so that goods could be sent without delay to the city directly by boat or in freight cars under bond.

On September 30, 1871, the first two bonded carloads of imported merchandise destined for Field and Leiter's store rattled into the Michigan Central station. On the freight platform, dignified and elated, stood Field and Leiter, with the junior partners and department heads flanking them. Nearby were the officials of the new customhouse and a pompous appraiser, together with members of the City Council and the state legislature.

"In honor of this first direct importation a dozen of champagne were opened and drank by the gentlemen present," reported the *Tribune* ungrammatically. "Toasts were given and responded to and, altogether, the 'opening' not alone of the wine but of the cars was a very pleasant one."

Chicago was delighted by this rather belated recognition of its commercial importance. It awaited with interest the unveiling of wares that had been brought so far with such fanfare. None had any way of knowing that before any of the dresses would be hung on the racks or the expensive French broadcloth bolts piled on shelves for sale, disaster would befall not only the big State Street store but the very city itself.

THE O'LEARY COTTAGE. IN A BARN AT THE REAR
THE GREAT FIRE STARTED.

HOSE CART NO. 6

STEAMER NO. 17

FIRE!

On a mellow evening in 1871, John Devlin sits with companions on the front porch of a cottage on Fourteenth Street. The autumn air is cooling, the beer schooners well filled, the talk pleasant and relaxing.

Someone is praising that new story by Bret Harte, the one titled "The Outcasts of Poker Flat," printed this very morning in the *Chicago Tribune's* Sunday supplement. "A corker," all agree. And another mentions the terrible fire on the far West Side the night before, the one nearly all of the city's 200 hard-working firemen were summoned to fight. "Too many of them fires these days, the mayor oughta do somethin'," is the opinion.

Now the talk is split by the sharp clang of a bell from a nearby fire tower. The tower lookout has sighted a streak of flame only two blocks north. The men strain to see the smoke.

Fire engines clatter past the cottage. More tower fire bells ring. The men say hasty farewells and leave.

Big John Devlin walks rapidly to his rooming house seven blocks away, toward the ever increasing billows of smoke. By the time he comes within two blocks of the place he is swept into a crowd of white-faced, terrified people, already heading away from the flames. He never reaches his rooming house, but lets himself be carried in the pressing throng.

As the red-tinged smoke moves closer, Devlin's thought is for the store. What if the fire should reach the Field, Leiter and Company store, with its wealth of new imports?

Devlin joins the crowd surging toward State Street across the Van Buren Street bridge. He hurries over the creaky structure, remembering later, with a shiver, that he was one of the last to cross before the bridge was eaten up by the flames.

It is now ten o'clock on the night of October 8, 1871, an eventful night for Big John, a fateful one for his employers.

II

Those smoke clouds had risen from a stable behind the home of Patrick O'Leary and his family at 137 De Koven Street. Perennial legend would have it that O'Leary's cow upset a lighted lamp, setting fire to dry hay. But all that was clear then was that at 9:25 P.M. Danny "Peg Leg" Sullivan, the O'Leary drayman, saw red-black flames shooting from the stable and limped down the unpaved street bawling, "Fire! Fire! Fire!"

Soon chunks of blazing wood torn loose from the stable were caught up in a sudden wind. They landed on other barns and flimsy cottages in the neighborhood, setting them aflame. The fire leaped into churches, mills, factories, homes, stores, then reached out for the big business houses to the north and east. Only a few months before the *Chicago Times* had boasted that Chicago had changed "from a city of shanties that would have been no credit to a camp town to a city of marble palaces that fills the citizens of the old metropolis of the East with mingled wonder and fear." Now these "marble palaces" were afire, soon to vanish like the lowliest hovels.

When John Devlin finally reached the store, he found Henry Willing inside, with a dozen other stalwarts. The flames were still far from State and Washington streets. Soon Leiter arrived and with him Higinbotham. They held hurried discussions.

Someone cried out that the flames whirring around Courthouse Square, a few hundred yards west, seemed to be pointing north. This led those in the worried little group to hope that the fire would ultimately miss State Street. One of the crowd observed that even if the flames did lick out toward the store, there stood the fireproof First National Bank Building on the opposite corner, surely a firm bulwark against destruction.

But more employees now rushed up with harrowing news of what was happening on Lake Street, a few hundred yards north. There the flames had swept down both sides of the thoroughfare, moving toward the lake. People crowded everywhere. They tried to clamber atop high fences, and the fences crashed. They clung to store awnings, and the awnings crumpled beneath the weight. They stumbled over furniture hurled into the street, and others trampled them in the mad rush eastward toward the "blessed lake shore." Men lugged boxes and women clutched babies, bundles, and housewares—blankets, toys, old picture frames. Some were yelling and cursing, others plodding silently, dazed; some were pushing, shoving, clawing; some were wailing, "God's will is done! Oh, wicked Chicago!" and others moaned, "God has punished us all!"

Already the looting had started.

Up and down Lake Street the mob surged. Some broke into whisky shops, smashing bottles and guzzling liquor. Whisky barrels were overturned, their contents spilling into the streets to mingle with the heat and fire so that long, thin strands of blue flame streaked in the gutters toward the sewers. Thieves were invading the dry-goods stores, hurling silks and fabrics to their accomplices on the sidewalks below. East of Shay's store, a ton of fancy goods was thrown into the street, to be stomped on by shrieking people. In front of the store itself, a man loaded a wagon with silks while employees howled at him. One worker drew a pistol, aiming it at the thief, but he, yelling, "Fire and be damned!" flicked his whip over his nervous dray horse and drove off, trampling half a dozen screaming men and women.

Urchins sported expensive white kid gloves stolen from stacks of merchandise the harassed storekeepers had piled on the sidewalks. Near the Clark Street bridge a grimy youngster, lying crushed to death beneath a slab of marble, wore two gloves on each hand and his pockets were crammed with gold-plated sleeve buttons. Down State Street shuffled a gaunt woman, her arms loaded with stolen dresses, her voice shrilling, "Chickey, chickey, craney crow, I went to the well to wash my toe!" Another old crone, laughing drunkenly, staggered along, leading a goat draped in dazzling silks that trailed in the mud.

Men did insane things. They smashed store windows, not to steal the articles for themselves but to scatter them into the streets or to hurl them high above the heads of the crowd. One man deliberately set fire to a load of costly furniture piled in front of a house on Michigan Boulevard's fashionable Terrace Row, between Van Buren and Congress streets, an area not yet invaded by flames. In the same block another man ran into the house of Deacon Bross, now part owner of the *Tribune*, pulled on several suits and ran out again to be met by a weary Bross returning from his office.

"You have a considerable invoice of my clothes, with the hunting suit outside," rumbled Bross. "Well, go along, you might as well have them as let them burn."

Men with coaches, buggies, costermongers' wagons, and drays were demanding fantastic prices for carrying loads toward the lake shore. "Cash! Cash! Let's see the color of your money!" they roared, as men and women cried out to them to take their last few belongings to safety. Some teamsters, after receiving as much as $150 for a load, dumped the contents into the street whenever anyone offered more money. Checks were refused, even those from the most reliable of men. "Pay as you

"CHICAGO IN FLAMES!" A contemporary artist's lurid conception of the 1871 conflagration. Starting at night, October 8, the fire finally burned itself out on October 10. Hundreds lost their lives; damage was $200,000,000.

go! Pay as you go!" was the cry. "Never," Horace White, the *Tribune's* editor, would comment wryly in a few days, "was there a community so hastily and completely emancipated from the evils of the credit system."

III

Back at the store a decision had been made and action taken.

Field, arriving in time from his home to hear the tales of the pillage, conferred quickly with Leiter and Willing. Then: "We'll save what we can. If the fire comes, it comes, but we will save all we can before that time."

Higinbotham hustled to the store's barns to summon drivers and their wagons. A salesman, H. B. Parker, was sent to the basement to smash boxes and hurl wood into the boiler, firing it up so that the steam elevator would go smoothly.

Then the men, working in bucket-style brigades, started to

remove the store's most expensive wares. From the top floor came bolts of Japanese silks, black satins, black velours, German mantilla velvets. While four of the huskiest men stood guard at the front doors, the others lifted the bolts of cloth into waiting wagons. Whips fell, the wagons rumbled off to the lake shore, there to be met by other strong-shouldered guards, to unload and return for more. Now came packing boxes filled with laces and heaps of Ristoni and Patti shawls, French cretonnes, Biarritz cloth, Empress Sultana and Tibet scarves.

At midnight a flaming brand flew into the tar house of the city's gas works out west, forcing the attendants to let the gas seep into mains to avert an earth-jarring blast. All the gas jets in the store flickered lower, then went out. The men lighted candles, stuck them on the window sills, and went on with the hasty job of carrying out loads of French bombazine, Irish poplins, wool cashmere, crepe mohair, expensive serges.

The heat grew fearful. The wind suddenly switched its course and blew south. It snared the flames and sent ahead deadly harbingers of its awful force. The courthouse, its mourning bell resounding from the wooden tower, was pierced by a big burning chunk of timber wrenched from a La Salle Street building, and now walls and bell toppled together. Burning embers cracked into the windows of buildings across from the store. Spurts of flame shot out over the cobblestone street, singeing workers and horses.

"Volunteers! Volunteers!" cried Field. "We must try to save the store!"

John Devlin, Charles Swartout, and seven others stepped forward. Up they hurried to the mansard roof where stood three huge water tanks. The basement pumps were turned on with greater force, and the men drenched the roof with water from buckets and played hoses on the walls of the store and adjoining buildings. Inside the store, their fantastic shadows huge on the candle-lighted ceiling, Field and six other men soaked heavy blankets and draped them out of open windows to keep the walls from overheating and crumbling.

IV

But the store was doomed.

By three o'clock in the morning, after some $200,000 of the best merchandise had been saved, the flames moved closer. Worse yet, at this very hour, the city's waterworks a mile north at Michigan Boulevard and Pearson Street were on the edge of ruin. All night sparks and brands had been whipped toward the structure, but now a twelve-foot brand from the blazing Lill's Malt House and Brewery across the street buried itself in the waterworks' slate-covered wooden roof. Within minutes the roof was aflame and caved in. The engines stopped. There was not a drop of water to fight the flames rushing north and west again, and south toward the store.

When this happened, many who had sought shelter near the waterworks became panic-stricken. Fearing the flames would reach the lake shore, thousands rushed down Wabash Avenue. The looting of wholesale stores along that street grew wilder by the minute. Only a block from Field, Leiter and Company, maddened men and women pushed along, stomping on oil paintings, books, musical instruments, mirrors, glassware. Again drunken hordes invaded the liquor stores and saloons; bartenders gathered in coins until the flames were at their very doors.

The fire continued to eat its way along State Street, too, and into the block where the store stood. Soon the Allen-Mackey Carpet establishment next door was swathed in flames. From this building and from structures across the alley on Wabash Avenue, flaming brands swept into the floors on which Field and his helpers were still feverishly hanging out their soaked blankets. In a few minutes each floor had its own spreading fire.

Devlin and his crew on the roof poured the last buckets of water over the side of the burning building. When they finally fought their way down the stairway through the burgeoning flames, their hair was singed, their faces soot-blackened, their eyes inflamed.

Their task was not yet done. To thwart the vandals, Field and Leiter gave orders to move all the salvaged merchandise on the lake front to a safer place. Devlin and two dozen employees marched to the spot where the goods were piled. Quickly, wagons and all other available conveyances—even the owners' buggies—were crammed with laces, silks, and shawls. Blankets, bedding, and inexpensive coats and wraps were left behind, to be turned over later to the Chicago Relief and Aid Society.

Past the shivering, moaning crowds huddled along the lake shore, the wagons creaked toward a fire-free area near Leiter's

White-faced, terror-stricken people, clutching a few belongings, crowded bridges, hoping to escape the spreading flames by crossing to the other side of the river.

home, at Twenty-third Street and Prairie Avenue. Part of the valuable load was stored in his house, part in an adjacent frame building, and the rest, covered with tarpaulins and guarded every second, in a nearby schoolyard.

The fire swept through the store, devouring everything. Shortly after dawn a series of explosions rattled the building. An hour later came a massive blast. Flames spurted out of all the windows. Millions of faggots, blazing hot, flew everywhere.

In another half hour the building dissolved in the flame and smoke. Nothing remained but red-hot ruins, twisted steel, and smoking lime into which the intense heat had powdered the proud marble.

v

By Tuesday, when the fire finally burns itself out, the heart of the city is a mass of blackened ruins.

Gone are stores, homes, banks, hospitals, public buildings, railroad stations, hotels, theaters. Nearly 300 have lost their lives. Nearly 100,000 are homeless. Almost $200,000,000 of property has been destroyed.

"Chicago is in ashes," a woeful citizen writes to a friend in Iowa. "Not one wholesale business left. Such a conflagration was never known on this continent. At present we hardly know the extent of the damage, only that it is terrible."

And amid the destruction of State Street, a twenty-year-old reporter, Joseph Edgar Chamberlin of the *Chicago Evening Post*, comes upon an old man staring at the devastation.

"Our capital is wiped out of existence," whines the old man. "The trade of the city must go to St. Louis or Cincinnati and to New York. We couldn't transact any business if we had customers, for we haven't got anywhere to transact it.

"Yes sir, this town is gone up, and we may as well get out of it at once!"

THE WATER TOWER AFTER THE GREAT FIRE

THE CASH BOY SIGN
AT THE STORE RUINS

OUR CITY
SHALL RISE AGAIN!

Chicago promptly set out to give the lie to the gloomy old gentleman; to those in New Orleans and St. Louis and Cincinnati who cried, "Chicago will never be the Carthage of old"; to those who fled the smoking ruins, certain in their fearful minds that the city's glory belonged only to the past.

Many bewailed their lot, but not the chubby little woman who, on that same Tuesday morning, trundled her handcart through the rubble to State and Randolph streets, flicked her apron over her wares, and called, "Apples! Apples! Who'll buy a nice juicy apple?"

Many counted up their losses and moaned. But not an eager young real-estate dealer who gathered a few friends and knocked together a wooden shack on Washington Boulevard off State Street, tacking to it the sign: "*Wm. D. Kerfoot, 89 Washington St. All Gone but Wife Children & Energy.*"

In Wednesday's *Chicago Tribune*, first since the fire had demolished its building, Joseph Medill proclaimed, "CHICAGO SHALL RISE AGAIN!" In the same issue appeared crude, brave advertisements: "We Still Live!" and "Resumed Business!" and "Keep the Ball Rolling!" and "Behold! Dry Goods and Clothing!" There were other sad little notices seeking missing wives, husbands, children, mothers, fathers. Dinky stores, selling goods that had been salvaged—groceries, liquor, clothing, tobacco, sewing machines, scales, stoves, furniture, pianos, crockery— all vowed: "No Advantage Taken of the Calamity!"

West on prim, stately Washington Boulevard, where the fire had skirted by, hundreds of sedate dwellers turned into fly-by-night merchants. They set up box-like structures in their front yards and loaded them with clothing not needed by their families. They draped dresses, skirts, suits, bedspreads, and underclothes on chairs in their living rooms. "The carelessness, even recklessness, with which Commerce has dropped down into dwellings," observed William Croffut, editor of the *Chicago Evening Post*, "is grotesque and whimsical to the last degree."

The boosters were soon rallying Chicago's thousands, promising a greater and more prosperous city. Medill, soon to be elected

Staring at these ruins of the Field and Leiter store, a discouraged citizen told a reporter, "This town is gone up!" But at that very moment the two partners were planning their horse-barn store at State and Twentieth.

mayor on a "fire-proof ticket," enumerated the losses and the damage. Then he declaimed, "Under free institutions, good government and the blessings of Providence, all losses will soon be repaired, all misery caused by the fire assuaged, and a prosperity greater than ever dreamed of will be achieved in a period so brief that the rise will astonish mankind even more than the fall of Chicago!"

Deacon Bross scurried to the East to assure the bankers and big merchants that Chicago would survive and surpass its former self. "Go to Chicago now!" he thundered. "Women, send your husbands! Men, send your sons! You will never again have such a chance to make money!" And George F. Root, one of the nation's favorite song writers, expressed the spirit in a new composition, "From the Ruins Our City Shall Rise!" that pealed:

"Ruins! Ruins! Far and wide
　From the river and lake to the prairie side.
　　Dreary, Dreary, the darkness falls,
　　While the autumn winds moan through blackened walls.
　But see! The bright rift in the cloud
　　And hear the great voice from the shore!
　Our city shall rise!
　Yes, she shall rise!
　　Queen of the west once more!"

II

Within an hour after the marble palace on State Street had crumbled, Harlow Higinbotham was at Leiter's home.

"We must start at once to think of the future," he said.

Leiter sighed and shook his head in despair. "Oh, no! Chicago is lost," he mumbled. "It's too early to make plans."

But Higinbotham pressed his point. Marshall Field, asked for his opinion, agreed with him. Field was certain that an inventory would reveal that much of value had been saved. All that was needed was a new place, more goods, and customers.

None of the other big firms—neither Farwell, Gossage, nor Hamlin—were ready to start up again. That very morning John Farwell had suggested to Field and the other merchants that they draw up a proposal for shearing off certain of their debts. Unless eastern creditors showed them special consideration, they could not resume business, Farwell argued. Field was not interested. It was clear that Farwell, their biggest competitor, was in no position to jump into the lead and grab sales and customers.

Now only the slab-town merchants, selling their cheap wares in pine-box stalls, were attempting to fill the hysterical needs of the people. The big store that opened first, Field reasoned, would not only make a lot of money and check the loss of wholesale customers to New York, Cincinnati, St. Louis, Milwaukee, and Detroit, but it would do a real service for the citizens.

A decision was reached quickly. Each man was assigned a specific task.

Field set out to find a suitable place to resume business. To avoid risk of theft, all the salvaged goods were shipped at once to La Porte, Indiana, and there stored in a railroad roundhouse and a paint shop until Leiter could make an inventory. Willing hurried to Valparaiso, Indiana, to hold shipments of incoming goods from the East until the new store location was found.

Higinbotham left the next morning, on his thirty-third birthday, for his mother's home in Joliet, where he set up the company's temporary offices. With him went his family and three bookkeepers carrying the store ledgers. He and his crew worked for several days on the books, finally establishing the firm's losses at $2,500,000. But all except $750,000 of this amount was, happily enough, covered by insurance.

For two days Field searched for a new business site. He found it at State and Twentieth streets, well out of range of the

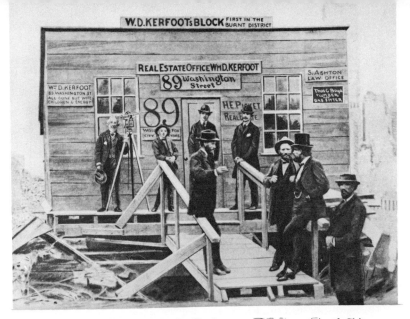

A young real-estate dealer, W. D. Kerfoot, typified the spirit of Chicagoans after the Great Fire. "All gone but wife, children, and energy," cried he.

smoldering fire, in the shape of a two-story, red brick barn in which the Chicago City Railway Company had once quartered its horses. He leased it instantly, then informed Leiter and the others. The next day work was begun to make it into a store.

Oat bins, stacks of hay, harnesses, reins, and blinders were pitched out. The walls were whitewashed and the floors varnished. In the horse stalls were placed hastily built pine counters. All the goods were rushed back from La Porte and Valparaiso and arranged in neat piles. A workman was sent to the old store's ruins, there to nail on a charred post this sign:

Cash Boys & Work
Girls will be Paid
what is due them
Monday 9 a.m. Oct. 16th
at 60 Calumet Ave.
Field, Leiter & Co.

The boys and girls responded. Told of the new horse-barn store, they hustled there to volunteer for new jobs. Clerks and salesmen came, too, and were quickly put to sweeping floors, arranging goods, and sprucing up wherever they could.

Orders went out to New York for more merchandise, which arrived in such quantity that bobtail horsecars were needed to help haul it from the railroad depot. A policeman, sighting such a load one evening, halted the driver to ask, "What are you carryin' there?" "Merchandise from the warehouse," the driver replied. Where, the amazed policeman wanted to know, where was it all going? "To Field and Leiter's horse barn on Twentieth Street." "Well," mused the policeman, taking another look at the streetcar on its unusual errand, "that beats all. Seems there's nothing impossible at Field and Leiter's."

By October 21, less than two weeks after they had seen the flames devour their magnificent store, the partners were ready to announce a fresh start. On the *Tribune's* front page they placed a modest advertisement, announcing calmly that they had now removed to the corner of State and Twentieth streets and would in a few days open a complete retail section. Soberly the announcement concluded: "We sincerely thank our friends for their many kind expressions of sympathy and hope soon to renew our former pleasant business relations."

III

From the opening day the store thrived.

First came the wholesale customers, shaking their heads in awe as they arrived through the ruined section of the city, full of sympathy and admiration for the way Chicago was rebuilding and hustling itself out of momentary depression.

Then came the women, not content with the meager offerings in the slab-town stores and makeshift stalls along Washington Boulevard. The horse-barn store, of course, had none of the elegance of that lost marble palace, but here were silks and shawls, linens and laces, even cloaks newly arrived from New York. And here was Marshall Field at the door to greet the ladies, to show them to the proper sections; here were salesmen, neatly dressed and courteous as usual, and department chiefs with flowers in their lapels.

Editor Croffut, continuing his tour of the resurgent city, found much to surprise and please him in the barn store.

"Here," he recorded, "are hundreds of clerks and thousands of patrons a day, busy along the spacious aisles and the vast vistas of ribbons and laces and cloaks and dress-goods. This tells no story of a fire. The ladies jostle each other as impatiently as of old, and the boys run merrily to the incessant cry of 'Cash!' Yet, madam, this immense bazaar was six weeks ago the horse-barn of the South Side Railroad! . . . .

"Here, where ready-made dresses hang then hung sets of double harness; yonder where a richly-robed body leans languidly against the counter and fingers point laces, a manger stood and offered hospitality to a disconsolate horse. A strange metamorphosis!—Yet it is but an extreme illustration of the sudden changes the city has undergone."

The rush of customers increased. So did the firm's orders to the manufacturers in the mill towns of New England and to the importers and wholesale houses in New York. Soon the *United States Economist and Dry Goods Reporter* disclosed: "At present we can learn of but one house who are buying and shipping goods to Chicago, and that is Messrs. Field, Leiter & Co., who, though among the largest sufferers, are yet the first in the field as operators, adopting the old maxim—'There is no better place to look for a thing than where it was lost.' "

Even the august *Harper's Weekly*, reporting on the burst of activity in Chicago as the city frantically sought to remove the rubble and rebuild, editorialized: "Fire nor flood can quench the indomitable spirit that made Chicago and will remake it greater than before."

IV

Within a month the partners were on solid ground again.

By Christmas, sales in the new horse-barn store had reached the gratifying total of $125,000. All other assets—the salvaged goods, money owed by merchants all through the Middle West, real estate, insurance—brought the partners' total to $2,750,000. Leiter, in a joyful letter to Joseph Field, could inform him, "You will see that we have left a very handsome capital to continue our business."

And the situation was sweetened by the fact that while Field and Leiter were announcing that they stood prepared to pay all debts promptly and fully and would continue to sell goods on approval, John Farwell was obliged to plead in the newspapers, "It is needless to remind our friends that their remittances will be very acceptable."

V

Only six months after the Great Fire, the *Chicago Dry Goods Reporter* surveyed the amazing business scene, then delivered itself of some windy rhetoric:

"Despite the fact that the heart of Chicago was burned out six months ago, and every business man was made penniless for the time; despite the severity of the winter and other multifarious difficulties in reconstructing the obliterated town; despite the legitimate efforts of rivals to make opportunity out of our misfortunes, and despite the misrepresentations and diabolical slanders of envious competitors, we are able to say today that trade was never so heavy as it is now in this market.

"There is a divinity that shapes our ends and it is this divinity that watches over the affairs of the ill-fated city, and is giving

The ruins of the great conflagration were still smoldering as undaunted citizens began rebuilding, determined to make the city "queen of the west once more."

back the millions of wealth snatched from us by a dire accident. The ordeal through which our business men have been compelled to pass has aroused an energy that will make Chicago more speedily than otherwise was predestined, the grandest inland commercial city in the world, and we warn our persecutors that the course they pursue toward us is not wisely designed to smother us in our ashes, but on the contrary, to stimulate us to extreme exertion, and to keep alive the sympathies and more strongly cement the friendship of our business friends.

"Chicago is not dead, but mingling with her glorious ruins there is today more life, more energy, and more business than is exhibited by any of her ignoble competitors!"

Field and Leiter were already translating into action the editorialist's wordy prophecy. Even while workmen were still whitewashing the walls of the Twentieth Street horse barn a few days after the fire, Field had negotiated for the construction of a more permanent structure, principally to house the wholesale division. He selected the northeast corner of Madison and Market streets, where, before the conflagration, the Garden City Hotel stood.

The neighborhood had been of low character. Along Market Street had stretched sailors' boardinghouses and groggeries; Madison Street had been lined with whisky mills and cheap stores. But those evils were gone now, and the site was a convenient one for buyers, who could reach it from most of the new railroad stations and from the North and West sides of the city without plowing through the burned-out districts.

Leiter agreed to this move. There was no possible chance at this time, he wrote to Joseph Field, to go back to State Street. "If a store were erected upon our old quarters or near it," he stated, "it would be of little or no value for occupancy for the coming year. The debris from the burned buildings is so great that it would prevent access of people, and the dust arising from it would destroy a stock of goods." Besides, the Market Street land was cheap, only $7.00 a square foot as compared with the $2,100 a front foot Palmer had charged them for the State Street property.

Now all the wholesale stocks were carried to the new building, constructed at a cost of $140,000. A retail division also was established in the Market Street building, and designated Retail No. 2, while the horse-barn store became Retail No. 1. Wholesalers were permitted to buy at Market Street as early as March 4, 1872, but the public was informed that the grand opening would not be held until the evening of April 25. Meanwhile, improvements continued at the horse barn. Workers wrapped pillars with red velvet draperies, hung rich-looking carpets on the walls, covered the deal counters neatly with oilcloth. In one section of the barn was created an elegant carpet hall, which swiftly became famous for its new blood-red, white-bordered Axminsters, and an upholstery and trimming department featuring brocaded terry cloth and blue satin lambrequins.

VI

No sooner had Field acquired the Market Street location than John Farwell also selected this area, building a massive store two blocks away, on Franklin Street between Madison and Monroe streets. "The Merchant Prince of Chicago!" some of the newspapers called Farwell as his advertisements invited all to the grand opening on Saturday night, March 30.

It rained heavily that night so that the formal opening had to be postponed to Monday. But a *Chicago Times* reporter who braved the downpour assured his readers the next morning that the Farwell establishment was "well worth going through a pelting storm to see."

Through credit purchases, Farwell had outdone all his prior efforts, it seemed. His basement was filled with carpets—$400,000 worth of French moquette, American and English velvets, Wiltons, Brussels, and exquisite heavy tapestries. Now he also was trying to snatch the retail trade from his rivals, luring one of their ace managers, George Livermore, to act as superintendent of his retail division. In this section, the variety and beauty of the camel's hair and India shawls—priced from $35 to $1,500—was, vowed the delirious reporter, "enough to make the ladies go wild!"

In the "enlarged mourning department" were grenadines, bombazines, black alpacas, and splendid cashmeres. And, in happier mood, directly across the aisle, were English and Irish poplins, calicoes, gay ginghams, Biarritz cloth—"all utterly beyond the mind of a male human being to recollect or enumerate!" The upholstery department, the reporter found, was "simply perfect"—Gobelin tapestries for piano and table covers; silk and satin damask for curtains; silk, terry, and coteline cloth, cretonne draperies "in endless and bewildering confusion." In aggregate or in detail, burbled the overwhelmed journalist, "the retail department of J. V. Farwell cannot be surpassed in the country!"

All this may have been true enough, but Field and Leiter were unworried. They were biding their time. Their reputation, they felt, was firmer than Farwell's, and they knew his financial position was not too sound. They declined to stretch their credit to match Farwell's flashy opening. They were confident that their established methods—goods on approval, prompt delivery, tested merchandise, sound credit policy—would meet any threat Farwell could devise.

Without much clamor, Field and Leiter opened the doors of their Madison-Market building to the public. Their modest

The charmer before this mirror is setting her hair in the popular "sausage curls." To make the curls, she spent hours with brush, mirror, and curler.

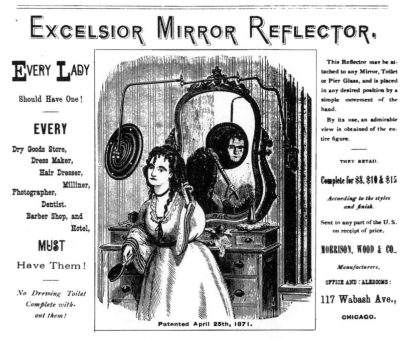

advertisement announcing a public display of retail goods was overshadowed by Farwell's blaring offer of a "Re-Opening Showing" that same night to allow the public "the opportunity of enjoying an agreeable evening among Dry Goods." But the people flocked to Field and Leiter's Retail No. 2, to be greeted at the door by a suave, white-gloved Marshall Field.

There were 30,000 visitors that night of April 25. As at that important opening four years back, when the partners stood by in their frock coats at the doors of the State Street store, Field noticed keenly how the customers, especially the women, paid scant attention to the four upper floors which were jammed with wholesale wares. Instead, they swept eagerly through the mammoth first floor, examining the imported laces, embroideries, trimmings, underthings, silks of most delicate shades, which smiling clerks held just right in the glow of the gas lights to bring out the subtlest worth. They ogled the imported gloves, shawls, and mantles in the center of the floor. They gasped at finery most of them could not afford: a dress of apricot silk, with train, for $300; a sage green silk-street dress, $250; a frock of grenadine moire, a watered silk fabric, which sold for $225. These luxurious gowns evoked so many attentive glances that a *Times* reporter commented wryly: "*Pater familias* may expect to be ruined in a few days, for every lady who goes will want one of these dresses."

The *Chicago Inter-Ocean*, noting that the John V. Farwell's "Re-Opening" caused no stir at all, was astounded by the thousands who came to Field and Leiter's Retail No. 2, and concluded: "The crowd was a little too dense for comfort, but everybody, especially the ladies, seemed delighted with what they saw and departed with happy hearts."

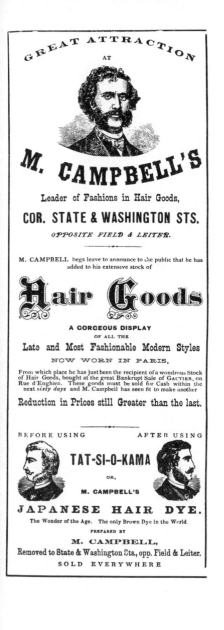

RETURN TO
STATE STREET

For a few months the ladies were happy at Retail No. 2. Chicago was rising again, and trade was brisk. The West prospered. Immigrants who poured into New York's Castle Garden by the tens of thousands moved on in rude railroad cars to help rebuild Chicago, lay more railroad tracks, plant crops where buffalo grass had grown. Wages were low, but entire families worked. These newcomers were soon among the buyers, clothing their families, furnishing homes, equipping farms.

From villages and towns freshly sprung up across the great plains more carloads of grain, beef, and pork rolled eastward to Chicago. More merchants boarded the passenger trains, bound on Chicago buying trips. More housewives and their husbands took advantage of $5.00 round-trip railroad excursions—all the way from South Dakota and Nebraska!—to spend a wide-eyed day in Chicago, seeing the sights, selling their pigs, buying new goods from Field and Leiter.

There was much to delight them: the usual staples—denims, ginghams, yarn, woolen and satin goods, outing flannels; the splendid silks, lace collars, embroidered handkerchiefs; an intriguing array of "Notions and Fancy Goods." From the Field and Leiter wholesale division the retail salesmen could swiftly replenish their stocks of ivory- or gilt-stick fans, sewing boxes and baskets, fine perfumes, writing sets, toilet ensembles, glove and handkerchief chests.

There were novelties and fineries: ornaments made of Russian leather, blown-glass flowers from Bohemia, Swiss carved bracelets, special holders for bouquet flowers, Parisian watch stands in gilt or silver, ash receivers, inkwells, match safes "in great variety of chaste and elegant design," carved jade, shell and ivory goods, wax dolls, China dolls, rag dolls, dressed dolls—and "astounding talking dolls!"

Wholesale trade flourished, with no sign yet of the panic to come from overproduction of grain on the western plains. Again and again the country merchants returned to the Field and Leiter wholesale floors at Madison and Market streets, still marveling at Chicago's revival and bent on favoring the plucky city with orders.

Field and Leiter, eager for profits from the booming West, expanded. Carpets were added to their growing stocks—cheaper domestic ingrains at 50 cents to $1.50 a yard, up to such expensive floor coverings as English Axminsters and Smyrna tapestries. With the peace following the Franco-Prussian War, foreign imports spurted, and the company could boast again of its French and Belgian laces. A new wholesale department of "Fine, Medium and Low-Price Furs" was started, to supply both the retail stores and the country trade.

As the wholesale customers made their rounds, they carried neat, gold-embossed order books cataloguing the merchandise. When the times grew more uncertain, prices were dropped from the listings, and Field and Leiter provided daily bulletins, setting forth the latest quotations, together with information on choice bargains and timely buys. Late in the year, when horses were dying by the dozens in Chicago, tying up delivery systems, the partners added this cheering news to the end of one such list: "We can assure our friends that there will be no

THE GREAT HORSE DISEASE
IN CHICAGO, NOV. 1872

When distemper decimated Chicago's horses in 1872, Field and Leiter used oxen. "All orders filled promptly and shipped the same day!" they boasted.

delay in shipping Goods on account of Horse Distemper, as we have secured a large number of Oxen. All Orders will be filled promptly and shipped the same Day as received."

But although the wholesale business thrived, Field saw, to his great dismay, that retail trade, once the novelty of shopping in a converted horse barn and in the new district around Madison and Market streets had worn thin, was falling thousands of dollars short of his hopes. Smaller houses were doing as well as both retail branches. Neither Retail No. 1 nor Retail No. 2 seemed to possess the allure for women shoppers that even some of the grubbiest stores closer to State Street had gained. After that first rush of business a calm settled over the ladies. No longer were there crowds too dense for comfort.

127

The sight of wholesale customers marching to Madison and Market streets no longer cheered Field after he had studied the thinning ranks on the retail floors. The ladies, he concluded, simply cared not a bit for traveling west or south to do their shopping. John V. Farwell, to his financial disadvantage, had already found that out and had given up the retail section he had opened a year earlier with such hullabaloo.

There was only one thing to do, Field told Leiter. Casting his cool, objective stare upon the ledgers that showed slipping profits, he said, "It's time we went back to State Street."

II

The chance to move soon came—and again the fortunes of Field and Leiter meshed with those of Potter Palmer.

When the Great Fire had ravaged Chicago, Palmer, visiting in New York, learned that thirty-two of his buildings had fallen. "I have particulars of the fire," he telegraphed to his sparkling-eyed young wife, Bertha Honoré Palmer. "Am perfectly reconciled to our losses. Be cheerful and do all possible for sufferers."

On his return he quickly set about selling much of his land. With customary gusto he made plans for a revived State Street that would have not only more splendid stores but a new Palmer House, the first wholly fireproof hotel in the United States. The plans provided for an elaborate facade, large rooms, statuary in the lobbies, and an amazing barber shop whose floors would be studded with silver dollars.

To finance this plan he disposed of one of his biggest pieces of property to the aggressive and tight-lipped men who headed the affluent Singer Sewing Machine Company. This land was the site of the old marble dry-goods palace where Field and Leiter had exulted, for a few brief years before the Great Fire, in their roles of the city's leading merchants. For this land the Singer officials paid Palmer $350,000, then spent another $750,000 to erect, in the spring and summer of 1873, a five-story structure with a huge glass dome in the center of its mansard roof.

Despite their eagerness to return to State Street, Field and Leiter balked at the $75,000 annual rental the Singer people were asking for the store. But when they heard that no less a personage than A. T. Stewart himself, New York's prime merchant, was planning to take over the building as a branch store, they ended their bickering and signed a three-year lease. They closed Retail No. 1 and Retail No. 2 and announced: "WE SHALL REMOVE our Retail Business to our new store, State and Washington Streets, on Monday, Oct. 6."

On the morning of the scheduled opening, fire broke out in the store's roof. It was soon extinguished, but the big opening had to be delayed. Finally, on October 9, the second anniversary of the disaster that had driven Field and Leiter from the "street of stately splendor," the doors of their new store were opened.

Following the Great Fire, Potter Palmer built a new, splendid hotel on State Street—"Finest in the West!"—with 650 rooms and a fireproof structure.

PALMER HOUSE, CHICAGO.

The crowds swept in, chattering excitedly about the glowing gas chandeliers and the frescoed ceilings. They stood in the light well on the broad first floor, staring up at the glass dome through which light fell on the strategically placed silk and glove counters. A force of 500 clerks smiled their best smiles while their dapper boss, C. P. L. Lyman, whom Field and Leiter had hired away from A. T. Stewart's Broadway emporium, flitted from counter to counter, brushing imaginary dust from his Prince Albert coat with a large silk handkerchief. "The building is a fitting tribute," decreed the *Chicago Mail*, "to the good taste and liberal judgment of Chicago's beauties, who are its patronesses."

Other inducements were offered these "patronesses."

A retail rug department, with choice items supplied by the Madison-Market wholesale house, featured domestic ingrains which were cheap and serviceable—and the ladies who could not afford better hastened to buy them. For the wealthier customers there were imported Aubussons and Wiltons, rugs with patterns of roses as huge as pineapples or flowers held together by gay ribbons. In the fourth-floor workrooms women turned out "Our Exclusive Products"—ties and collars and scarves, from the best Italian silk, and underwear and hose. For those women—still in the vast majority—who made their clothes at home by hand or on sewing machines, there were bolts upon bolts of yard goods. Popular then and for some years to come was red flannel, favored for underwear principally because it was supposed by many to contain certain medicinal properties that safeguarded its wearers from ever becoming rheumatic.

To make of these visitors steady, contented, and pleased customers, Field and Leiter issued to all clerks and salesmen their first official set of rules, printed in a folder.

"Never misrepresent an article, or guarantee wear or colors," the employees were warned.

"Be polite and attentive to rich and poor alike, courteous and agreeable to all those around you.

"Have patience in serving customers, showing goods willingly and pleasantly, without asking too many questions as to price, quality, width, size or colors wanted.

"Taking an address, be careful to get initials, names, numbers, street or destination correctly. Make record of all transactions, as required by general rules, remembering you are responsible for your errors and omissions and their results.

"Report at once any complaints from customers, of whatever nature, relating to the business of the house."

The clerks were warned against using tobacco and eating candy, fruit, nuts, or lunch in the store. And they were advised not to gossip with their visiting friends.

All clerks were expected to report at half-past seven in the morning, half an hour before the doors opened to customers. They were required to stay until six o'clock every night. They were responsible for the good order of the stock in their care. Salesclerks working overtime received no extra pay except "supper money," usually about 50 cents. Many went supperless and pocketed the money, adding it to their $10-a-week pay.

To these rules, and all other injunctions issued to employees, was appended the important and constant reminder that goods could be exchanged, or the customer could request a full cash refund. "Satisfaction guaranteed!" was still the store's motto.

III

While the partners concentrated on regaining and holding the glory of their first State Street store, the country was being swept by a new financial panic.

It came as a thunderbolt in September, 1873, when Jay Cooke—the financier many had hailed as "the pillar of the nation" during the War between the States—clanked shut the doors of his big New York banking house. Cooke, trying to underwrite the Northern Pacific Railroad, had been caught, like lesser men, by the overexpansion of the railroads, the overproduction of western farms, frantic speculation, and general inflation of credit. Banks in many cities toppled. Stock prices collapsed. More than 5,000 business firms, short of money and unable to get credit, smashed up. In a single day, at the height of the frenzy, five New York merchants committed suicide.

In Chicago five banks failed. Mercantile firms with shaky credit ratings were swiftly ruined. Some wholesale houses, badly frightened, abruptly cut off all their customers in the country towns unless they were able to pay their bills in full at once.

Field and Leiter were not among them. As in earlier periods of financial stress, they had few debts and ample cash reserves, despite the opening of the new store. Their customers were as solid as merchants could be, worthy of trust. Even as the Chicago Clearing House sent notices to country bankers, temporarily suspending payments on any sudden, large demands for cash, the partners dispatched letters informing their customers they would continue to conduct business in the usual manner.

"We see no cause for general alarm," they wrote, "and advise merchants and others to keep on in the even tenor of their way.

"The partial failure of crops in Europe, creating such a large demand for our breadstuffs and provisions, warrants us in assuring you of our belief that no action of bankers can long retard their movements, and as the business of the West is almost wholly dependent on the money realized for its products, it cannot suffer to any great extent.

"Importations have been very light this season, and stocks of American merchandise have at no time since the close of the war been sold up so close.

"We do not at present anticipate any immediate change in values or merchandise."

Field and Leiter returned to this State Street building erected after the Chicago Fire. A force of 500 clerks helped them to regain their old glory.

America was, in fact, headed for five years of hard times. But Field and Leiter were sustained by their faith in the vitality of the West, by their strong financial standing, and by the accurate reporting of their European buyers. Their attitude sowed confidence in the Chicago trade territory. Buyers, somehow getting money or able to convince Leiter of their credit worth, continued to come to town and to place orders with the two partners. And Chicago, despite its jobless and hungry, fared better than other cities.

IV

Ten days after Field and Leiter opened their new store, they were visited by a reporter from the *Chicago Times*. Assigned by his rip-roaring editor, Wilbur Fisk Storey, to tell the world that no panic could ever whip Chicago, the reporter had been touring the city interviewing bankers, stockbrokers, industrialists, and merchants. He sought out Marshall Field to ask, "How's business?"

"Trade is fair," Field replied. "It is quite as good as we have any reason to expect. We are doing about as well as we did last October, but we are not doing as well as we expected to do when the season opened."

"Will prices be affected?"

"Not at all up to the present time. But I think they will within thirty days unless there is a change for the better."

"Will that suit you?"

"Yes," replied Field, with a sly grin. "We like to sell cheap. It pleases our customers."

All was not so well with the rest of Chicago. Lake Michigan traffic, the reporter found, was at a standstill. The Union Stock Yards and the Board of Trade were in "a rather bad way." Many of the country merchants who came to town were unable to arrange for credit and could not buy.

Storey, nevertheless, was firmly optimistic, seeing in the somewhat dolorous replies to his reporter's questions a significance not as readily evident to other readers. With typical vigor, Storey set down his conclusions:

"Notwithstanding the panic . . . . the city is generally more prosperous this Fall than ever before. Business circles are more animated and business men more cheerful than they were two weeks ago. Except for a few old croakers who are always predicting a storm even under a clear sky, everybody now believes the panic is over and business is fast resuming its former activity."

The streets, Storey's *Times* pointed out, were filled with busy strangers. The hotels were crammed with visitors. The theaters were packed. The grain elevators were shipping wheat, by railroad if not by boat. On the lake front, Chicago was staging its first big exposition in the garish, triple-domed Inter-State Industrial Palace, with exhibitors from all over the Middle West displaying their products to enthusiastic throngs.

Chicago, bragged Storey, was still "key city to the West." It stood ready to take over new trade that other cities, prouder and older, were too timorous to handle. The nation is growing, the West is growing! chanted Storey. Chicago was the town to grow with the West, Chicago and her merchants and manufacturers. "In New York, Philadelphia, Boston, St. Louis and Cincinnati trade is stagnant," wrote the gruff editor. "There money is scarce and people disheartened. Chicago does not glory in the misfortunes of her rivals. Neither can she be blind to the prosperity which the Fates shower down upon her."

Despite Storey's rosy words and the excitement of the Exposition, Chicago's situation was better only by comparison with that of her rivals. The lines of the jobless increased. The Greenback party, campaigning for a new money system, won adherents. Knights of Labor organizers found men who had little to do but listen. Wages dropped. There was discontent and rumors of trouble among workers and farmers.

For two dangerous years Field and Leiter nursed their new store and their big wholesale business. Their conservative financial policies were enabling them to survive. They had no patience with the new discontent, the labor unions, the Grange movement among the farmers, or even a proposal to liberalize the bankruptcy laws. Hard work, they believed, would pull everyone through. That some had failed to lay by cash reserves was not their fault. Leiter cracked his credit whip over those who welshed on their debts. Often the house rumbled with the roar of his voice as he shoved a defaulter from his office, shouting, "You promised to pay and you did not do it! Get out or I will have the porter throw you out!"

A merchant possessing what Leiter considered a "bad record" could not buy a handkerchief in these times, or any other. Not even if he had the cash to pay! "It makes no difference," Leiter would roar at the welsher who now had the effrontery to return. "We don't want your money. We don't want your business! Your record is bad, sir!"

Yet to hard-pressed smaller merchants of good standing the partners often showed kindness and consideration. To many caught in the panic they were downright benevolent. They invited some country merchants to come to their wholesale offices to talk over their problems with Leiter's aide, Harlow Higinbotham, an expert at easing credit woes. They instructed their salesmen to keep calling on nonbuying customers and advise them. In some instances they dispatched a star department head or general salesman to a country store to aid the owner in solving his problems.

Field and Leiter replaced delivery boys with delivery carts in 1873, then by 1897 Field's was using this famous fleet of "glass window wagons."

There was no neglecting the retail trade either. The most notable improvement in the State Street store was the expansion of the delivery system. Before this time deliveries for retail customers were rare, except when errand boys carried packages to waiting carriages. Now boys were hired for the specific job of toting bundles and packages to outlying homes. For $2.00 a week, these youngsters—most of them thirteen or fourteen— slung their package-filled khaki bags over one shoulder and made deliveries to residences in an area within a few miles from the store. Later, as the store and the city grew, the force was augmented by dozens more who used the cable cars on new routes stretching into outlying neighborhoods.

More horses and wagons were added. The barns on Pacific Avenue (later La Salle Street) were rebuilt and expanded to make room for fifty horses and canvas-topped wagons. These wagons went into some of the new suburbs and also were used for wholesale deliveries to other Chicago merchants.

Strict orders were issued at the barns for the care of the horses. Any driver who brought back a horse with whip marks was severely reprimanded and often discharged. The best horses worked only half a day. If a driver found himself on the far South Side at noon, he was directed to leave the horse and wagon at a neighborhood stable, return to the store by foot and cable car, and finish his day's deliveries with a fresh outfit. And on all the walls of the main barns, and others built in the next few years, were constant reminders that the animals were to be well treated. One sign read: "DON'T WHIP THE HORSES!" and another, titled "The Horse's Appeal to his Master," pleaded:

> "Of water stint me not,
>   Oh, whip, lash me not.
>   And don't forget to blanket me."

BEFORE DRAWN UP

MADAME DEWEY'S DRESS ELEVATOR

TO THE PRICE WARS

Difficult times continued to plague the country after the Panic of 1873, especially in the East where hard-hit railroads and industries sought to retrench by cutting the wages of their remaining workers, most of whom received little more than $1.00 a day. There were strikes and riots. Pitched battles raged in the streets of some cities, resulting in the death of many men and the destruction of nearly $10,000,000 in property. But the more resilient West made quicker recovery. More villages and towns leaped into being all over the stretches of plains beyond Chicago. Farm production bounded. Texas longhorns, driven north to fatten on the grasslands of Nebraska and Montana, were shipped to the Chicago market. And Europe, as Marshall Field had predicted, required much of its provisioning from America's western plains.

The dugouts and cabins of pioneers in the Dakotas, Nebraska, Idaho, Iowa, and Kansas blossomed into busy hamlets and cowtowns, each with a Main Street, a livery stable, a church, a corner saloon, and—most important for Field and Leiter and other wholesalers—a general store. These merchants read closely the circulars and letters sent out by the Chicago dry-goods houses. While money was short for them, too, and they took up the cry of Congressman Richard "Silver Dollar Dick"

Bland for free coinage of silver, they were still able to buy. Chicago, taking the produce of their farms and ranches, sent back farm machinery and dry goods.

Between them, they largely ignored the East. Chicago factories turned out for Chicago jobbers cowboy chaps, buckskin cowboy gloves—big-cuffed and ornamented with studs and embroidery—cowboy boots, farmers' work clothes, harness, buggies, wagons, plows, and, of course, reapers. Together with these shipments to the West went household wares, linens, gingham, curtains, mattresses, laces, suitings, and dress goods. And, as hunters slew bison to feed railroad builders on the wide plains, Field and Leiter were advertising "Buffalo robes, newly arrived from the West."

Soon the eastern manufacturers and wholesalers, beset by the long-lingering depression, stirred themselves and invaded the lush new territories. They set up their own jobbing houses in the districts dominated by the Chicago wholesalers. They sent glib traveling men into the new towns, urging retailers to buy from factories and save money. They sold cheap and shoddy goods, but their prices were low and tempting.

This touched off a price war with the Chicago crowd. Field and Leiter still refused to embark on such a campaign or expand their small force of traveling men. "I will quit the business first before competing on the road with these small jobbing houses," Field stormed. "I would rather have my business go under than have to peddle it out on the road."

He obviously had no real intention of doing any such thing. Events were moving too speedily for him to disregard or withstand the price-cutters. So he cut his prices too. And when eastern wholesalers, who looked the other way if their neighbors cited prices lower than those of the upstart Chicagoans, complained about the price-cutting of the firms in the Middle West, Field burst from his calm shell with bitter and angry retorts.

While some drummers carried calling cards backed with jokes and cartoons, Field and Leiter salesmen's cards featured chubby cherubs and mythology.

Above the battle boomed the voice of that inveterate home-town booster, Deacon Bross. He urged Europeans to bypass the eastern ports and ship their goods directly to Chicago by way of the Great Lakes. "Here," he cried, "customs duties can be paid and goods will be free from the exactions of New York sharpers. No country merchant in the North nor in the South-west need now go to New York!"

II

In the midst of the strife, Field and Leiter were confronted with a new threat—and in the very heart of the community where they had established their commercial supremacy.

On a sultry August day in 1876, a short, brisk man named Sabin Smith hustled into town. His arrival brought to a quick climax scores of rumors about new invaders from the East, for

Sabin Smith was the general manager of the mighty A. T. Stewart enterprises which now included, in addition to the famed and prospering Broadway retail store, a dozen mills, factories, a vast force of traveling salesmen, a staff of foreign buyers, and even hotels and resorts in upstate New York.

Stewart himself had died the previous April, but plans for this invasion, Smith blatantly assured reporters, had been laid long before then. Now, said Smith, he was acting in behalf of Stewart's successor, Judge Henry Hilton, the pioneer merchant's lawyer who had been bequeathed $1,000,000 and the power to carry out this and other plans. Judge Hilton, smiled Smith, hoped to surpass even the one and only Stewart. And it was indeed true, he added, that the Stewart Company would soon open a wholesale house in Chicago, a "handsome and commodious one" to compete on a grand scale with Field and Leiter.

Engaged on this new front in the struggle for profits and power, Field and Leiter fought back. For one thing they were instantly grateful: Smith approached Harlow Higinbotham with an offer to double his salary if he deserted Field and Leiter for the new firm, but the lanky credit genius smiled and shook his head. Several of the partners' best salesmen, also approached by Smith, likewise decided to remain.

For a time after Stewart's started operations on September 23 in three large buildings at Wabash and Washington, only a short block from the partners' State Street store, there were brief skirmishes. Field and Leiter had already announced to their customers that they would no longer be required to pay the cost of crating goods. Now Stewart's announced, "No charge for cases, no charge for baling, no charge for cartage." Stewart's promised low, easy prices, while Field and Leiter advertised, "Strangers visiting the city are cordially invited to look through our store and inspect our goods whether desiring to purchase or otherwise."

Chicago spurted ahead as hundreds of new factories were built to compete for the trade of midwestern farmers. Among the manufacturers who set up shop in Chicago was J. V. A. Wemple, builder of threshing machines, corn shellers, and carts.

Soon Stewart's began underselling Field and Leiter. "You will see," Field wrote to Lorenzo Woodhouse, head of their New York office, "that it is getting to be pretty mean competition." He vowed to give Stewart's "no great advantage" and told Woodhouse that in order to avoid complete chaos, he and Leiter had arranged an agreement with this new rival not to cut prices beyond reasonable limits.

Stewart's held to the agreement only until Smith and the other officials realized that they had neither the organization nor the reputation in this section of the country to compete with Field and Leiter on fair terms. Then unlimited price-slashing was renewed. "We shall stand none of their nonsense,"

Field informed Woodhouse once again. "If they desire to do a fair business they must talk less and behave better." Vexed by his foe's methods, Field was, by turns, depressed—"Business very slow," he scrawled on a letter in November to Woodhouse —and optimistic—"I still hope for better things."

This competition shoved Field closer to the practice he considered so distasteful, that of sending more and more commercial travelers out on the road. He still insisted that the best way to buy was for the customer to come into the city twice a year, be squired about by a general salesman, examine the goods he wanted, and place his orders. "As desirable goods can always be bought cheaper in the open market than from samples as shown by agents at your place of business," read a circular, "we again urge you to protect yourselves by waiting until you can personally inspect quality and prices."

But increasingly merchants were finding it easier and cheaper to stay home and select what they wanted from salesmen's samples. The trend toward a mass system of traveling salesmanship was too strong for even as mighty a house as Field and Leiter to stop. Still Field found the idea repugnant. When Dixon Bean, head of the company's carpet departments, told him of the great success a Philadelphia rug manufacturer had on the road during 1876 with only a single satchel filled with samples, Field shook his head sadly. When Bean went on to predict that in two years their own house would have men from every department out on the road with their samples, Field muttered, "No, I would close up first."

Persistently Bean pressed for a chance to see what results he could get on a selling trip. Field reluctantly allowed him and two other men to make a try at it that winter. "If you're not successful," he warned, "I'll want you back here."

The men were successful, sending in more orders than could have been achieved by the older method. Within a few months

After a disastrous fire in 1877 had destroyed their second State Street store, Field and Leiter moved to the Crystal Palace, built for the 1875 Fair.

additional salesmen were on the road, and in the spring of 1877 they were traveling to towns where the august name of Field, Leiter and Company won them orders promptly.

Whether or not he knew then of the far-reaching implications of this move, the tension of Field's battle with the Stewart group had eased. Not only was he meeting each price cut and holding and even gaining customers, but Field was also being helped—although he was unaware of it at the moment—by the basic weakness of the entire Stewart organization. Judge Hilton, a proud and imperious man who fancied himself a greater merchandising genius than Stewart, had expanded too quickly, had taken on too many new rivals. He himself had no ability, it soon developed, for such complicated endeavors; nor did he have an organization of experienced, devoted men to rely on. Each month saw new defections from the ranks of the old Stewart executives as Judge Hilton put into motion grandiose ideas that

145

were doomed to fail or suddenly slashed salaries to make up for his unexpected business losses.

By April, 1877, Field could see a way out of the fight with Stewart. The enemy, he reported to Woodhouse, was befuddled and wavering: "Stewart's people do not know what they want, in short, they want some business, have no idea more than a child unborn how to get it. . . . . Meantime, we have no idea of learning them how to get it, our interests are in keeping prices up and shall do so as far as can but have no notion of losing our trade, let it cost what it will. . . . . If they are mad we can't help them—it will do them good to know how it is. . . . ."

Soon Stewart's once-mighty business vanished, and Marshall Field was requesting reporters to stop referring to him as they had done with Palmer, as the "A. T. Stewart of the West."

III

Before the end of 1877 and the ultimate triumph over their rivals, another calamity befell Field and Leiter.

On the rainy night of November 14, a citizen saw smoke rising from the roof of the State Street store. An alarm was turned in, setting off a tragicomedy of errors. The first firemen to arrive misjudged the source of the smoke and took their hoses all the way up the stairway of the adjoining Burley and Tyrell crockery and glassware store. Other firemen hooked up their hoses but were unable to throw streams of water high enough to reach the blazing roof. Two dozen salesmen and clerks who lived in nearby boardinghouses rushed to the store's upper floors, squirting water from fire extinguishers. But before special hoses on each floor could be connected and the basement pumps started, the fire spread down the elevator shafts and drove all the fire fighters—amateurs and professionals alike—to the lower floors. At the height of the blaze a huge water tank fell, killing two firemen and injuring a dozen others.

As in the holocaust of 1871 the store's employees worked desperately on the lower floors to save the stock. Wagons, rushed from the Pacific Avenue barns, stood in the muddy streets while silks, shawls, and rugs were piled into them. By two o'clock the next morning, when the last flickers of flame were snuffed out and only the store's outer walls were still standing, some $200,000 of the store's merchandise had been saved and hauled away to the barns and to nearby lofts. Another $800,000 had been destroyed, but this loss was more than amply covered by $1,000,000 insurance.

All that day, solemn crowds hovered near the ruins. "The destruction of St. Peter's at Rome," the *Chicago Tribune* noted, "could hardly have aroused an apparently deeper interest than the destruction of this palatial dry goods establishment. It is questionable whether the death of the Pope or the burning up of the Vatican could have excited such a keen local interest. . . . . This was the place of worship of thousands of our female fellow-citizens. It was the only shrine at which they paid their devotions."

When reporters asked Field, "How soon will you reopen?" he retorted, "Give us time to breathe!" But he followed with quick assurance, as they pressed him for news of his plans: "We will announce that as soon as we are ready."

In two days he was ready. Quickly he arranged with the managers of the Inter-State Industrial Palace—Potter Palmer among them—to rent the huge structure as a temporary store for $750 a month. Workmen toiled day and night to whip the place into shape. Most of the salvaged stock not damaged by smoke, together with new wares from the wholesale section, were arranged in a central circle and on rickety wooden counters. Water-soaked and flame-singed goods were piled high outside the building, to be sold at drastically reduced prices or in wholesale lots at auction.

For three days before November 27 when the "Exposition Store" on Michigan Boulevard opened, Chicago was deluged by rain. On opening day, the rain was heavier than ever. Yet, despite rain, mud, and bedraggled goods the crowds poured in. "Womankind," gasped the *Tribune*, "was excited. Fathers and families complained of the cooking at breakfast. Children were hustled off to school with their shoestrings untied and their noses untouched by the maternal apron. And at nine o'clock, there were two processions on Michigan Avenue marching in opposite directions toward the same point—the main entrance to the Exposition Building."

Hour after hour, in the driving rain, the crowds of women grew bigger. Guards at the main doors allowed the avid shoppers to enter in groups. As each detachment pressed inside, the doors were slammed shut again. Each time the doors opened to admit another batch, people shouted and roared and shoved. "*FEMININE FOLLY*," next morning's *Tribune* headed its account of the big opening.

By the end of the week, the crowds had thinned out. The rains ceased and even the merchandise soaked in the opening-day torrents was dried, refolded, and auctioned off. From the wholesale house came new wares so that by December 10, as the Christmas shoppers swarmed through the long building, the partners were able to state, "Every department in the retail has been replenished with New and Elegant Goods." As a special inducement for shoppers inclined to linger on State Street, free omnibuses ran every five minutes from the corner of State and Randolph streets to the Exposition Store.

Special features of the wholesale house were soon displayed at the lake-front emporium.

In keeping with the current movement in women's dress reform, especially against tight corsets—"Avoid tight lacing as you would a black snake," the fashion writers hinted—the corset section displayed the famed Madame Foy's Skirt Supporting Corset and the Good Sense Corset Waist. An indication that the price war was still on was the firm's claim in this department: "We guarantee to undersell any manufacturer that finds it necessary to go to the retail trade."

Another favorite was a new line of Jessie Oakley soaps, now in such scents as golden hyacinth, tonquin musk, wood violet, and spring flowers. The J. and P. Coats sewing cotton, winner of first prize at the Centennial Exhibition in Philadelphia the year before, was another excellent seller.

But the season's novelty rage was men's paper collars, offered in a variety of tricky ways. One was the William Reilly collar, which got its name from a popular song of the day, "Oh, Rise Up, William Reilly, and Come Along With Me!" The George Washington collar came in a box with a small gilt hatchet "to be worn by the truthful as a charm." The Moss-Covered Bucket collar was put up in a solid wooden bucket,

Little girls who wore Ferris Brothers' Good Sense Corset Waists, sold by Field and Leiter, grew up to fill out these fetching Madame Foy's Corsets.

"handsome for a toilet article." The Arkansas Traveler—
"greatest novelty of the season"—came in a Zoetrope box that
contained a series of comic revolving pictures. And the Cunard
collar was in a small tin pail. All these specialties, the shoppers
were assured, were "entirely new, being worth alone, as attractive novelties, more than double the price without collars."

IV

A few weeks after the rubble and smoldering ruins of the
burned State Street store had been cleared away, the Singer
Company officials started to build a new one. They assumed,
from the beginning, that Field and Leiter would be overjoyed
to return to their original site. But they were only half right in
their thinking.

Field did want to re-establish the retail store again—and in
bigger terms and scope than ever before. But Leiter had lost
interest in this phase of their business. He tried to persuade
Field that they must concentrate on their wholesale trade, what
with the price battles, competition, and growing markets. The
big money, Leiter pointed out with assurance, still lay in wholesale. He could cite figures for his case—retail profits for the
six years since the Great Fire totaled some $300,000, while
wholesale profits added up to a soaring $5,286,000.

But Field was stubborn in his purpose. Wholesale, obviously,
did yield the greatest revenues; but whatever drama and showmanship and prestige existed in the routine dry-goods business
were all concentrated in the retail store. Here the basic purpose
would be to get as much profit as possible but with the equally
vital motive of service to the community—and especially to the
community's women.

Besides, Field emphasized as he examined the cold figures,
retail trade was rising even as the city rose in population,
dwellings, and enterprise. Even in the grotesque surroundings

of the Exposition Building and in temporary quarters on Wabash Avenue through 1878, retail profits had leaped to more than $160,000 for the year, almost $100,000 above the previous year.

Grudgingly, Leiter assented. He even promised to undertake negotiations with the Singer people for the purchase—not the mere rental—of the new store building. But while Field was in New York, these negotiations reached near-disaster proportions early in 1879. Singer demanded $700,000 for the building. Leiter offered $500,000—"And not a penny more! If we don't take the building, you won't find another tenant in Chicago for it!"

Rumors spread that other companies intended to move in, such New York merchants as Arnold Constable and the prospering combine of Lord and Taylor. Still Leiter refused to budge from his position. Suddenly the Singer executives made a startling announcement. The store had been leased, at $70,000 a year, to the industrious Scotchmen who headed the firm of Carson, Pirie and Company, they who did a comfortable business at Madison and Peoria streets and had been advertising, "It Pays to Trade on The West Side."

Field arrived in time to hear the news and thwart the plan. He conferred days on end with the Singer officials and with Sam Carson and John T. Pirie. He upbraided Leiter for not carrying through the original plan for moving back to State Street. At the conclusion of the fuss and fury Field and Leiter got the store. But they had to pay not only the $700,000 the Singer officials had asked for, but an additional bonus of $100,000 to the wise Scotchmen to give up their lease.

At last, in spite of the trouble and wrangling and ill-feeling, the partners were headed back to State Street, never again to leave it. And the hardest days were behind them.

LOTTA BRAID

GOSSAMER CRIMPS

GOSSAMER WAVE.

CALKINS' CHAMPION WASHER.

THE NEW WOMAN
ARRIVES

"Home again, eh?"

The clerks nodded and the salesmen smiled. Once more, on a warm April day in 1879, crowds celebrated what had become a civic rite, the opening of a new Field and Leiter store. This establishment was the grandest yet.

The aisles were wider, the carpets softer, the displays fancier. There were still only two elevators, but each had colorful upholstery and expensive wood and mirrors. A grand staircase twenty-three feet wide led from a broad middle aisle to the second floor. On the third floor lay piles of carpets for the new homes of the newly-rich, on the fifth floor sat 300 women stitching dresses for the wives of the city's magnates, and on the top floor was another workshop producing "exclusive" laces, suits, and cloaks.

Signs of class and elegance were clearly evident. At the entrance stood John Muir, a uniformed official greeter, who bowed and held the doors wide for the ladies stepping from their carriages. No longer did clerks and ushers call each other by their last names only; now it was "Mr. Clark" and "Miss O'Brien" and "Mrs. Townsend." No longer was that little section at the rear of the first floor to be called "Gents' Furnishings"; it was "Gentlemen's Furnishings." No practice here of calling customers, as in other less dignified stores, "Dearie" or even "My Dear." "Yes, madam" was the fitting address.

Even the cry of "Cash! Come Cash!" was heard no more. Each cash boy now had a number. As of old, he sat stiffly on a bench in his tight-fitting uniform, but instead of clerks yelling for him or tapping impatiently on the solid counter tops to get his attention, he was dispatched by a man who watched as a counter number was flashed on a board near the bench. Boss of these lads now was Mike Ford, who had been Marshall Field's footman until a day when he whipped a few young toughs who had thrown snowballs at Field's carriage. Impressed with Ford's efficiency, Field had assigned him to take charge of the cash boys with the warning, "See that they act like little gentlemen." Ford insisted the youngsters dress neatly, scrub their faces, and comb their hair. Despite such hardships there were many seeking these jobs that paid $2.00 for a six-day week. This soon became an axiom: "When you get a cash boy's job at Field and Leiter's, you start shining your shoes every day."

II

A "New Chicago Woman" could be found in the new Field and Leiter store, selecting from the splendid displays, roaming through the aisles, or settling herself in the second-floor waiting room among potted palms and ferns.

She was a member of the "society set," a new elite that, developing after the Great Fire, set the modes, fashions, and moral concepts for most other women of the city. The New Woman, whose husband inevitably was doing well, made a pilgrimage to Europe at least once every two years and came back prattling of the extravagant splendors of Paris and the "aesthetic" movement led by Oscar Wilde in England.

Her home, new and enormous, was usually a garish monstrosity modeled after some French mansion she had seen. She either was, or longed to be, a member of the Chicago Woman's Club, formed in 1876 with the lofty objective of "mutual sympathy and counsel and united effort toward the higher civilization of humanity," or the Chicago Society of Decorative Art, dedicated to "art and its refining and elevating influences."

She was able to afford costly dresses and splendid carriages because her husband was a meat packer or a dry-goods merchant, a manufacturer of horseshoe nails or a dealer in grain. She tried hard to forget the source of her income. She was an exponent of "taste," a refined appreciation of the artistic and elegant, for which her husband had neither interest nor comprehension. She loved art for art's sake at the very moment when astute merchants and manufacturers had discovered means for the mass production of art objects and furniture.

As the ladies continued to appear in growing numbers, Field and Leiter supplied their wants and needs. Field set about diligently to educate western taste—his conception of a merchant's task. Yet he was ever the realist. If the American woman yearned to imitate the wealthy classes of Europe and the society leaders of the eastern cities, she would be indulged with imported originals or, where necessary, with factory "modifications" of European styles.

The lady, happily, was never sated. New fashions constantly whetted her appetite. Fine family heirlooms, once the pride of the American home, went to the attic or the trash heap to make room for glittering goods. The lady doted on gilt Eastlake chairs, horsehair chairs, fragile chairs in blue velvet elaborately carved and inlaid with ebony, ivory, rare woods, or mother-of-pearl. If she could not afford an original, she bought a factory imitation for as little as $1.00. The horsehair sofa and the overstuffed chair had a prominent place in the parlor, or perhaps a gay set, upholstered in green damask, with a puffing of yellow satin and a black walnut frame.

Chicago's New Woman gave considerable attention to beauty and adornment. By carriage, train, or trolley she stormed to the Field and Leiter counters when arrivals of goods were announced. Having abandoned the cumbersome crinoline, an impossible garment in the fast age of railroad transportation, she wore a bustle and tight-fitting skirt that forced her to take mincing steps.

She was fond of the low, wasp-waist bodice, pleated skirts of flowered material, velvet jackets, plumed hats, watered silks and satins, laces, fringes, and gewgaws. She made petticoats of a new muslin, so sheer, according to the Field and Leiter advertisements, "that it outrivals the finest web ever spun by the cunningest old spiders, having embroidered all over its frail surface the brightest of small red and yellow butterflies."

She had her choice of dozens of "beauty aids" to make her more attractive and hundreds of skilled and expensive modistes to mold the yards of material into the most fetching dresses and frocks. "Ladies' Trousseaus a Specialty," said Madame Myra, a State Street dressmaker who catered to the best families.

Less prosperous but equally romantic young women could acquire their trousseaus for only $50 through the shoppers' service section of Martha Louise Rayne's *Chicago Magazine of Fashion, Music and Home Reading*. This sum, said Mrs. Rayne, would provide six muslin chemises, four pairs of drawers, four tucked white shirts, four nightdresses, two flounced skirts, one linen suit, one delaine wrapper, one traveling dress, one pair of slippers, one pair of kid gloves, and a bottle of cologne.

A lady shopping at Field and Leiter's usually visited Campbell's Hair Store across the street. "What," demanded Campbell in his newspaper and theater program advertisements, "would even the highest type of beauty be without heavy braids and flowing curls?" Campbell's big business was in switches, puffs, curls, chignons, and his own creation—French Crimpees.

The favorite of the time was the hair style used by Lily Langtry, the actress who charmed kings, millionaires, and even the irrepressible Oscar Wilde. "Ladies!" cried Campbell. "Bring in your old faded hair and exchange it for new! Our $3.50 Langtry bangs is the greatest bargain on earth!" Women hastened to make themselves as alluring as the "Jersey Lily," with her bangs, her charms, her smile that, according to the advertisements, was made more tempting by her use of a toothpaste called "Sweet Saponax."

For those denied the shapely figure of Miss Langtry, a boon was available at Hood and Severn's shop a few blocks from the Field and Leiter store. "It is a lamentable fact," chorused Messrs. Hood and Severn, "that all American women, or with few exceptions, lack the full figure which is requisite to perfection of form, and as they are in need of assistance from art to supply the deficiencies of nature, we are glad that the inventive genius of

The New Woman had a new look, too, thanks to such boons as the elastic bosom (which could also serve as a life preserver in case of shipwreck, its makers claimed) and trim, stylish boots.

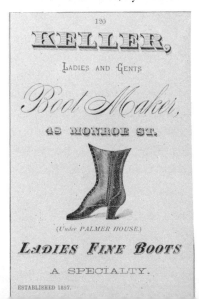

our country has supplied a substitute that is comfortable and at the same time helpful." They thereby offered to the curveless ones the "American Elastic Bosom," a popular item of apparel referred to by scoffers as "the gay deceivers."

Salves and tonics concocted to erase wrinkles and remove warts, and such nostrums as "Hair Revivum—the Great Hair Restorer," were among the best sellers. Women in delicate health found many panaceas available: "Radway's Ready Relief"—popularly known as R.R.R.—promised "A cure for every pain." Collins' Voltaic Electric Plasters were hailed in printed testimonials as "The Curative Marvel of the Age." Dr. Dohme's Sulphide of Arsenicum was described simply as the "Supreme and Wonderful Skin Remedy and Blood Purifier." No woman with a few dollars to spend had reason to lack beauty of face and figure and the bloom of youth.

The New Woman was handsomer, much more daring, and a lot giddier than the ladies of a decade ago who had come to the first Field and Leiter store on State Street. Some were emancipated enough to puff "Cocarettes," made of Virginia tobacco and Bolivian coca leaves, and acclaimed as a "Nerve Tonic and Exhilarator, Absolutely Not Injurious." A few had taken to reading French novels and to serving cozy Sunday breakfasts of French delicacies: chicken livers *en brochette*, *café noir*, and *omelettes aux fines herbes*.

Shopgirls and housewives giggled with delight at the account of the amazing housewarming in the marble mansion built by Perry H. Smith, along Millionaires' Row on the Near North Side—a stately palace with black-walnut woodwork, high ceilings, a ballroom, and a theater. Mrs. Smith, it seemed, had startled her guests on the occasion by leading them to the butler's pantry, there to turn on each of three faucets. From one poured hot water; from the second came cold water; from the third—iced champagne!

CROQUET DRESS   WALKING DRESS.

Madcap ladies, going all out for exhilarating sports, wore daring, form-fitting costumes like these to provide freedom of movement in a smashing game of croquet. Men, scoffing at the garb and antics of "the new woman," often were beaten by these sports-loving girls.

III

To supply Chicago's women with what they demanded or were persuaded to demand—whether $1,500 shawls, fragile gilt chairs, or artificial bosoms—a flock of other stores had sprouted to compete with Field and Leiter.

Carson and Pirie, soon to move to State Street, were the closest of the competitors, appealing to the same class of shoppers that patronized Field and Leiter. These careful Scots had as a partner Andrew McLeish, who had scorned a job in Potter Palmer's Lake Street store back in 1854 because he believed Palmer's venture had no profitable future. Now Carson and

Pirie were prospering on the West Side, where the store had been set up after the Great Fire.

Nearby were two young men, Leopold Schlesinger and David Mayer, who had gone into partnership in 1872 when Schlesinger was twenty-six and Mayer only nineteen. They sometimes tried to draw wealthy shoppers to their establishment on Madison Street, but their widest appeal was to the vast masses. "Popular Prices!" was their cry although they liked to think of themselves as a "fashion center" occasionally as they sang loudly of their laces, ribbons, silks, and dress goods.

A formidable competitor of Field and Leiter's was the pioneer, Charles Gossage, whose stately establishment a block away on State Street was fronted by two brass lions. On land owned by Field, three brothers—Simon, Leon, and Emanuel Mandel—carried on a busy and profitable dry-goods trade. They had started in 1855 shortly after they came from Europe. Their first store, at Clark and Van Buren streets, had vanished in the Great Fire. Like Field and Leiter, they had set up business in a makeshift way on the South Side in the days after the fire, but by 1875, encouraged by Field's liberal rental arrangement, they had moved back to State Street. All these merchants staunchly considered themselves dry-goods dealers, as did Field and Leiter. Their establishments, they insisted, were primarily dry-goods stores, despite the widening range of other wares.

The only one who conceded he was the owner of an out-and-out "department store" was a German-born newcomer named Edward J. Lehmann. In 1875, he had started business in a one-story frame building on State Street, featuring cheap jewelry, notions, crockery, kitchen utensils, and hardware. He called his store "The Fair," and blared that every item—"Everything for Everybody Under One Roof!"—was cheap. His low prices snared the interest of the hard-pressed, depression-ridden citizens, who came to his store in such numbers that in four years he was able to buy out several bankrupt merchants and expand his store to four times its original size.

Along with the kind of stock offered in less flashy stores, he piled high on tables on the sidewalk in front of The Fair goods from auctions, bankruptcy sales, fire sales, and similar disasters. He staged Odd-Cent Sales at which a Chicagoan could buy a gold-tipped toothpick for 28 cents, a ten-carat-gold band ring for 88 cents, a gold-plated sleeve button for 22 cents. At his Losing Sales, a rocking chair was 50 cents, undershirts 15 cents, men's collars 5 cents, cuspidors 10 cents, books 44 cents, candies 10 cents a pound, and a "fine oil painting, in an extra furnished gilt frame," $2.25. At his popular Four-Cent Counters one had his pick, for this slight amount, of earrings, veil pins, neck charms, and scarf holders.

IV

Industrious though the competitors were, their profits fell short of those gained by Field and Leiter. Nor could they match the partners in sheer prestige, for the State Street store, with its air of genteel elegance and qualities, and simply as an exposition to be seen and admired, had become a sort of civic possession—a symbol of rowdy Chicago on its best behavior. Here were no undignified sales methods, no hint that anything savored of meager quality. The tone was not that of a hard-driving store, with clerks tugging at sleeves and yelling into a customer's ear the alleged merits of this coat or that scarf. Here was a place, of course, where profits were as eagerly sought as in the crasser establishments. But never, warned Field in his cold, careful way, was anyone to consider a mere sale more important than holding a customer. Again and again, he affirmed, the customer had to be pleased. There, Field was certain, lay the way not only to a good reputation in the community but to increasing profits.

WHOLESALE BILLHEAD

MARSHALL FIELD
& COMPANY

Oddly, relations between Field and Leiter grew more frayed as the store prospered.

Leiter never had cared for the retail end of the business. "Costs too much to make any real profit," he grumbled. Field had greater imagination and felt genuine enthusiasm for the retail store. He wanted State Street to become one of the world's great shopping centers. "If we bring the people here, then it is up to us to win them to our house," he liked to say. "First, we must get them to State Street."

Having lured the Mandel brothers with reasonable rental for land he owned, Field also sought to encourage Schlesinger and Mayer to move. He had confidence in his own powers as a merchant. If some of the trade funneled off to rivals, Field and Leiter would command their share from the increasing throngs. Field and Leiter would be first, setting the tone, garnering the cream of the sales. As for spending money on improvements and costly merchandise, he always maintained, "There is nothing too good for retail!"

A clash was inevitable since Field insisted more firmly than ever on running the business his way, and Leiter adhered grumpily to his own ideas. Field believed that although Leiter's credit policies had served to pull the firm through its worst crises, his

Watchdog of the credit department was Levi Z. Leiter, whose bite inevitably matched his frequent bark. Leiter grudgingly aided wholesale customers in distress but often denied goods to cash buyers because he did not like their looks or reputations.

burly partner alienated too many people with his ferocious ways. It was essential, Field conceded, to carefully investigate credit-seekers, and to reject some applicants. But Leiter often was unreasonable and eccentric in determining the reliability of a potential customer.

Once, while striding toward his office, Leiter spied a visitor with graying hair and a jet-black mustache. "What do you want, sir?" Leiter bellowed. The man replied, "I've come to buy some goods." Peering intently at the mustache, Leiter roared, "No you don't, sir! Your mustache is dyed and you are obviously a thief. Get out of here, and good day, sir!"

Again, a young salesman who had sold $800 worth of goods to a customer happily brought the bill and buyer to Leiter's office. Leiter took one look at the name on the tab and shouted, "No, sir, you cannot have these goods." "But I'm going to pay cash," insisted the customer. "That makes no difference," Leiter replied. "Your credit record with us is bad, and you cannot have these goods!"

Despite the differences in their temperaments the two men had managed to accumulate between them some $6,000,000 in real estate. Of this, $1,700,000 was owned jointly. Each had bought much land on State Street and the surrounding areas during the years following the Panic of 1873. But despite these successes the relationship of the two became so strained in the months following the return to State Street that neither spoke to the other for days at a time.

Each man now had accumulated a sufficient fortune to buy out the other. There were rumors that this would happen, but both Field and Leiter were careful to brush them aside. Finally, the break came. It was Field who made the first move.

II

Field had ready allies in his plan to sever his long partnership with the irascible Leiter. They were the junior members of the firm: Field's brothers, Joseph and Henry, and three others— Harlow N. Higinbotham, Leiter's protégé; Henry J. Willing, who had come far from his early days as a messenger boy at T. B. Carter's; and Lorenzo Woodhouse, the head of the busy New York office. Each found Leiter a hard man to deal with even in the most routine problems. Nor were they pleased by his persistent refusal to give them a greater share of the profits and a bigger role in running the business.

For weeks before the first of 1881, Field approached each of the juniors partners and most of his other key executives. To each he posed the same question: "Will you stay with me if I should buy Mr. Leiter out?" In each case the reply was "Yes."

Armed with these promises, Field confronted Leiter. Coldly and politely he informed him that he no longer wished to continue their partnership. "It's time we part," he said.

Caught by surprise, Leiter cleared his throat and tugged at his beard. Before he could reply, Field continued. He offered to name a figure at which either one could buy or sell the entire business, wholesale and retail. The figure was only about $2,500,000, a preposterously low one for an enterprise that had total sales of nearly $25,000,000 in 1880.

"You have first choice," said Field, acting superbly the role of the shrewd Yankee trader. "Buy or sell."

Although Field knew the position he had put Leiter in, he agreed to Leiter's request for twenty-four hours before giving an answer. In that time Leiter contacted the junior partners and the important executives. Then he knew why his partner had set such a low figure, for, as Field expected, each man to whom Leiter spoke told him he had given his word to stay with the organization only if Marshall Field remained as sole owner. Without these key men, Leiter realized, the business could quickly decay, as had the mighty house of A. T. Stewart.

So he returned to Field, a glare in his eye. "You win, Marshall," he said. "I'll sell."

III

In great secrecy the details of the sale were worked out after the new year started.

By January 26, the news had leaked sufficiently for the newspapers to send their reporters to the firm's offices. By this time the partners presented a calm front to their visitors. Both, reported the *Chicago Tribune*, were attending to business "with just as much sangfroid as if their protracted interview had relation to the extension of a customer's note, or the drop of a quarter cent of a yard in domestic cottons."

The ex-partners were affable but closemouthed. Their reluctance to discuss the deal drew tart comment from the *Tribune's* editorial writer. Chiding Field and Leiter for their "timidity" about informing the citizens, he reminded them of the store's standing in the community.

The first store to bear the name Marshall Field & Company—this building was the third structure on the State and Washington site, built in 1879.

"When the public goes abroad," he wrote, "it boasts of Field, Leiter and Company just as it does of the Stock Yards and the Crib, and the wonderful attractions of Chicago as a place of summer resort. It has felt a great pride in them. It takes its rural cousin down there to show him the great pile, with its marvelous contents, and the least humble of its army of clerks who has plied the scissors and yard measure on its counters, or even the smallest cash boy who has listened to the spiritual manifestations all over the building until he has learned to distinguish its own, has felt his bosom swell with pride as he reflected that he belonged to one of the great institutions of the city."

The silence continued. Marshall Field had taken 46.5 per cent interest in the business, allocating 17 per cent to Wood-house, 14 per cent to Willing, 10 to Higinbotham, 5 to Henry

Field, and 7.5 per cent to Joseph Field. But these details he stubbornly refused to disclose to the public.

Wild talk and rumors increased. A report that Leiter had yielded to the pleas of his wife, Mary Carver Leiter, who felt her husband's business connections hampered her social aspirations, was denounced by the *Chicago Times* as "the senseless vagaries of the gossipy world." Another piece of gossip had it that Leiter intended to start a rival store after he returned from a long European vacation. Years later he would build such a store on State Street for a pair of merchants, but now he took the trouble to deny this story. "I have retired from business," he insisted. "I am going trout fishing."

The only official word to the public of the end of the seventeen-year partnership appeared in formal advertisements: "Marshall Field & Co., Successor to Field, Leiter & Co., EXTRAORDINARY BARGAINS!"

But one of Wilbur Fisk Storey's enterprising reporters, Frederick Francis Cook, did inform the readers of the *Times* about some of the juicier details of the sale and the extent of both men's real-estate holdings. In a long, statistic-filled account of the deal Cook told of the growth of bad feeling between the two partners and the wishes of the younger men for larger interests in the firm. "Individually and collectively," wrote Cook, "they are the largest real estate owners in the city." Then he went on to itemize what Field and Leiter each owned.

In the agreement ending the partnership, Chicagoans were informed, Field turned over to Leiter for his share of the business several chunks of land and buildings on State Street, including the handsome one at the corner of Madison Street to which the enterprising fellows, Schlesinger and Mayer, had finally moved from the West Side and were paying a comfortable rental. Field retained the major interest in the store that had been leased to the Mandel brothers.

When Field read Cook's story, he was aghast. He asked Storey to send Cook to his office.

"Mr. Cook," said Field, with a frown, "what possessed you to give those details about our business?"

"I saw no reason for not doing so," replied Cook. "It was certainly legitimate news matter."

"Well, you shouldn't have done it," snapped Field. "We have been large patrons of the *Times*, and the paper should have considered our interests more."

Cook bristled. "Mr. Storey," he informed Field, "doesn't expect us to consult the counting room when it comes to a matter of news. Why do you object so to publicity about your real-estate holdings?"

"Well," said Field, "I do not care being made a target for socialists to fire at."

This fear of what "socialists" might do was one of the few common beliefs Field and Leiter had held in the closing years of

Chicago's society women and their hours for receiving callers were listed in the Bon-Ton Directory, published in the late seventies. Most such ladies maintained their reputations as leaders of fashion simply by ordering their carriages to the Field and Leiter store on State Street, where they instructed the clerks to "charge it."

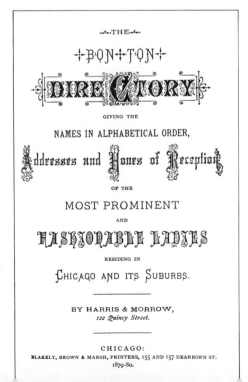

THE

BON-TON

DIRECTORY

GIVING THE

NAMES IN ALPHABETICAL ORDER,

Addresses and Hours of Reception

OF THE

MOST PROMINENT

AND

FASHIONABLE LADIES

RESIDING IN

CHICAGO AND ITS SUBURBS.

BY HARRIS & MORROW,
122 Quincy Street.

CHICAGO:
BLAKELY, BROWN & MARSH, PRINTERS, 155 AND 157 DEARBORN ST.
1879-80.

Field's was not a big advertiser in early days, but its copy appeared consistently, except on Sunday. Sunday ads, Marshall Field held, were a sacrilege.

their relationship. In 1877, in the wake of the depression, Chicago had been the center of activities of various radical groups that fused into the Workingmen's Party of the United States. When local newspapers began reporting the clashes between striking railroad workers and policemen in Pittsburgh, Leiter, at Field's urging, had led a committee to see Victor F. Lawson, whose *Chicago Daily News* had doubled and quadrupled its circulation by front-paging the stories of the strike and riots. They asked him to suspend publication because the "Strike Extras" were "inflaming the masses." Lawson refused.

In the weeks that followed, the strike did spread to Chicago. The city seethed with armed clashes between strikers and police.

Through the terror, Field and Leiter armed their clerks and workers in their big wholesale house with rifles, deadly certain that mobs were preparing to invade the district. No mobs appeared and soon Army regulars marched through the streets of the excited city to help break the strike. The company's rifles were stowed away, and the owners concentrated on taking due advantage of the good times that were slowly starting to return.

IV

Leiter became a changed man, once the pressure of business was off his mind.

He and the stylish Mrs. Leiter traveled to Paris, London, and even Moscow, returning with a samovar from which they served tea to twittering matrons and their bored husbands in their big house on Calumet Avenue. At Lake Geneva, Wisconsin, Leiter built a $200,000 house, Linden Lodge, which became a showplace among the showplaces of that fashionable summer community. Here he had a Dutch windmill, an icehouse, and his own trout pond. He got wealthier by the year from his real-estate investments; he joined more clubs, headed the Art Institute, and collected rare books and art masterpieces.

He never lost faith in Chicago as a place where fortunes were to be made. Only a few months after he had left the business world—later he would return for a brief, dramatic scene with his old partner—he was ready with counsel to a young man who was pondering the possibility of doing well in Chicago.

From Paris, where he and Mrs. Leiter were visiting the Louvre and the sidewalk bookstalls, he wrote to a young New Yorker who contemplated opening a jewelry store in Chicago: "It would be a well advised enterprise and could not fail to yield you a handsome profit. Chicago, you will remember, has a pre-eminent position in point of distribution for the entire Mississippi Valley. . . . . There is money to be made there."

The

GENUINE

Alexandre Kid Gloves,

For Finish, Durability and Fineness
of Skin are the Best in the World.

The Cut of the "ALEXANDRE" is
such that when on, its perfect fit gives
the hand a more graceful appearance
than any other glove.

MARSHALL FIELD & CO.

Cor. State and Washington Sts ,

CHICAGO.

PORTRAIT OF A MERCHANT PRINCE

Now Marshall Field stood alone as the city's first-ranking merchant prince, and for the rest of his life he would prosper as his fame and reputation and that of his State Street store flourished. Chicago paused in its tumult of expansion to take a closer look at Marshall Field in his moment of victory.

He was forty-six, a few inches under six feet, and spare of figure. His eyes were cold and bluish-gray, topped by heavy dark eyebrows that contrasted boldly with the hair and mustache, once chestnut-brown, that had turned gray suddenly in his fortieth year. His cheeks still retained the pinkness that the ladies back in Deacon Davis' store had found so charming.

In repose, his features were sad; his smile, when it appeared, was quick. His hands were rather thick. The forefinger of his right hand was crooked slightly, and he habitually kept this hand in his right vest pocket, hiding the stiffened finger. In this pocket he also kept a roll of one- and five-dollar bills, with larger ones in the other pocket or in linen-lined envelopes in his coat. He was slightly bowlegged and a little stoop-shouldered, but he affected the walk of a military man, stiff and firm.

His greatest joy was in business, and his home life was somewhat less than happy. He lived with his ailing wife, Nannie, and their handsome children, Marshall II and Ethel, in a red brick,

On Prairie Avenue, Chicago's "street of the stately few," the home of Marshall Field, shown at the right, was one of the grandest. Its cost was $100,000.

French-style mansion on genteel, wealth-laden Prairie Avenue. The house had been built for him at a reputed cost of $100,000 in 1876 by Richard Morris Hunt, a noted architect who had also designed the luxurious dwellings of William H. Vanderbilt, John Jacob Astor, and other New York millionaires.

Although the exterior of the Field house was less ornate than other mansions rising on this "street of the stately few," its walls were covered with yellow satin, and one room was furnished in the style of Louis XVI. There were many shelves of richly bound books, their pages cut but largely unread.

Nannie Field often spent months in Europe, principally in the south of France. Sometimes Field and the children accompanied her, traveling always on the "Baltic," a White Star liner, in a set of rooms known formally as the "Field Suite." His letters to friends were filled with reports on his wife's health, sometimes sad and rather bitter, occasionally flashing with hope that she would improve and that her chronic headaches might vanish after a stay in France.

Field himself made other trips alone to Europe, principally to see Joseph Field in the Manchester office. He too went to France, but more often on business than on pleasure. On one such trip he had the satisfaction of having his firm appointed sole agent in the United States for the famed Alexandre kid gloves, an important privilege that had been held by the once potent house of A. T. Stewart.

He was now a trustee of the First Presbyterian Church, sitting each Sunday in a front pew. An irreverent reporter for the *Sunday Herald*, assigned to do "pen portraits" of some of the members of this affluent congregation, has left a flippant sketch of the millionaire merchant when he was consolidating his position as the head of the biggest retail store in the city and largest wholesale business in the country.

"Gathered with the faithful this morning is Marshall Field," he wrote. "The wonderful executive ability of this man is reposed in a figure compactly built, firm and of medium weight, some five feet nine inches in height, with an excellently developed head over which has blown more than two score winters. His bright-blue, restless eyes, his keen, bargain-driving New England nose, his erect carriage, quiet manners, impressive silence and stylish get-up have made him for years a remarkable man.

"Wealth, truly, he has accumulated, but he has not forgotten to lay claim to treasures beyond the prey of the spoiler. His partnership with Mr. Leiter is said to have been dissolved because Mr. Leiter insisted on singing 'Over the Garden Wall' in business hours and Mr. Field made sarcastic remarks about Mr. Leiter's upper register."

Most of Field's tastes were simple for a man of his means. He was fond of fine horses, but kept no more than three or four in his stable. Some of them came from his Stanton Breeding Farm near Springer, Nebraska, which he owned jointly with Joseph Field. But the carriages pulled by these bobtail horses were considered merely respectable by society men who took a more intense interest in such matters.

Potter Palmer, for instance, then investing thousands in a new project—called a "crazy scheme" by many—of building up the north shore of Lake Michigan, typified those who lavished far more money on their steeds and carriages. In the annual Derby Day parades to Washington Park, Palmer and his beautiful wife always rode in an elaborately carved, highly polished French coach, with coachmen and footmen in full regalia and leopard skins thrown over the seats.

Despite this reluctance for spending, Field made regular contributions to his church and to charities; eventually it was his grant of land and cash that provided ground for the new University of Chicago. With his checks, especially for church funds, he affixed notes ending, "I beg you will not allow anyone to know that I send it to you."

II

Field's daily routine in the city rarely varied. Each morning he ate breakfast promptly at eight o'clock, then glanced over the financial columns of the newspapers. He always rode only part of the way to the State Street store in a carriage. Five or six blocks from the store the conveyance stopped, and he alighted, waved to his driver, and walked sturdily down Michigan Avenue toward the Washington Street entrance. A policeman at Michigan Avenue and Washington Street always spied him coming and hurried down the street to inform Eddie Anderson, who had taken over the job of official greeter. Word swiftly passed through the store, not yet open for customers.

At the door, Field handed Anderson the gray plug hat he habitually wore. If he wore a silk hat, he took it with him to his office, set it atop his desk, and used it to hold the day's most important letters. On normal days he stayed at the retail store for two hours, but in the months after the dissolution of the partnership with Leiter, he spent more time there in perfecting a smooth-working organization.

He lunched more often than not at the Chicago Club. He walked there alone, finding his place at the "millionaires' table" in the august dining room. Flanking him were such moneyed magnates as George Pullman, the inventor of the railroad sleeping car; John Crerar, the maker of railroad supplies; N. K. Fairbank, the club's venerable president; Lyman J. Gage, the cool-willed banker; and Judge Lambert Tree, whose son Arthur would one day marry Ethel Field.

These men were good talkers, witty and penetrating. They spoke of world events and of doings in the city; they told robust jokes and even gossiped. But Field never indulged in this talk.

In 1889 stately dwellings still lined elite Terrace Row on Michigan Avenue.

While the others lingered over their coffee and cigars, Field usually left early, walking either to the Merchants' Loan and Trust Bank, in which he owned most of the shares, or to his wholesale house at Madison and Market streets. Sometimes he did take a companion to lunch, such a close friend as Robert Todd Lincoln or General Phil Sheridan.

In later years his luncheon habit was peculiar; his companion then was Robert Fair, one of the top executives called "Dusty Bob" because his clothes were always dusty and rumpled. Together the men left Field's office; together they strolled silently to the club; together they entered. But once inside, Field and Fair always parted company at the door of the dining room. Field then went to his regular table with the other millionaires, while Fair ate alone. When lunch was over, the two walked out together and back to the day's business.

III

Field's offices in both the retail and wholesale houses were no more distinguished than those of the average lawyer on Clark Street. Each was equipped with only the most essential furniture—a stark contrast to John Wanamaker's office in his Philadelphia department store. Wanamaker, one of the few merchants of the day on the same level of wealth as Field, had a suite of six magnificently furnished rooms, with books, flowers, paintings, and even statuary. Field's office in the retail store, a visitor noted, was "a plain box of a place, fenced off in a corner of the store." Nor were his wholesale quarters much fancier.

In both he talked with his partners or executives, or rather, let them do the talking. They said of him over and over again: "He can ask you more pertinent questions with a few words than any ten men alive." Mostly he visited his department heads in the store or wholesale house, striding suddenly into the section with eyes flashing everywhere. He would ask a question or

The main hall of Marshall Field's French-style, red brick mansion was elaborately furnished with valuable possessions from many lands. Richard Morris Hunt, a noted architect of that day, designed the residence.

two about plans for the season, or about a particular purchase, listen hard, then usually shrug and say, "Well, use your own judgment." He was trying hard, now that he ran the store from the very top without any interference, to distribute responsibility to his executives.

Twice each week he made a complete tour of the wholesale house, carrying in his left hand a small writing pad on which he scribbled notes with a 10-cent Dela Mine Alberta pencil. He always stopped in the cashier's office to compare a day's sales, cash received, returned goods, and bank balances with the same day a decade earlier. Mostly he mumbled to himself and made a note in his little book.

Sometimes there came a surprising outburst, as when he once noted an entry showing a merchant overdue in paying $25,000.

179

"What's this? What's this?" he asked excitedly. "Oh, they're just a little late, they're good for the money," he was assured. Field's eyes narrowed. "Nothing is good, sir," he informed his bookkeeper coldly, "nothing but cash in the pocket!"

When he strode through either the wholesale house or the retail store, he passed out pieces of advice and aphorisms that he expected his workers to take to heart. He always stressed the store's keystone idea, the right of the customer to do almost anything. "Don't ever lose a customer," he said, "for he's always right." And again: "Quality is remembered long after price is forgotten." And, of course: "Remember, the customer is always right."

He advised his executives, as always, to keep their wares turning: "A starved stock doesn't pay any dividends." He told Harlow Higinbotham that the secrets of success in business were "the four C's—character, courage, courtesy, and capacity." He hoped, he added modestly, that he possessed all four and trusted that Higinbotham and the others had them too. To a clerk who had lied about the quality of some goods, he said that another such incident would mean instant dismissal and added, "This store, remember, sir, does not knowingly misrepresent its goods."

Although Field burst with benevolence when an old worker was in distress and was paternalistically interested in keeping his 2,000 employees content, to most of them he seemed cold and majestic and unapproachable, skimpy with praise and skimpy with wages. Beginning salesmen in the retail store got down early and stayed late, performing the "last man" chore of sweeping and dusting; and for this they were paid $8.00 to $10 a week, plus bonuses.

Advanced salesmen in both wholesale and retail divisions received better salaries—if they showed results. If they did not, they rarely stayed for very long. Those who got bonuses also found in their envelopes a note advising them to consult the company cashier for advice on investing this extra largesse in solid stocks or bonds.

Other salaries, except those of higher-ranking personnel who bargained individually with Field for specific salaries in contracts, were equally low. Elevator operators received $4.00 a week as a starting wage. Women in the upstairs workrooms got $9.00 to $12 a week. A salary of $25 a week for most of the employees was considered "the limit."

All this was in accord with the theory of the times and with wages paid in other stores. There was little complaint from the workers then, for just as the little twelve-year-old cash boys started to shine their shoes when they went to work for this store, so did most of the others feel that the low wages were worth the reputation of working for Field's. "You were considered very respectable," many veteran employees recalled years later, "if you told your neighbors you worked at Field's store on State Street."

Field himself not only was a fervent advocate of low wages, but he also hoped that his workers tried to save something of what they earned each week. He believed that a man who received too much salary too quickly would be ruined for the future unless he had shown evidence that he was an unusually thrifty fellow. "Remember," he sometimes said as he paused to speak with a wide-eyed clerk, "the five, ten, or fifteen cents a day that is squandered, while a mere trifle apparently, if saved would amount to thousands of dollars in a few years."

IV

If, as some of his social acquaintances said disapprovingly, Field's first passion was business, his interest in investments followed close behind. He seemed to have the magic touch when it came to putting his money in the right ventures.

His early investments in Pullman's company were paying

fat dividends. Moreover, he had an arrangement by which Pullman annually bought many thousands of dollars worth of mattresses, pillows, slip covers, draperies, and other goods needed for his sleeping cars. Field held shares in half a dozen banks in Chicago and as many in other cities. He was a big stockholder in railroads which served the city where he had accumulated so much wealth.

Soon he would put more cash into plans that would yield more, such as the purchase with John D. Rockefeller of 20,000 acres on the Vermilion iron range in Minnesota. He kept his stocks, bonds, and securities in a black iron strongbox that weighed over 150 pounds and had an elaborate and complex lock, plus a false lock to fool burglars who might break into his office in the wholesale house.

His real-estate holdings were extensive and growing more valuable by the year; people said he was "property hungry." Within two years he was carrying out the interesting plan by which he owned completely the building and land occupied by the retail store so that the firm paid him personally a rental of $50,000 a year—a sum that would rise to $1,000,000 in twenty-five years when he would own all the land in the square block filled by the store.

He was rich and growing richer. As might be expected, he was politically conservative, with a formidable fear of "anarchists" and "socialists"; into either class he often threw those who might simply be calling for shorter working hours or higher wages. A strict individualist, he was nominally a "Cleveland Democrat" who invariably voted Republican. He shunned local politics and rarely interfered publicly or privately with the machinations of the aldermanic boodlers in City Hall.

Reserved in his private life, he was removed from many of the problems and worries that affected other people; yet he was sometimes quick to show kindness and courtesy to any

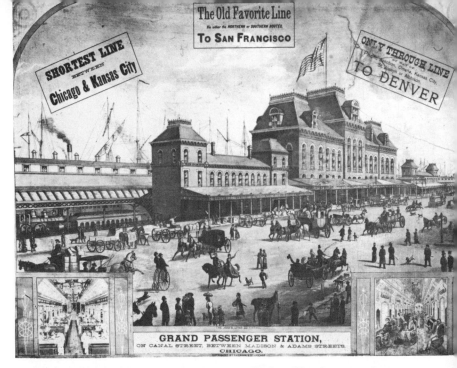

This poster touted Chicago's Grand Passenger Station. The depot was later destroyed to make room for the Union Station, one of the largest in the world.

number of unfortunate or indigent individuals. The only group to which he gave the same attention and consideration he often showed to a man or woman in need was, naturally enough, his customers. Laborer's wife or society *grande dame*, Idaho general storekeeper or rich retailer, the customer was to be catered to, pleased, and gratified.

v

His partners and executives shared this feeling.

With Leiter gone, Field had an organization of men who believed that the best way to remain supreme was his way. His company of partners, once Leiter agreed to resign, was announced by Field at a dinner in the Calumet Club at the end of 1880, a few weeks before the public became aware of developments. This set a precedent that continued for years, not only for partners but for major executives. By this method, Field would invite chief officials to a dinner in his home or his club, feed them terrapin or duck, then stand, clear his throat, and announce, "The firm next year will consist of . . . . ." Then would follow the names of those who were to remain and those who, for one reason or another, were no longer affiliated with the firm. Those who retired in this way, or of their own free will, were given dividends accumulated over their years with Field, plus bonuses. Their final take-home earnings then were never less than $1,000,000.

As the company now entered its most glowing years, Harlow Higinbotham was credit chief, Henry J. Willing was in charge of the wholesale branch, and Lorenzo Woodhouse retained his post as head of the New York office. Joseph Field was to remain in Manchester, England, building the foreign trade and seeing to it that the firm's buyers were routed to the appropriate manufacturers of desirable goods on the Continent. A new office was opened in Paris, where a Field representative watched for shifts in styles and placed orders accordingly.

Besides the partners there were others who, in the typical Field tradition, had started in menial jobs and risen through the years. Most of these executives received salaries of only $6,000 a year, but their bonuses and percentages of annual sales boosted their yearly pay to six or eight times these amounts. In the next few years, many would themselves be partners, destined to retire with fortunes.

The McWilliams brothers—Lafayette and John—were prospering, although John, the gayer of the two, was said to drink too much and Lafayette impressed people as too glum. Thomas Templeton, a deeply religious Scot whom the workers called "Tamas," was the firm's treasurer. A rigid man with red sideburns and a "head for figures," he could reduce statistical reports to understandable proportions. "Dusty Bob" Fair was a spark plug in the wholesale division, a master salesman who greeted customers with mighty handshakes and laughed uproariously at country merchants' witticisms.

Field was as wise a merchant of men as he was of goods. Once he secured the services of a man he considered able, he gave him unusual authority and responsibilities, supplying him with the best merchandise obtainable for him to sell. For the most part these men responded to this treatment with vigor and ability, an attitude sharpened by Field's practice of giving each a handsome percentage of profits at the end of the year.

Although Field paid less attention to the details that had occupied him in the earlier days of the firm, his presence and personality continued always to hover over all, from the lowliest clerk to the highest executive. He would be called on for major decisions and, sometimes, to settle petty squabbles that threatened to weaken the organization. "His hand," an observer wrote later, "was upon everything. From infallible intuition as well as from long experience, he knew whether aught was well or ill done."

As the fame of Marshall Field & Company broadened, these men contributed their various talents. If they proved to be devoid of such skills, they no longer remained. And none had more to give in the years that followed than two men as different in temperament and ideas as they were in size and appearance. One, a former farm boy with a high-pitched voice and a taste for the exquisite, had profound ideas about wholesale; he was John Graves Shedd. The other, a hustle-bustle fellow with dashing sideburns and dashing ways, turned over a million ideas in his head about retail; he was Harry Gordon Selfridge.

WINDOW CURTAINS WITH
DRAPED LAMBREQUIN.

LACE—AND—RIBBON *Gilet.*

JOHN SHEDD:
I CHOOSE QUALITY

John Shedd fitted snugly the pattern of those who had become successful in the organization molded by Marshall Field. A New Hampshire farm boy, he left the plow and fields near his home town of Alstead at seventeen. His first job then was in a general store at Bellows Falls, Vermont. He received $1.50 a week and room and board and managed to save nearly all of his annual earnings of $75. Then he worked in other such stores in his native state and in Rutland, Vermont, always carefully putting away part of his earnings in a bank.

At twenty, he was a short, angular youth, with a broad nose and big ears. He could have become a successful storekeeper in Rutland, for he was already getting a munificent clerk's salary of $175 a year. But this was 1871 and the fever of expansion and adventure beyond the confines of New England toward the great West was as infectious as it had been for Marshall Field nearly twenty years earlier. Already three of Shedd's older brothers had joined the westward exodus, going as far as the Pacific coast to seek gold.

With $300 savings, Shedd set out for Chicago, a frankly ambitious youth bent on working for the best store in the city. His quiet ways belied rugged determination, for, without hesitation, he tramped into the wholesale house Field and Leiter had opened at Madison and Market streets after the Great Fire. He managed a meeting with Field himself and asked for a job.

"Are you a salesman?" demanded Field.

"Yes, sir," replied Shedd in his high-pitched voice.

"What can you sell?"

The reply was quick. "Anything!"

Field stared hard at Shedd. "If that's the case," he said, "I think we have a place for you."

Field sent Shedd to the wholesale department where linens, laces, hosiery, gloves, and men's underwear were sold. In his memorandum to Henry J. Willing, then head of the department, Field instructed that Shedd be paid $10 a week for three months and "if suits" should be raised to $12. At first Shedd worked as a stock boy. In an age when a ten-hour day and a six-day week were considered normal, Shedd's working habits were faultless. The wholesale house became his life. He spent little money, went to church regularly, studied a book called *Daball's Schoolmaster's Assistant*. No clock-watcher, no time-waster, he packed goods, arranged stock, ran to fetch the general salesmen for customers. He was a youth dedicated to his job. Naturally, such a youngster could hardly fail to make progress in a firm whose master believed in every virtue shown by this stock boy.

Within five months Shedd was allowed to try his hand at selling, and his salary, instead of the specified $12, was $14. In the next seven months, having sold $10,000 worth of goods, he was raised to $17. Moreover, at the end of this first year he informed Marshall Field that he had managed to save $5.00 a week. Even Field was amazed at this feat. When Shedd asked if he wanted to see his bank book, Field replied, "No, I believe you." But John whipped out the book and pointed to the page showing his total deposits of $260.

Shedd was a prize salesman. Because he looked even younger than he was, some customers in the wholesale house grumbled

John Shedd was a farm boy from New Hampshire, but he had a keen taste for fine things. "I love good quality," he often said. After Marshall Field died in 1906, Shedd took over The Founder's duties and led the store to new fame.

about being waited on by a mere boy. But they quickly learned that young Shedd knew as much about the wares in his section as did some of the older salesmen. Although he was a farmer's son, with no training or education in such matters, he had a fine taste for the exquisite things in life—and, to him, the best things in life could all be found in the place where he worked. He enjoyed feeling the expensive tablecloths and laces, and when he afforded himself the rare luxury of dining out, he tested the fabric of the napkins and tablecloth. "I love good quality," he explained shyly to those who stared at him.

II

Shedd had little intention of remaining a salesman. "When I came, my first ambition was to make a living," he said later. "Then I wanted to become an expert salesman. Then I had the ambition to become a department manager."

That ambition was realized in record time. Under Willing's tutelage Shedd combined his love for selling with management.

He studied books and manuals and watched keenly all that went on around him. Soon he had evolved a plan that he was sure would save time and money for the firm. He noted, he told Willing, that there was always an accumulation of odd sizes in such merchandise as hose, gloves, and collars, while the more common sizes always sold out quickly. He believed that this was because the buyers simply used their own judgment, or personal whims, instead of any precise method for determining how much to buy each season. A more scientific way would be to plan purchases on how much was sold in the previous season, Shedd suggested. Willing gave him permission to go through the firm's books to check sales in various lines for several years back. From this study Shedd evolved a systematic method for planning purchases on the basis of sales. "Now," he said, "we can base our buying on what the public wants and needs."

Willing took the plan to Field, who studied it and pronounced it workable. He permitted Shedd to try the system for a year in the ladies' neckwear and laces section. In that year sales doubled. Shedd's future was assured.

In 1883 Willing retired, having enriched himself in his years with the firm by over $1,000,000. Shedd took his place not as a partner but as head of the department, with a salary of $5,000 a year, plus a bonus if sales were kept up. Despite a momentary business recession, Shedd performed as expected and received a two-year contract at higher salary. And at the end of the contract period he was made general merchandise manager of the wholesale division, and he sighted ahead for new goals.

III

As careful as he was to emulate Field, Shedd did not hesitate to press ideas that the head of the firm still found unpalatable.

After he succeeded Willing, Shedd became aware of the greater need to send additional traveling salesmen on the road.

In 1887, with Field's business booming, Henry Robson Richardson, the famed architect, designed this big wholesale house, covering a downtown block.

Except for the few who had been dispatched after the crises of the late 1870's, the only traveling men who ever left the wholesale house were the "general salesmen." They went into the new territories twice a year, to visit and chat with regular customers, see that shipments were coming as ordered, and gather gossip and facts to convey to Field. But they carried no samples and took no orders.

Other firms, Shedd argued, had not stood still. That pattern of the 1870's, when there was such competition for growing trade of the Northwest, had become fixed now. All other Chicago wholesalers had men swarming over the western territories. John V. Farwell, Shedd reminded Field, even hired bill-posters to come into cities in advance of his salesmen and slap against walls red-lettered announcements: "Our Travelers Will Soon Be Here!"

Quietly, but logically, Shedd pointed out that Field had to keep pace with the changing times and with those wholesale competitors if he wanted the trade of the new towns along the railroad stretches and in the plains and valleys of the West. The retailers in the small towns were growing more reluctant to make the long trips to Chicago or even to order from the catalogues sent by the firm twice a year. They liked this system of being visited by the traveling men. Some even enjoyed having their wives help them pick out their stocks for the next season.

Field still considered such methods cheap. But he was smart enough to know that Shedd's reasoning was sound. He gave the word to dispatch more salesmen to the new areas, arrange specific routes for them to follow, order them to report regularly on conditions in their districts, crop prospects, political doings. And he hammered away at his demand that the customers to be acquired in the new regions had to be those who could appreciate the quality he had to offer.

"The business of a salesman is to sell," Field told Shedd. "But I want to sell to the best merchant in every town, and if I cannot get the best merchant in every town, then I want to get the next-best merchant in every town. And if I cannot get him, I do not want to sell in that town."

So the salesmen from Marshall Field & Company, their ranks doubled and redoubled, took to the roads, broadening and strengthening the trend that would prevail for nearly four decades more.

The general salesmen and the specialty salesmen—the "linemen"—each had specific territories and specific customers. Both groups carried swatches of fabrics and materials and all manner of samples. The salesmen went as far as the Pacific coast by 1890, the general road men taking orders for any types of wares, the others handling only certain items, whether handkerchiefs or oilcloth. The specialty man sent colorful cards announcing his coming. He hired hotel rooms and set up his displays. Then the town's merchants trooped in to be greeted by this bustling fellow with a handshake, a clap on the back, perhaps even some liquid refreshment. He covered his district twice a year, taking a few months to visit every merchant on his route.

They were gay, energetic, and smooth, these new drummers. They told their rollicking stories and, when they were finished, they whisked out their sales books and asked offhand, "Now, Mr. Smith, how many dozen of these you gonna need this season, eh?" They were welcome in many communities for more than the goods they sold; William F. Hypes, for one, who traveled in the Dakotas, staged concerts and sang at prayer meetings and country socials.

There were the fellows they called "whizbangs." They, like the drummers of an earlier time, knew all the jokes and funny sayings of the day—and could sell thousands of handkerchiefs in a two-day stay in Detroit or hundreds in a few hours in a Nebraska town. They had to improvise sometimes, too. Once Howard Durham, assistant to the firm's cashier, received a three-page complaint from a salesman in Michigan that he was unable to sell anything because it was raining too hard. "Sell umbrellas," Durham wired him. The man took the advice and snared orders for $3,500 worth in a single week.

A lineman covered about thirty towns on his semiannual tours. He did it mostly by train, sending his trunks ahead; but if trains were not available, he did it by sled or on horseback or in carts. He received a 2 per cent commission plus a salary—and if he sold less than $80,000 worth of goods in a year, he was not considered worth keeping. The best salesmen averaged $100,000 in sales a year. If they topped that amount, they received an additional 10 per cent bonus.

Besides taking orders, the salesman also was expected to pick up all the information he could, for Field, as in his earliest days, still adhered to the wise practice of firing questions at a returning traveler. So that he could be kept aware of prospects in a specific area, he would ask: "How is the governor?" "How do people like him?" "Is he honest?" "Will he be re-elected?" "What are the crop prospects?" "Are the banks sound?" "What do you think of business conditions?" "How is the weather there?" "Is there new immigration?" "Are the people hard working and honest?"

IV

Soon there was not enough room in the old wholesale house at Madison and Market. When wholesale sales continued to grow—$20,921,000 one year, $21,650,000 the next—Field shuttered this building after commissioning the famed architect, Henry Robson Richardson, to build a new one. This bulky structure of granite and brownstone, covering the square city block bounded by Adams, Quincy, Wells, and Franklin streets, opened on June 20, 1887. Not only was the customary merchandise that had made the company rich and famed displayed, but a wider assortment of wares that reflected how it was keeping pace with shifting tastes and needs of its customers—carpet sweepers, rubber diapers, baby buggies, opera glasses, atomizers, harmonicas, machine oil, wire mattresses, magic lanterns, accordions, even violins and guitars.

At the door of the new house stood two official greeters, Joe Girard and Lou Bachus. When a customer entered and asked for the head of a department or a top salesman, the greeters snapped an order to one of half a dozen "on the bench" boys seated inside the door, and the lad scurried off to bring the man asked for. The department heads were the real elite in this establishment. All were called "Mr." by their underlings, except for Steen Billow, a big, rawboned man in charge of cottons and ginghams, who insisted that everyone call him simply "Billow."

Dan Hill, in charge of the silks, was fat and jolly, with a flair for the sensational that seemed strangely out of keeping with the conservatism of the firm. A typical exploit of his was to buy

--◆◇◆--••◦✳ INTERIOR ◦ VIEW ◦ JEWELRY ◦ DEPARTMENT, ✳◦••--◇◆◇--

MARSHALL FIELD & CO.,

ADAMS, QUINCY, FRANKLIN, FIFTH AVENUE, CHICAGO.

Gems, clocks, and cutlery were found in Field's big wholesale jewelry section.

5,000 pieces of silk and to advertise it at his own expense, sending to the merchants powerful exhortations that concluded with the call, "Come and Get it!" The method was frowned on, but not the fact that he sold every shred of silk in less than three days at excellent profit. Another happy sort was Roland P. Marks, who did $2,000,000 a year in black-cotton and silk stockings that came from Saxony, wore flashing diamond rings and had a string of actresses as girl friends. Head of the prosperous carpet section was Franklin Ames, a grumpy man who rode a horse to work each morning.

Next to these department heads, the chief general salesmen were the aristocrats. They wore, when in the city, silk hats and Prince Albert coats and always carried canes. They knew all the gayest spots, the finest restaurants, the best shows. John Devlin, who had been with the firm for so many years—later he would be the first to retire with the longest service record of sixty-five years—had developed into one of the best of these salesmen, a man who knew all the art of getting on with people. Then came the specialty men, who handled a single line, or perhaps two.

Whatever a man's work or position, he was required at all times to fulfill every want of the customer. If an out-of-town merchant yearned to see the town, he was escorted where he wished to go. Should he come from a Swedish village in Minnesota, or a Polish or German community in Wisconsin, and spoke no English, he was taken through the wholesale house by a salesman who knew his language. If he desired instruction in storekeeping methods, he got it from James Lindquist, a specialist in training methods, or from John Shedd himself.

In each department was a city buyer whose task it was to fill orders with items not regularly handled by Field's. This type of accommodation-buying sometimes entailed special effort and great patience, but it yielded much in good will. The city buyers were adept at locating lost relatives or rare bric-a-brac or even cheap goods sold at some of the lower-priced State Street or West Side stores. Many of their customers took advantage of this service to get articles for relatives and friends at wholesale rates. But when department chiefs, tracing some such sharpster, complained to Field, he waved them off. This chicanery, he emphasized, cost little when compared with the over-all profits derived from the service. "If it causes trouble," he said, "you'll have to accept the trouble. We're in business to give service."

Many would-be merchants appeared at the new wholesale house seeking financial backing for stores in new towns. Since the end of the partnership with Leiter, the credit system had relaxed slightly. But it still was one of the tightest in the city, for Higinbotham was a fervent Leiter disciple. Yet a young, earnest merchant with a good reputation and sound prospects found it easier now to buy goods on longer terms. Before granting a line of credit, Higinbotham's staff made thorough investigations. Field's had five men looking into the backgrounds of potential creditors but required only two to make collections, while most other wholesalers used only two investigators and found it necessary to employ a dozen collectors. Higinbotham usually extended a credit for $5,000 to a merchant intending to carry a $20,000 stock and gave him a year to

As Chicago continued to grow, the railroads stretched new lines of steel toward the bustling town. This poster was displayed all over the city after the "New Wabash Depot" opened for business in the early 1880's.

pay. The system won customers, many of whom did 90 per cent of their buying from Marshall Field's.

V

In his job as general merchandiser during these years when Field's climbed to a position second only to H. B. Claflin's of New York in world-wide wholesaling importance, John Shedd was always alert for chances to make improvements. He was confident enough in his standing with the company to institute the unheard-of practice of giving employees in various departments a half day off on slow Saturdays. He approved and encouraged the policy of allowing wholesale workers to buy anything they wished in the house at wholesale prices, or from the retail store at a discount of 6 per cent. He worked his salesmen hard, but was acknowledged to be a fair, if slightly uncommunicative, executive.

Shedd fought for wholesale profits, demanding and getting a credit for wholesale on all goods that went into the retail store even if a buyer there took it direct from a manufacturer. If Shedd made an unusual buy at a great bargain, he did not necessarily pass the benefits on to retail, but took all the profit he could get, a few times as much as 100 per cent. The retail buyers objected furiously to this when they learned of it, but Marshall Field refused to interfere.

Mostly, Shedd was doing everything he possibly could to mold himself in the image of Marshall Field. Did Marshall Field regard salesmen highly and office workers as "nonproductive"? "If we'd burn down, we could pick up somewhere tomorrow and the customers would come," cried Shedd. "But if we'd lose our staff of salesmen, the customers wouldn't come back!"

Did Marshall Field worry about overloading stocks? "Surplus stock must go! Keep merchandise moving!" piped Shedd. Did Marshall Field demand a splendid variety of wares? "We want the best assorted stock in America!" Shedd insisted. Did Marshall Field emphasize the importance of money in the pocket? "Surplus stock in distress is worth only half a dollar at best," said Shedd. "Sell before it's surplus and you have a whole dollar in your pocket!"

He also perfected his practice of jotting down on odd scraps of paper any business maxims and ideas that came to his mind during a day's work. All sounded as if Marshall Field had helped him write them:

Aim high and pull the trigger. You are pretty sure to hit something, but if you don't you will have made sufficient noise to attract attention.

The man who is continuously at work is the man who is happy and continuously successful.

Always be up and doing. Activity cuts a very much greater figure than it is usually given credit for in the success of a young man.

Hitch your wagon to a star, but be sure it is a star of the first magnitude.

Learn the value of time. It is a precious asset. To waste it in indolence is a crime.

Many men of his time spouted such platitudes for the sonorous sounds they made. But Shedd really believed in every word, and acted accordingly. More and more Field relied on his judgment and intelligence in the wholesale division until, at the end of 1892, he gave Shedd a partnership. The share was infinitesimal—exactly 2.5/88 of profits—but Shedd was more than content. His ambitious, carefully planned career had reached an important point, and from now on there was no other direction to travel but upwards.

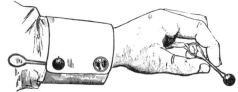

Perfection Cuff Holder

Gents' Boston Garters.

GENUINE
YANKEE SOAP,
Manufactured at
MANCHESTER CONN,
WILLIAMS & BROTHERS
CHEMISTS AND APOTHECARIES,

MILE-A-MINUTE HARRY

While Shedd was contributing his solid talents to the success of Field's wholesale division, Harry Gordon Selfridge swept through the retail store with the dash of a circus promoter and the fervor of a revolutionist.

Selfridge started with the company in 1879. In later times he pared a few years off his age and insisted he was only fifteen when he began. Actually he was twenty-one, a bright-eyed young man from Jackson, Michigan, where his widowed mother taught school. After high school he had hoped to enter the United States Naval Academy, but he was too short. So he worked in a Jackson dry-goods store for $1.50 a week, then later as a bank clerk for $20 a month.

He came to Field with a letter from the merchant's cousin, Leonard Field, a Jackson businessman, commending Selfridge as an unusually alert and intelligent fellow. Field gave Selfridge a job as a stock boy in the wholesale house for $10 a week, but within a year the quick-tongued youth was a salesman, first behind the counters and then up and down Illinois.

Selfridge had a feverish imagination. His education had not halted with the end of formal schooling. He read books and newspapers, especially stories of merchants and merchandising. At night he often lay awake imagining what he would do if he had the power to make changes in the firm. By 1883 he was ready to leap ahead. There was a better job waiting for him in the wholesale division, but he asked to be assigned to the retail store where he was sure his ideas and imaginative theories could be put to fruitful work. For a time he was a mere clerk, noticing everything. Within a year he was appointed an assistant to J. M. Fleming, the haughty head of retail who believed devoutly in letting well enough alone and grudgingly installed innovations only if Field or one of the senior partners proposed them.

Selfridge teemed with ideas, but those he offered to Fleming were waved aside. This twenty-five-year-old fledgling, sniffed Fleming, was too brash, too imaginative, too impulsive. Selfridge argued that retail was too dependent on the whims of wholesale, that retail had to set out on its own because Chicago was bursting with new people who wanted a type of merchandise different from that desired by country-town dwellers. It was the business of a retail manager, he loftily told his boss, to create a demand and constantly nourish that demand. Fleming looked down his cold nose at the enthusiastic upstart and informed him that most of his ideas were unworkable and expensive.

They called Harry Gordon Selfridge "Mile-A-Minute Harry" in the days when he ran things in the Field retail store. Later, when he went to London, he set up the first American-style department store there and was known for years as England's prime merchant prince.

Selfridge overcame this obstacle in characteristic style. He went to Field with his ideas. A natural conservative, Field might have been expected to agree with Fleming and urge Selfridge to bide his time. Yet he now saw in Selfridge a man almost in the same position he occupied when he was the impulsive partner of John V. Farwell or when Levi Z. Leiter had stood so steadfast against retail improvements.

He decreed that Selfridge be given his chance. There would be but one test for the success or failure of his schemes: they had to bring profits.

II

Now the "revolution in retail" was on its way.

Field's had been the first big store in the city to use electric globes in 1882; Selfridge installed many more so that additional light was thrown on the merchandise displays. Until 1883 the store had only five telephones; Selfridge tripled that number immediately, installing a central switchboard with lines into every department. At the Washington Street entrance he placed greeter Eddie Anderson, who slicked down his hair over his forehead and affected a Boston accent as he met the refined ladies at the doors of their carriages. He started a system of "annual sales" on the wise and profitable theory that shelves could be cleared in this way for new goods. He ripped out counters and high shelving for piece goods, piling up the assortments on tables in the center of the first floor so that the women customers could get at them more quickly.

It was Selfridge's idea, too, for the store to print souvenir booklets in 1884 when the Democrats and Republicans held their Presidential conventions in the city. These contained information about past conventions and space for tallying votes, together with the happy proposal that the delegates visit the store where they might have their packages checked free, see a model dining room, India shawls, or "650 feet of glass cases filled with the newest Paris articles." And, whether they bought or not, they would receive "polite and courteous attention."

His most impressive ideas during this bustling period came in 1885. For some years part of the store basement had been used as an outlet for goods and articles that had been marked down in price because they had either gone out of fashion quickly or, for some other reason, had not sold well. Now Selfridge urged the expansion of this basement into a vast "bargain center" for customers who usually stayed away from the store because they could not afford some of the higher-priced wares.

Always the persuasive talker, Selfridge convinced Field that such a move would not only bring crowds of purchasers, but these newcomers would make a habit of shopping at Field's; and when they or perhaps their grown-up children could afford to, they would buy in the departments upstairs. No stigma need be attached to the idea of the bargain basement, Selfridge insisted. "We must give the shopper there the same service and honest representation of goods—and she will come back again and again!" he cried.

Although Fleming snorted, "Cheap!" Selfridge was permitted by Field to try out his plan. Again Fleming was proved wrong, for the delighted shoppers came by the thousands in the first week after the basement salesrooms opened to grab for the cheaper silks, dress goods, embroideries, housekeeping linens, white goods, underwear, hosiery, handkerchiefs, gloves, ribbons, cloaks, and shawls. "Specially Attractive Bargains!" shouted the newspaper advertisements. Field's, read the ads, was keeping up with the times, meeting the "growing demand for lower priced goods and the wants of our rapidly increasing business."

These advertisements themselves marked a radical change in the store's methods. Under Fleming, the retail advertising had been mild, conservative, and dignified. Selfridge visualized the

This *Chicago Tribune* page in 1883 featured advertisements of some of the big stores of the era. Several besides Field's are still in business in 1952.

The "hello girls," like these in Field's, had brought the cause of Feminism a long way from the days when women had clamored for the right to work.

newspaper display as another avenue into which to pour his exuberant showmanship. In this same year he persuaded Field to spend $25,000 on newspaper space, a boost of almost $20,000 over Fleming's appropriation the prior year. Selfridge himself wrote much of the copy, and instructed department heads how to play up the features of their sections. In time he placed at the top of the greatly enlarged advertisements his own "inspirational" messages on the delights of shopping in the store—flamboyant and wordy essays which those who disliked him came to call "H. G.'s Declaration of Independence."

The advertisements, insisted Selfridge, must not only be eye-catching and informative, but completely honest. If goods were seconds or slightly damaged, the people had to be told of that. "We allow no misstatements," became a Selfridge admonition of major importance to department heads who brought the rough drafts of their proposed copy for his inspection. "It is our intention that every advertisement which we publish shall be absolutely true and correct in every particular." Later he even offered a cash prize to any employee who found any statement in an advertisement that exaggerated quality, listed the wrong price, contained a misspelled word or grammatical error. The prize: $1.00.

In time, too, the bargain basement shunned the use of the words "cheap" or "lower priced" in referring to its wares. To quiet the apprehension of those partners who feared that the all-important idea of high quality might be weakened as the basement continued to thrive and grow, Selfridge kept changing the name. It became known, at various times, as the "Annex Department" and "Branch Department" with goods that were "Trustworthy" and "Less Expensive But Reliable." Ultimately the basement, largest single salesroom in the world, acquired the permanent name of "Budget Floor" and grossed $25,000,000 of sales yearly.

III

By 1887, Field became convinced that Selfridge, however theatrical his methods, was a man who loved merchandising and the service the store gave to the people—and the profits he produced. So Selfridge was given Fleming's job, with the title of "retail general manager." And his revolution rolled on and on.

"Mile-a-Minute Harry," the employees called this handsome young man with the long sideburns, carefully trimmed mustache, and cameo face. He loved to go through the store a dozen times a day, but he seemed to fly rather than walk. He wore pinch-nose glasses on a gold chain hooked to his lapel and an expensive frock coat. When he swept through the aisles, his imperious head held high and his eyes taking in every detail about him, the gold chain flew from side to side and the ends of the coat flapped breezily.

As his salary changed for the better, his way of life became more luxurious. He took a neat apartment on the sedate Near North Side and moved his mother from her modest Jackson home. He furnished his office far more elaborately than Field's. Each morning a barber came into the office to shave him. Sometimes he changed his clothes two or three times a day, but he always wore wing collars and gleaming patent leather shoes.

Selfridge, however, was more than a mere fancy dresser. He took a deep interest in everything that went on in the store—from the welfare of the cash boys, who regarded him as another Marshall Field, to the exact wording of the linen department's advertisement for the week. He stayed in his office until long after the store closed each night, yet was one of the first to arrive in the morning.

He never criticized workers in the presence of customers or other clerks. If his eye caught dust on a counter top, he said not a word but paused long enough to write "HGS" with his fingertip, then strode away to give the frightened clerk time to polish and polish the offensive grime away. On his trips through the store he always stopped to talk with customers, as Field had done in the earlier days; but, unlike Field, he seemed to relish these encounters. If a crank harangued him about some trivial error at such times, he listened patiently and promised, "We will see that it doesn't happen again, madam. You are absolutely right." Any customer, whether her mission involved a small purchase or one that ran into the thousands of dollars, was assured a personal interview with Selfridge if she desired it.

Nor was Selfridge less solicitous about his employees, whether they worked for $2.00 a week as errand girls in the stationery department or served as top salesmen. Once, a twelve-year-old cash boy found a purse, but when he returned it, the owner reported $20 missing. Mike Ford, then head of the cash boys, took the youngster into one of the locker rooms and ordered him to strip. Tucked between the lad's toes was the $20 bill. Between sobs, the boy said that his mother, a scrubwoman in the store, and his father, a loader in the wholesale division, were both ill and needed money for food and medicine.

Lindsay T. Woodcock, Selfridge's assistant, insisted the boy be fired. But Selfridge, hearing of the lad's plight, kept him on the payroll and explained the case to Field himself. Ford was directed to buy food and medicine for the parents with $400 given by Field. He followed his orders and carried the supplies in a company delivery wagon to the family's home in "Little Hell" on the north branch of the Chicago River. As he was hauling the cartons into the house, he bumped into another man entering the building. It was Selfridge, carrying a basket crammed with more food and household necessities.

This personal interest in the employees paid dividends. In keeping with the company's axiom, "Office boy today, partner tomorrow," Selfridge was always on the lookout for clever young men to be promoted to better jobs. One of them was a West Side youth named Homer J. Buckley, who toiled in the store's shipping department—a musty, stuffy room known more familiarly as the "stink hole." His experience was typical of Selfridge's methods, which benefited not only the alert employee, but the firm too.

One day, when Buckley was crating a final order, the telephone rang. Most of those who worked in the shipping room shied from answering any calls near the closing hour because it invariably meant they had to work overtime without pay to fill a late order.

But Buckley did answer, to find Selfridge on the line. A good customer in the Englewood district, he told the boy, had called to complain that a photograph he had sent for framing had not been delivered. It was a picture of the customer's Yale University graduating class. He wanted to show it to some fellow-alumni who were coming to his house that very night. The picture was ready, said Selfridge. Could Buckley arrange to have it delivered to the Yale man?

"Yes sir!" promised Buckley. But when he put in a call to the delivery-wagon barn, he was told roughly, "We're down for the night. No more deliveries."

Instead of calling Selfridge and telling him of this, Buckley waited a few minutes, then, deepening his voice, he telephoned the delivery barn again. "This is Mr. Selfridge," intoned Buckley. "That photograph has to be delivered tonight, you understand? I want you to do me a favor and get it to our customer!"

The delivery man responded swiftly, picked up the parcel, and carried it to the delighted Yale man in time for the reunion.

On the next day Buckley told Selfridge what he had done to insure delivery of the photograph. "Very good," said Selfridge. "You come up to my office. I want to talk to you."

Buckley scrubbed his face and polished his shoes and presented himself upstairs. Selfridge waved him to a chair.

"Tell me, Homer," boomed Selfridge, "what do you think of the business?"

Buckley replied that in the four years he had worked in the shipping room he had noticed a disconcerting development. "We don't ship merchandise out to lots of homes we once did. I wonder why. I can never find anybody looking into it."

"You get on it, Homer," said Selfridge, "and I'll take you out of shipping."

Buckley asked a few questions. He learned that among the customers who had stopped dealing with Field's was the wife of a local banker. He asked the officials of the credit department what they knew of this case, and they promptly rebuked him for his effrontery in interfering with their affairs.

"You write her a letter over my signature," advised Selfridge.

In reply, the woman scrawled, "You know very well why I don't trade with you!"

Selfridge directed Buckley to write the woman another note over his name asking her to drop into his office to see him when she was shopping on State Street one day. She appeared soon enough, filled with indignation over the incident that had led to her cancellation of all relations with the store and curious about this important man who would go to such lengths as to ask her to state her complaint in person.

"Mile-A-Minute Harry" was all charm and concern. Why, he asked softly, had she stopped dealing with this fine store?

Two years before, the woman related, she had ordered an expensive dress made by Field's. "While I was being fitted, your salesperson differed with me about the style. I insisted on getting what I wanted. But when the gown was finished, it was finished not the way I wanted it, but the way the salesperson wanted it! Well, I paid $275 for that dress. But I left it right here in the store, and I never came back!"

Selfridge's look was one of extreme grief. "Madam," he said, "we were so wrong! If we credit you in our accounts with the money you paid, will you be our customer again?"

The woman rose, holding out her gloved hand. "I will come back," she declared. "Thank you, madam, thank you!" he cried.

Although Selfridge could not take so much time or enact such a role with every angry customer, he was persuaded by the

Late in the 1880's aesthetic-minded ladies placed these statues "of chaste design" in their parlors, and women of fashion were happily wearing fancy bustles again.

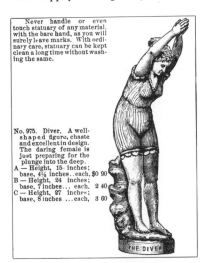

Never handle or even touch statuary of any material, with the bare hand, as you will surely leave marks. With ordinary care, statuary can be kept clean a long time without washing the same.

No. 975. Diver. A well-shaped figure, chaste and excellent in design. The daring female is just preparing for the plunge into the deep.
A — Height, 15 inches; base, 4½ inches..each, $0 90
B — Height, 24 inches; base, 7 inches... each, 2 40
C — Height, 27 inches; base, 8 inches ...each, 3 60

THE DIVER

incident that there might well be hundreds of others who had stopped buying at Field's for real or imagined injury. He removed Buckley from the shipping room and put him in charge of a follow-up system that became the model for similar measures in other stores throughout the country. Buckley rose steadily in the organization to become a close aide of Selfridge's and stayed for many years until he left to form his own mail-order advertising business.

IV

Selfridge's zeal for keeping customers and employees happy spurred him always as he strengthened his position in the store. He constantly planned new departments and new advertising techniques. He devised a simpler method of making out sales slips. He rearranged displays. When the products of William Morris' artisans in England enchanted the ladies of Chicago, he opened a special room in which the poet's designs and fabrics, wallpaper and furniture were shown and sold. He opened a small gallery where "art linens" and paintings in gilt frames were for sale. He set up workrooms where a woman shopper might leave her glasses to be ground, her gloves to be cleaned, her jewelry or shoes to be shined.

Selfridge moved fast to catch and surpass any other stores in the city which expanded their range of merchandise. In March, 1889, he established two departments for which he had long agitated. In the same week in which an addition to the store was being completed—"Nine thousand feet of space has been added," crowed his announcement, "with a view toward making the store greater, more interesting and more satisfactory as a shopping centre!"—he opened a children's clothing section, then followed a few days later with a "Fine Shoe" department.

The first served boys and girls from two to eighteen a variety of apparel from the immensely popular Little Lord

Fauntleroy hats and overcoats to silk bonnets for young ladies. The second carried shoes in dozens of styles. It evoked such a quick response that in a few months it was enlarged, and the firm was obliged to advertise for more clerks to handle the rush of business.

For several years Selfridge had sought permission from Field to open a restaurant in the store. But Field shunned the idea. "This is a dry-goods store, we don't feed people here!" he invariably replied. Yet Selfridge persisted, and in April, 1890, was successful in setting up a tearoom on the third floor near the fur section.

There were fifteen tables, with eight waitresses and four women in the kitchen. On the first day only fifty-six patrons were served, taking their choice from a menu that offered corned beef hash, chicken pie, chicken salad, orange punch in an orange shell, and Field's Rose Punch—ice cream with dressing. There was a red rose on each plate.

The tearoom had sudden appeal for women shoppers. In a year it was enlarged and serving as many as 1,500 each day. It featured not only the items on the original menu, but specialties like gingerbread cakes and a delicious chicken salad, both of which were devised by a young woman named Harriet Tilden, later to become the wife of William Vaughn Moody, a Chicago poet and professor. Miss Tilden, through her orders directly from Selfridge, was thereby enabled to start her Home Delicacies Association, supplying freshly cooked foods and tidbits for society dinners, lunches, and parties. Some of the other specialties, such as codfish cakes or Boston baked beans, were cooked in the homes of the women chefs and brought to the tearoom's kitchen hours before the first hungry shopper seated herself at one of the tables. Eventually, this tearoom became one of several restaurants and dining rooms on the store's seventh floor, some decorated with palms, some filled with heavy oak tables and carved chairs, some with open grills where chops and steaks were broiled in sight of the customers, some serving sandwiches in tiny baskets with bows on their handles—all of them catering to thousands of shoppers every day.

V

It was time, Selfridge decided one day in 1889, for another step forward. Confronting Field, he abruptly asked to be made a partner.

Field was startled into an angry flush, for never in the history of his firm had anyone dared to utter such a demand. He and he alone decreed who would be his partners, and he distributed the partnerships as he saw fit to those he thought deserved them. Yet, as he reflected on this, he obviously realized that few in the organization were more deserving than Selfridge since annual sales had risen during this young man's first six years in the retail store from $4,000,000 to $6,700,000 and the profits from $370,000 to $570,000.

"You will be a partner, Mr. Selfridge," he curtly told him.

As the new year started, Selfridge was on the rolls—a junior partner, with 2/85 of a share in the total profits. Field himself advanced the $200,000 needed to buy the partnership, with the

The Central Music Hall was a gathering place for Chicago's lovers of music and oratory. Here, too, is where Selfridge held his wedding, complete with a stage banked with flowers and a chorus of fifty voices.

provision that Selfridge would repay this sum out of his earnings, which promised to be heavy.

Selfridge was elated, but not so the older and more conservative members of the firm. Even Shedd, who admired Selfridge's flair for selling and merchandising, sometimes criticized him. "John Shedd wears too small a collar," was Selfridge's response. There were others who actively opposed Selfridge. Charles Ward, head of the upholstery department, had purchased a huge amount of blankets and was holding them back, refusing to draw up a draft of an advertisement. "I don't believe in advertising," he muttered. When Selfridge heard this, he wrote a huge advertisement himself and inserted it in all the newspapers. Ward, reaching his department the next morning, was stunned to find thousands clamoring for his clerks to start selling the "special price" blankets. Even Selfridge came down from his office to help the clerks in the rush.

The executives in the wholesale house, sensing a foe in Selfridge, what with his talk of a need for retail buyers to shake themselves loose from wholesale's grip, often sought to ridicule his flashy methods. They mocked his grandiose ways and his fashion-plate dress. They chuckled at the fact that when Selfridge married Rosalie Buckingham, a society debutante, in November, 1890, no less a place would do for the ceremony than the imposing Central Music Hall at State and Randolph streets—its stage covered with chrysanthemums, floral pillars of smilax and white roses, and a great screen of rose branches, while organists, harpists, and a fifty-voice chorus joined in the nuptial music. Subtly and openly they sought to disparage Selfridge in the eyes of Marshall Field.

But Field, at such moments, pointed a thick finger at the firm's ledgers and gave Selfridge's critics a sharp answer: "He may not be doing things to your liking, gentlemen. But he's making a lot of money for us. Are you?"

RIBBON LABEL
BEARING TRADEMARK

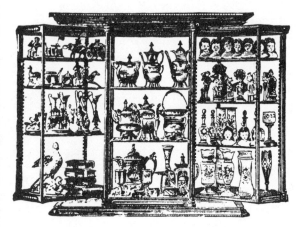

WIRE BUSTLES

PUG-DOG DOORSTOP

GIVE THE LADY
WHAT SHE WANTS!

If Selfridge's critics expected him to slow down his razzle-dazzle methods or money-making ways, they were disappointed. Chicago was approaching a period when a man with his vigorous flair for the dramatic would thrive as never before and when Field's store would acquire fame beyond any it had yet achieved. For the hustling city had snatched, through windy talk and booster promise and an outlay of hard money, the honor of staging the World's Columbian Exposition in 1893. Gleefully it swung into this mammoth task.

Along the south shore of Lake Michigan sandy, clay-filled tracts were transformed into the "White City" of synthetic marble exposition palaces and exotic carnival streets. Cried Daniel Burnham, the White City's go-getting director of construction, "Make no little plans! Aim high!"

Selfridge, excited and enthusiastic, nodded his handsome head. This, he saw, was his big chance to dramatize Marshall Field's great store before the world, to provide a special thrill in State Street for the thousands upon thousands of visitors expected for the fair. They must come, stare, and buy, then go to their homes speaking the wonders of Marshall Field's.

The store, boomed Selfridge as he reveled in the preparations for the big event, must be as much an attraction for the out-of-towners as the amazing Ferris wheel whose cars climbed 265 feet high; or the Columbus Caravels that had sailed from Spain; or the great telescope built with Charles Tyson Yerkes' traction riches for the new University of Chicago; or the Arts Palace, the gilt Transportation Building, the creamy Agriculture Hall, the high-domed Administration Building, or the Wooded Island with its dainty Japanese house.

The store was soon expanded to the north and east, and across Holden Court, which separated the main building from an addition on Wabash Avenue. The world's rarest goods went on display—a $20,000 Persian rug, costly gems, Sheraton and Chippendale furniture, exquisite Paris gowns, Indian shawls, Chinese rugs and jades, Japanese curios. There was a splendid new restroom for the ladies, and comfort rooms equipped with marvelous American plumbing.

Marshall Field's, trumpeted Selfridge's advertisements, "is an exposition in itself." He cited its vast size, the 23 large elevators, 12 separate entrances, including new-fangled revolving doors, the 100 different departments, 3,000 employees, the world-wide imports, special rooms, styles, fashions and luxuries, and the "low prices." "Our Retail Store," Selfridge concluded, "owing to its enormous size, its perfect arrangements, its wonderful variety of merchandise, and its great stocks is a continual and ever-changing exposition."

The Fair had its attractions, and so did Field's. Mrs. Bertha Honoré Palmer, the city's social queen, dedicated the Woman's Building in White City by driving a golden nail with a silver hammer. She helped to dedicate Field's new addition by treading the red carpet Selfridge had stretched across Holden Court.

At the Exposition one could see gems from Russia, the ten-ton cheese from Canada, the watches from Nuremberg, the $120,000 French Gobelin tapestries, and the statues by St. Gaudens and Taft, or the glittering Midway, with its raucous barkers, its cooch dancers, and its German, Irish, Algerian, Tunisian, Chinese, and Japanese villages.

At Field's there were bright silks from the Orient, filmy laces from Belgium, daring French lingerie, sheer French hosiery, incredible French hats. There were Irish linens of exquisite artistry, ingenious novelties, ornaments and glass from Bohemia, huge rugs and draperies, and the newest in household wares.

It was the perfect time for a perfect showman. Again Selfridge's methods proved themselves. The store sparkled at precisely the right moment in its history, and more people than ever before were made aware of its splendors and merits. The sales remained high, the profits good. Even in the bleak depression that followed the World's Fair, with thousands of men and women roaming the streets looking for jobs and hundreds of homeless sleeping in the City Hall, the company carried on as handsomely as any of its two competitors combined.

From Marshall Field there soon came a reward for Selfridge; not a gush of praise, since this was not the old man's way, but a larger share of yearly profits. Selfridge used his new bounty to build a summer home at Lake Geneva, Wisconsin, which he

A view of the "White City," Chicago's World's Fair of 1893. From everywhere visitors came to see the cultural exhibits—and the sights on the gay Midway.

named Harrose Hall for himself and his wife, and invited cash boys, errand girls, clerks, and executives to a gala picnic.

II

Harry Selfridge was hardly one to rest placidly on the achievements of the World's Fair year. Month after month, as the century ran its course, he whirred and stirred the activities of the retail store.

More than ever he concentrated on implanting the "Marshall Field & Company Idea" into the minds of all employees. He posted instructions, proverbs, mottoes, exhortations, and rules on bulletin boards throughout the store. He called on them to consider themselves "part of a great force," reminding all that they, as had others, could advance to new positions and better salaries. "Merit Will Win!" he cried. "The Idea" itself read:

"To do the right thing, at the right time, in the right way; to do some things better than they were ever done before; to eliminate errors; to know both sides of the question; to be courteous; to be an example; to work for love of the work; to anticipate requirements; to develop resources; to recognize no impediments; to master circumstances; to act from reason rather than rule; to be satisfied with nothing short of perfection."

Such a call to service sounded like an appeal to members of some mighty army of crusaders. Indeed, at one of Selfridge's many conferences with his department heads, he once proposed that employees don uniforms, adding, "I wouldn't mind at all wearing a general's uniform!" The innovation was not put into effect, but the spirit that moved Selfridge to make the suggestion was reflected in his other actions.

Although Selfridge, like the other executives, frowned on unions, he believed in trying to keep workers reasonably happy. Wages were not high, but many women preferred to work for a lower salary at Field's because, as one of them later stated,

"You were considered low class if you clerked in some other store. If you worked at Field's it was all right. You were a 'point-out' in your neighborhood. Besides, it was pretty nearly true—as our bosses kept telling us—that if you worked for Field's for half an hour you could go to New York or Philadelphia and get a job almost at once." Women workers, by a courtly rule, were not required to stay as late as men so that they might return home before dark. "We endeavor," read a Field's statement, "to throw about our young women an atmosphere of protection."

There were special restrooms and lunchrooms for employees and a school for cash boys. Selfridge tried to keep morale high by methods other than picnics and occasional salary boosts. At the outbreak of the Spanish-American War, John W. Hughes, head of the special service force, came to him with a plan to have a party for all volunteers and make the promise that each would regain his job at the end of the conflict. Selfridge assented, but was quickly overruled by Robert Fair, a senior partner. Selfridge stomped into Marshall Field's office and spoke to him. In fifteen minutes he was back, beaming. "It's all right," he told Hughes. "We'll go ahead with your plan."

Any clerk who sassed a customer was reprimanded and, in many cases, dismissed. "You had to look respectful," related Ellen Bredin later of her many years in the exclusive stationery department, "and wait on her as quick as you could and never, never push her. If she didn't seem eager to buy, you said, 'See if you need it when you get home and come back tomorrow, madam!'" This admonition against "pushing" was a distinctive feature of the store, for in most others at the time employees were specifically directed to do a fast selling job. A young University of Chicago sociologist, Annie Marion McLean, spent two weeks in department stores and reported that clerks rushed madly toward elevators as they disgorged their customers, grabbing them by the arms, shouting, "What would you like, madam?" or "Something I can do for you, sir?"

While Selfridge deplored the "push" tactics of other stores, he warned against a lackadaisical attitude. "It is recognized in this store," he declared, "that the undue urging of merchandise upon customers is not desired. But this does not in any way mean that indifference in the slightest degree is to be permitted. Salespersons must be alert and will, under no circumstances, allow any of their actions to be such that the customers can interpret them to be actions of indifference."

Even in their dealings with fellow-employees, Field's workers were advised to be circumspect. They were to use "dignity, respect and care" in addressing each other while on duty: "A careless word or an act of familiarity may, in the mind of some passing customer, cause a reflection to the discredit of those who are responsible for same, or allow customers to wrongfully interpret words or gestures, and this we wish to avoid."

Nor were employees, within customers' hearing, allowed to discuss the store's business. "It has been suggested by one who has overheard such a conversation," read one fastidious bulletin, "that any of the saleswomen who may be using the toilet rooms which are also used by the customers should not discuss business of the house, as it is complained that . . . . matters have been referred to which included the mentioning of customers' names."

Direct criticism of any patron was a ghastly sin: "We are sorry to have it reported that employees occasionally make remarks derogatory to customers after they have left the counter or department; for instance, suggesting that the customer is a crank or making some equally uncomplimentary remark. Language of this kind should be avoided, and we must insist that our people refrain from using anything of the kind."

In his passionate pursuit of customers, Selfridge was acting in the rigid pattern established by Marshall Field. Always Field had yearned for "tone," and his own set of rules in the 1870's formed the basis for Selfridge's code. Even those who could not always afford to buy what Field's store offered appreciated the service and the elaborate courtesy. Many who made only one small purchase every six months came to consider the store a place where the customer was always right, and this became an unofficial maxim in these years. Another motto stemmed from an incident in which Field, while strolling through the store, came upon Lindsay T. Woodcock, assistant retail manager, speaking heatedly with a woman customer.

"What are you doing here?" asked Field.

"I am settling a complaint," replied Woodcock.

"No you're not," snapped Field. "Give the lady what she wants!"

III

More than genteel tone and courtesy drew the shoppers.

For a decade and more after the World's Fair the firm imported nearly $3,000,000 in foreign goods every year. Its retail and wholesale buyers ranged the world. In Europe, after checking in at Joe Field's chilly little set of offices in Manchester, they set out to buy silks in Lyons; lace curtains in Nottingham, Brussels, and Calais; woolens in Bradford; Swiss handkerchiefs and embroideries in St. Gall; hosiery and gloves in Chemnitz; bronzes, ceramics, pottery, and novelties in half a dozen cities and towns in Bohemia, Slovakia, Austria, and Italy. Stiff, swishing dress fabrics then in vogue were sent by the quickest routes known. So were wares bought in Turkey, India, and Japan; a great fashion had developed for Japanese art and bric-a-brac near the close of the century.

By 1895, Field's was the country's largest importer of laces. The rage then was for fancy lace curtains, and a wealthy shopper at Field's could buy a pair of curtains of Brussels point lace for $500. Imported gloves continued to be popular with the ladies. A pair of the best, made from goatskin by French artisans, was only $2.00. No item was too small to import if the customer showed a desire for it; a typical "popular seller" ordered by Hilton Thorpe, an Englishman who was Joe Field's assistant in these years, were egg-timers, miniature hourglasses to measure the cooking of three- or three-and-one-half-minute eggs.

The craze for Oriental rugs, developed in the 1880's, was still strong. In charge of Field's department was Albert H. Dainty, a Pittsfield, Massachusetts, youth who had been with Field since the Great Fire. He sent buyers deep into the Orient, into the very homes of the weavers, to procure the best rugs the natives could produce. In his section were displayed century-old carpets and others woven especially for Field customers on Kashmir looms. There were Bagdad carpets, Mecca prayer rugs, and camel bags from the Arabian deserts.

To enhance the effect, Dainty hung lanterns made by Moorish ironworkers and Cairene hammocks and placed about the floor ancient chests from Persia. He delighted in selling exotic and expensive floor coverings; but Dainty did a lively business in the section where he piled rugs and carpets, less romantic but highly serviceable, for customers who could not afford the luxuries.

Under Selfridge, the store's window displays entered a new and colorful phase. For years no one had paid much attention to the way in which wares were shown to passers-by; Field and Leiter, after dissolving their relationship with Potter Palmer, had abandoned his far-seeing practice of making windows attractive. For the most part, porters or employees with an artistic bent were the store's window trimmers—even in the year of the World's Fair. It was enough, decreed the older partners, that strong light came into the windows and shone on the goods that were displayed.

But Selfridge, of course, could not hold with such a theory. Like Potter Palmer, he knew the real value and lure of a beautiful window. In 1895, a salesman told him of the remarkably fine windows which were being created by a young man named Arthur Valair Fraser in a little dry-goods store in Creston, Iowa. Selfridge sent for Fraser and hired him.

Quebec-born Arthur Fraser turned out to be a display genius, and at Field's his show windows became world famous, helping to launch the frenzied vogue for red—the "Red Epidemic," style experts called it in 1897. The color was favored in new fabrics and trimmings from Paris. Fraser responded by giving over to it six entire windows: in one he placed red silks; in others, gowns and wraps, ribbons, millinery, even red petticoats. "No stronger proof of the fashionable quality of red need be given," commented the *Chicago Dry Goods Reporter*, "than such a display made by this conservative, reliable house."

Alertly Selfridge watched for every opportunity to expand Field's prestige and services. When Chicago schoolteachers were first paid by check instead of currency, Selfridge installed a special assistant cashier near the State Street entrance and advertised that the store would cash teachers' checks free. This gesture was greeted by the *Chicago Tribune* in precisely the

"Republic" stood watch over the Court of Honor at the Columbian Exposition.

way Selfridge meant it. "Given a school teacher," wrote an editorialist, "who finds herself in the downtown district with a check in her possession which makes her feel like the man in Mark Twain's story of the 1,000,000 pound bank note; given also an easily accessible spot where the check may be cashed without trouble and without delay; given, too, certain surroundings to that spot, consisting of all the alluring fabrics and bewitching knick-knacks most dear to a woman's heart. What will be the result? Certainly it will not end in the sudden death of trade. Foully beset by temptation is the woman who has eyes and can see and ears and can hear, when she attempts to pass unscathed through the devious ways of the stores which deal in all things having to do with the world, the flesh, and the devil. And though the small boy may tremble at her nod, the school teacher is but a woman."

Selfridge hated to see sales missed and was ever ready to grab them. For some years imported and high-priced furniture had been on display in the upholstery department; but prospective customers, so the comment went, "came to look at our stuff and then went to buy at The Fair." William H. Miller, who had been an assistant buyer in the bedding section, and W. E. Clarke, head of upholstery, were dispatched to Grand Rapids, where new factories were turning out lower-priced goods. They sent back box couches, heavy oak chairs and sofas popular in the period, colonial-style desks and tables.

Marshall Field objected strongly to this move, but the goods sold. Subsequently Miller was sent to Europe to bring back traditional Sheraton, Hepplewhite, and Chippendale, which were then modified according to his instructions to the Grand Rapids manufacturers. After 1900 the furniture section earned big profits and grew larger until it was handling every type—from antique to modern—that could be found in establishments that dealt exclusively in furniture.

IV

Always, whatever his innovations, Selfridge watched carefully for the response of the feminine trade. The ladies came, and continued to do so—awed visitor from the farm towns and lofty society matron alike.

Monday was the favored shopping day although some society ladies appeared two or three times a week. The wealthier shopper always drove up to the Washington Street entrance in her carriage, an open victoria in the summer, a closed hickory phaeton in colder weather. Eddie Anderson or Charlie Pritzlaff, the doormen who knew each by name, greeted the lady as she stepped out of her conveyance. Her coachman, a husky in white buckskin breeches and boots, with silk hat and coat matching the carriage upholstery, found his place in the double line of vehicles from Michigan Avenue to State Street. All day two street cleaners did nothing but sweep that stretch of pavement with long-handled brooms.

Charlie, who had been a coachman for F. J. Kennett, a friend of Selfridge's, was always on hand an hour before the store opened, sweeping the cobblestone streets in front of the entrance. He soon got himself a notebook and in it wrote the name of the customer, checked it in the society Blue Book, then memorized all he could about her so that he might greet her in a more personal way the next time she came shopping.

And there were many names for Charlie Pritzlaff to inscribe.

Mrs. Palmer, erect and proud, was a regular shopper, driven in a coach surmounted by two attendants in maroon livery. The Infanta Eulalia of Spain, who had created such a furor at the opening of the World's Fair by refusing to be gracious to Mrs. Palmer—"After all," mewed the Spanish princess, "the wife of an innkeeper!"—came to see the sights at Field's.

So did other society leaders. Grover Cleveland and Theodore Roosevelt came, as well as hard-eyed Hetty Green, the richest woman in the world; and Prince Henry of Prussia, who spent his evenings at the Everleigh Club drinking champagne toasts to the denizens there. And even his hostesses were regular customers at Field's, arriving in handsome equipages with their choicest, best-behaved girls, sweeping grandly to the section where they might obtain the most luxurious silks.

Not only did the Everleigh sisters shop here, but so did their friends and rivals from the rip-roaring Levee. Frankie Wright and Vic Shaw, prime madams both, bought the best frocks, while Carrie Watson, soon to forsake the fleshpots for the hushed retirement of a suburb, always stopped to chat with Charlie Pritzlaff or to hand a dollar to a passing beggar.

When Mrs. William McKinley, whose husband had won the Presidency in 1896 through the good work of his pudgy friend, Mark Hanna, needed a gown for the inaugural, she decided that fitters and dressmakers at Marshall Field's should make it for her. The President-elect came with her for the fitting, and he shook Pritzlaff's hand and signed his book near where Carrie Watson had scrawled her name.

The newspapers used a two-column picture on the front page, informing the eager readers that Mrs. McKinley would wear—it was her own design, at that—"a dress of silver wrought brocade of Parisian texture combined with *point d'Alençon* lace and silver passementerie threaded with tiny pearls, with lace edging and a taffeta skirt and many frillings and French shirrings."

Another customer in these years—not famous then but destined to reach a sort of immortality later—was Isadora Duncan, newly arrived from San Francisco, seeking a job as a dancer. "Get some frilly stuff to go with that Greek dance you do," the manager of the Masonic Temple roof garden told her. With no money to buy a frilly dress, Isadora glided into

Potter Palmer and his lovely wife, Bertha Honoré Palmer, were leaders of Chicago society after he retired from business and built his lake-shore "castle."

Field's and asked to see the manager. Selfridge cast his blue eyes over her, smiled, and told her tenderly she could have anything she wanted. She chose some white and red material for petticoats and some lace frills, pressed Selfridge's hand in hers, then flitted back to the roof garden manager to score a success with both her Greek dance and her frilly gown.

Whether the shopper bore the name of Bertha Honoré Palmer or that of an unknown dancer, or if a woman came in a hansom cab, on the cable car, or one of the West Side trolleys marked "Field Special," she was treated courteously. The instruction was invariably the same to the doormen, the clerks, and the dapper floorwalkers who strutted about with their 5-cent carnations in their lapels: "Utmost courtesy is required. . . . Under no circumstances allow the customer to leave the store dissatisfied."

Such was Field's reputation for grandeur that on the streets of the far West Side children who had yet to pay their first visit to the big store sang a ditty—

"All the girls who wear high heels,
  They trade down at Marshall Field's.
  All the girls who scrub the floor,
  They trade at the Boston Store."

V

Not always was it easy to treat all customers with the required courtesy.

There was the woman who put her coat in one of the store's fur vaults for the summer season. She valued it then at $200, but when the coat somehow was lost, she claimed $600. John W. Hughes, special service chief, refused to pay the claim. The woman's husband appeared, threatening to punch Hughes. When Hughes dared him to do it, the man said, "OK, I'll take $400." Hughes paid this amount and later was glad to hear that the woman told her friends and neighbors that the store was fine to do business with—a fact that led him to conclude such word-of-mouth advertising was worth the extra payment.

There were always those who took undue advantage of the return policies. Field himself figured in two such incidents.

One involved an expensive tablecloth imported from Italy by A. L. Bell, head of the linen department. When Bell told Field he was asking $800 for it, Field said, "Too much. You'll never sell it." A week later Field sent for Bell. "I was wrong," he said. "Your judgment was better than mine. I dined on that tablecloth at a friend's house last night." Bell blushed and replied, "Sorry, Mr. Field. She took it on approval yesterday morning and returned it today."

The other concerned a society woman who returned a cape on the day after a fashionable ball in the Auditorium Hotel. Because the cape was expensive, the case was brought to Field's attention. The woman insisted she had not worn it at the ball and Field took her word. But when he examined the wrap more closely after she left, he found an expensive lace handkerchief tucked into one of the folds. "If she said she didn't wear it," he sighed, "then she didn't wear it. But I guess we'd better send her handkerchief back to her."

There were the cranks and the customers who demanded the impossible. One woman wanted $10,000 because she had slipped on the polished floor; another woman disliked the gaudiness of Fraser's windows; a man protested that Field's delivery wagons made too much noise. A Mr. S. E. Hurlbut wrote that in his twenty years of dealing with Marshall Field he had found only one thing of which to complain: "The elevators at the south end of your store are too low in the door to admit a man of full stature. I have broken and spoiled two good silk hats there and am tired of the sacrifice. I am 6 feet 1 inch in shoes."

And there were the inevitable shoplifters, most of them women drug addicts who stole to obtain money for opium or morphine, the narcotics then most widely used. Two detectives from the agency of McGuire and White kept sharp eyes out for these thieves as they traveled through the store. Whenever one was spotted, the detective sidled up to her and whispered politely but firmly, "Now get the hell out of here."

One shoplifter, an old-timer in the business, paid the store as much of a tribute as any regular customer. Seized by the detectives as she was heading for an exit with a fur coat, complete with hanger, stuffed into a special "booster skirt," she was brought to Hughes' office.

"Now look, Millie," said Hughes, "every time you're caught, you're in this store. Why do you keep bothering us? Why don't you work the other side of the street?"

The grubby little woman drew herself up. "Me work the other side of the street?" she blared. "I'm no jitney thief boosting cheap stuff. I work your store because you got all the best stuff in the city!"

CHILDREN'S TOYS, 1890

FAREWELL
TO SELFRIDGE

Toward the close of the century Marshall Field had a final, dramatic reunion with his old partner, Levi Leiter.

The two men shared a disappointment in their sons. Neither Joseph Leiter nor Marshall Field II showed fondness or aptitude for the business that had yielded their fathers such riches. Young Field, a sensitive man who enjoyed good books and good music and liked to hunt and ride, did work as a $15-a-week clerk in the wholesale house, but he found the tasks there dull and uninspiring. After he married Albertine Huck, daughter of a local brewer, in 1890, he spent most of his time touring Europe.

Leiter's son was a man with the soul of a gambler. He played high-stakes poker and took daring risks in the stock market with his father's money. In 1897, Joe had been given $1,000,000 by his father to spend in a happy year traveling around the world. Instead Joe set out to corner the world's wheat market. He bought all he could get on margin and by May, 1898, almost accomplished his purpose. But when he refused to sell any of his holdings to P. D. Armour, who sorely needed 9,000,000 bushels in a hurry, he was doomed. Armour rushed a fleet of ice-breaking tugs to Duluth and in his big grain boats brought back not only enough wheat to deliver to his accounts but an additional 9,000,000 bushels which he poured into the market.

Leiter's corner was smashed. His $10,000,000 of paper profits were wiped out, and his debts shot to almost $20,000,000. The elder Leiter, by selling property and stocks, was able to raise all but $2,000,000 to cover the claims. He had yet other land to sell, including that at State and Madison streets, occupied by Schlesinger and Mayer, which he now proposed to surrender for quick cash; and he knew the man who had lots of it.

Leiter sent an emissary to Field asking if he would buy the property.

"He'll have to come himself!" said Field.

On the next morning, Leiter shuffled into the office, his derby hat down over his eyes and his collar turned up so that none should see him on his embarrassing errand.

The two men conferred for less than half an hour. Then Field emerged from his office. "Make out a check to Mr. Leiter for $2,135,000," he told John G. Rowe, the cashier. "I've just bought the Schlesinger and Mayer site."

II

Poignant as this transaction was, there were other real-estate dealings of greater importance. In rapid order Field made the moves which eventually would enable his store to spread over an entire block in the heart of the city. He bought the rest of the buildings stretching north along State Street, including Central Music Hall. He gave Hetty Green $350,000 for another chunk of property on Wabash Avenue, next to the addition built in the World's Fair year, and he started negotiations for other real estate in the block.

Selfridge was pleased. For months he and Shedd had been urging Field to do exactly this so that a further addition to the store could be built. Expansion was necessary, for Selfridge contemplated new departments and new services to attract more customers. The city's development was strong and steady, and as Chicago grew Field's needed to grow. Field agreed readily to these plans, showing far more inclination for such moves than he had when the Wabash Avenue section was first proposed; then, until the upper floors of that building were finally rented, he had called the structure "Selfridge's Folly."

In 1900, a permit was granted for a twelve-story building north of the original store and extending the rest of the block to Randolph Street. The Central Music Hall was demolished and so were the smaller intervening structures.

For a year while the building was going up Selfridge kept the public aware of the progress and his ambitions for the store. Everyone knew how deep the caissons were, how high the ceilings would be, where the Corinthian columns would be made. This was to be "Everybody's Store," roared the advertisements. "We have built this great institution for the people, to be their store, their downtown home, their buying headquarters, where their best interests might be considered!" There was new emphasis on lower prices. "We wish to wipe out completely any thought," said Selfridge, "that merely because this store includes in its great stocks some of the finest merchandise made that it is necessarily a high-price store."

Again, the throngs pressed into Marshall Field's. Originally the grand opening was planned to last three days—from September 29 through October 1, 1902—but so many thousands insisted on accepting Selfridge's invitation that it was extended through the rest of the week. In the first three days more than 150,000 people showed up, carrying away not only visual memories but $10,000 worth of special souvenirs—from silver pin trays to gold-plated bowls.

They saw new rooms for checking packages and clothes, a library with Oriental rugs and green leather mahogany furniture, restrooms with green willow rockers, a first-aid room with a trained nurse, and an information bureau that helped settle any

An employee with an idea or a customer with a complaint was always welcome in Harry Gordon Selfridge's office, where he planned his store promotions.

difficulties—from getting theater tickets to finding a hotel room. Nearly all the cash boys were gone, what with child-labor laws and the pneumatic cash carriers installed by Selfridge, but the greeters and the well-clad ushers were on hand. Through the store glowed electric bulbs in pink globes, softly lighting the cut-glass *objets d'art*, the Tiffany lamp shades, the furs, and the latest corsets "designed to fill out slim figures."

"Cultivating New Ties and Strengthening Old Ones," the advertisements claimed. Merchants all over the country read learned discussions in their trade papers about the notices heralding the opening, devised by Selfridge and Waldo P. Warren, his advertising manager. They read carefully the advice offered by the *Chicago Dry Goods Reporter*: "Every dealer has the opportunity to make his own store the leading trade center of his community by following out the spirit and methods that have built up Marshall Field's."

Even the employees were treated with greater care. Selfridge opened for them a special restaurant, recreation rooms, a gymnasium, locker rooms with separate shower baths, and a library. He devised a three-day training system whereby new workers were taught the ways of the big store, how to display goods, how to make out sales slips, and, most important of all, how to deal with customers.

"We wish," he advised all employees, old and new, "to make important the point of receiving merchandise which has been returned, without going through the unnecessary or unpleasant questions or remarks, which remarks make the customer ill at ease and really accomplish no good. We would much prefer to be occasionally imposed upon than to feel that we have made any errors in the other direction. The employee is not the loser by the returning of goods, except in a very slight way. The house is the loser, and if we prefer to stand the loss cheerfully, please let us have corresponding cheerfulness from employees."

One of the visitors to the store was John Wanamaker, whose Philadelphia emporium was one of the world's largest and who now looked for new places to conquer. Led on an extensive tour, he showed great interest in the store's fur workrooms on the upper floors. Here, in what was believed to be the largest factory of its kind in the world, were made muffs, hats, caps, and gloves. On the top floor of the new building was a cold-storage vault with room for as many as 20,000 fur coats.

Wanamaker also visited with Field in his office.

"I like this city," Wanamaker told Field. "I think you could use another store here."

Field grinned. "Probably. But I've been thinking of expanding too. You come here and I think we'll open in Philadelphia."

Wanamaker smiled weakly and shook hands, promptly forgetting about his idea of competing with Field's.

III

The new sales figures were impressive indeed. In 1901, before the addition was built, the retail gross had been $14,000,000, and the net profit $989,000. Net profit had slipped the next year because of the expense of the new store, although sales rose by over $3,000,000. But by 1903, retail sales were up another $3,000,000 and profits stood at $1,445,000, greatest in the history of the retail store.

Selfridge, however, was unhappy. He did not get the recognition he felt he deserved. Wholesale continued first in the affections of Marshall Field. When the company was incorporated in 1901, Shedd, Joseph Field, and even "Dusty Bob" Fair received 6,666-2/3 shares each—Selfridge only 6,000 shares. Even after retail's record-breaking year in 1903, Field listened less to Selfridge and more to John Graves Shedd.

Selfridge brooded. On a cool day in May, 1904, he walked into Field's office.

"Mr. Field," he said, "I have decided to go into business for myself. I am going to buy Schlesinger and Mayer's interests."

Field blinked. "Very good, Mr. Selfridge," he replied. "I hope you are successful."

"I can stay till the end of the year if you wish, Mr. Field."

"No, you can leave tomorrow if it suits you."

The financial arrangements were soon made, Selfridge receiving over $1,000,000 for his Field holdings. Friends and relatives supplied $4,000,000 more to enable him to buy the store of Schlesinger and Mayer.

"I have severed my connection with the house where I have been working for nearly 25 years," Selfridge stated formally. "I have done so only because of a great desire to become head of a business of my own. If I were not absolutely confident of success in my new enterprise, I should not have taken this step."

Marshall Field had not a word to say to the reporters. Selfridge the showman had done more than any other man, except Field himself, to make the name of the company world famous. But Field preferred a merchant to a showman, and he regarded Shedd as the greater merchant. And there were others to help— Stanley Field, his nephew, who had come from the office in Manchester to learn the business; James Simpson, the eager Scotch lad who had risen from office boy to become Field's private secretary; John McKinlay, the solemn office manager of the retail store; and several more.

"Well," Field grumbled when the Selfridge resignation was announced, "we'll have to get another office boy."

IV

Selfridge's career as sole owner of a department store in Chicago was brief and unsatisfying.

By 1905 women were favoring again the fashion known as the "Grecian Bend." This stylish advertisement stressed the appealing qualities of refinement, exclusiveness, individuality.

He opened with a typical flurry, emblazoning huge medallions bearing his initials on the front of the building. On the first day he ascended to the roof, clad in morning coat and silk hat, and ran up the flag. He sought to keep up with the styles and fashions as he had at Field's. He featured sales of automobile ulsters for men and women; ordered sports dresses for women now engaging in athletics to a greater degree; he arranged, as at Field's, children's days and special exhibits; he wrote glowing advertisements and issued high-flown bulletins.

But it was in vain. "There are so many things to do," he soon was complaining, "and no one to do them." The Schlesinger and Mayer employees had neither the spirit, pride, nor ambition he had found among those in the big store down the street. He was uncomfortable about fighting with Field's for customers. "I feel I'm competing with my own people," he said. "I just can't rid myself of that feeling."

Within two months Selfridge was ready to sell. He called on John Shedd, telling him of his financial woes. Shedd promised to find a buyer. His choice was Carson, Pirie, and Scott. These merchants had finally moved to State Street from the West Side, only to discover that their lease on the building at 106-110 State Street would not be renewed. No other good sites were available, and Marshall Field feared that such excellent competitors might return to their former neighborhood. Shedd telephoned Sam Pirie, who was incredulous. Why should Marshall Field be so solicitous, he wondered, after having to surrender a $100,000 bonus to get the Singer building away from Carson's years before? Besides, the twelve-story Selfridge property was a larger responsibility than Pirie cared to incur.

Shedd assured Pirie that Field felt no antagonism because of the Singer deal. Marshall Field wanted good merchants on State Street. Shedd would guarantee an agreeable bargain with Selfridge. Pirie was ready to listen further. He came to a secret meeting in the consultation rooms of the Illinois Trust Safe Deposit Company. Pirie was in one room, Selfridge in another, while Shedd, as intermediary, took a room between them. Selfridge wanted a bonus of $250,000 for his store. Pirie offered $150,000. Shedd worked out a compromise—$200,000. Pirie was ready to accept, but his partners were not. They conferred with Shedd, who urgently pointed out the advantages of State Street and emphasized that it might be the last chance Carson, Pirie, and Scott would have to remain on State Street. Finally, the partners agreed to pay Selfridge a bonus of $150,000 and to assume the obligations of the store, somewhat less than $50,000. Selfridge accepted.

For a time Selfridge lingered in Chicago, taking part in various civic ventures. Then he left for London, where, he decreed, a progressive and modern department store was needed. Shops there were too conservative, treating the customers with disdain. In 1909, he opened the doors of Selfridge and Company in London. At first the customers stayed away, while he was called an outsider, a barbarian, a cheap showman. But those few who were lured into Selfridge's spoke well of the courteous clerks and the service. Slowly, Selfridge prospered, bought out rivals, became the first merchant of Great Britain.

He lived on until 1947, a portly man with a manner of dress reminiscent of those days when he flew through the aisles of Marshall Field's store. He was a social lion, a first-nighter at the theaters, a collector of rare books and paintings; a boon companion of industrialists, artists, beautiful women, statesmen, and monarchs. Regularly he sent members of his staff to Chicago to study Field's store. Behind his desk there always hung a picture of the man who had given him his first job in Chicago. He made and lost three fortunes; and when he died, he left an estate of only $6,000, obviously having lived a full and satisfying life.

GLASS-WINDOW DELIVERY WAGON

FALL 1902

THE FOUNDER'S
FINAL YEARS

In Marshall Field's final years, his massive firm flourished on such a successful scale that its wealth, as one awed observer put it, "would add luster to the dreams of the fabled Croesus."

Men came to learn how he had achieved his triumphs and gained his riches. One was a gawky young writer named Theodore Dreiser, then preparing a series of articles for Orison Marden's popular magazine, *Success*—"An Up-to-Date Journal of Inspiration, Encouragement, Progress and Self-Help."

Dreiser had already interviewed bankers, meat packers, traction barons, and railroad magnates. In his mind he had tucked away ideas and impressions for novels that would stir the world, but to the readers of Marden's magazine he imparted the powerful men's secrets and formulas for success.

Fidgeting in his chair, he asked Field about his early days in Conway ("They were hard") and the money he saved ("A dollar looked very big to us boys in those days") and his first sight of Chicago ("The town had plenty of pluck and ambition, but the possibilities of greatness were hardly visible") and the lessons of panic and depression ("I learned what I consider my best lesson, and that was to do a cash business").

Honesty, energy, frugality, and integrity—these, said Field, were the prime requisites for success. "Practice these virtues and do the best you can. Any good fortune that comes by such methods is deserved and admirable."

There was more talk—of the firm's revival after the Great Fire, of the first $5,000 Field had saved, of flush times and hard times, of the need for perseverance and good judgment—and Dreiser unlimbered himself from the chair and returned to his office to write an article that overflowed with enthusiasm.

"No more significant story, none more full of stimulus, of encouragement, of brain-inspiring and pulse-thrilling potency has been told in these columns," he rhapsodized. "It is grand in its very simplicity, in its very lack of assumption of special gifts or extraordinary foresight.

"The Phoenix-like revival from the ashes of ruined Chicago is spoken of by Mr. Field as an incident in the natural and expected order of events. In Marshall Field it was no doubt natural and to be expected, and it touches the very keynote of character of the celebrated Western merchant, sprung from rugged Eastern soil, whose career is an example to be studied with profit by every farm boy, by every office boy, by every clerk and artisan—yes, and by every middle-aged business man, whether going along smoothly or confronted by apparently ruinous circumstances, throughout our broad land."

Another writer, Charles Gleed, in his series on "Captains of Industry" in *Cosmopolitan* magazine, found Field as "quiet and undemonstrative as a country preacher" and doubted that "any millionaire's influence in this country is better and more thoroughly salutary than that exercised by the modest gentleman." Even William T. Stead, the rambunctious British journalist who had rocked Chicago with his revelations of crime, sin, vice, corruption, and exploitation in *If Christ Came to Chicago*, admitted that as a businessman Field stood "near the top of the tree, if not at the very top" and that his store was to Chicago what "the Louvre and Bon Marché are in Paris."

Field's benefactions rose too. His original gift to the fledgling University of Chicago was augmented by some $300,000 and land to be used for an athletic field; for years the students called the tract "Marshall Field." After much persuasion he had finally agreed to give $1,000,000 to keep open the Columbian Museum, built during the World's Fair. Now he gave hundreds of thousands more, and the name ultimately was changed to the Field Museum of Natural History and remained so for many years. Another benefaction was a library in Conway; at the dedication Field, slowly and carefully, made his first public address, brief and solemn. By 1901, his total contributions in the decade came to nearly $3,000,000, and many paid him homage for being a public-minded man of wealth.

II

But there were vexing problems, in both his business and personal life.

For years, there raged a fight against what many called the "Department Store Octopus." Small merchants and their spokesmen cried angrily that the big stores were strangling them with "ruinous competition" and "fraudulent advertising." In this clamor against bigness such stores as Field's, Mandel Brothers, The Fair, Carson, Pirie, and Scott—all in Chicago— as well as similar establishments throughout the country were accused of conspiring to crush the small trader by concentrating all retail business in their smooth hands. The critics cried that they were tempting women to buy articles they did not need: "Women have to be protected from the allurements of the bargain counters!" And others inveighed, "It is better to have 1,000 storekeepers fairly prosperous than two or three millionaires and 997 bankrupt tradesmen!"

Field and his fellow-merchants returned argument for argument. They defied the "agitators" to prove they had crushed small businessmen. Marshall Field's wholesale division, as a matter of fact, had financed the opening of many hundreds of new dry-goods stores, and the wholesale division made twice the profits of the retail store in selling to those very merchants who supposedly were being crushed. If the small merchant failed, said the big-store owners, it was because he failed to cater properly to the public's needs.

"The public is in favor of our stores!" chorused the department-store owners. "The women do not have to be tempted. They like to come to us."

Eventually the fury of the fight waned as the country became aware that bigness was a symptom of the constantly growing economy and that the department stores, despite their foes' claims, were less detrimental to the well-being of the average citizen than a good number of really gigantic trusts in steel, tin, tobacco, and other commodities against which lasting and solid legislation was devised.

III

Another stormy aspect of the changing times, the rise of labor unions, brought worry and woe to Field. As a leading exponent of the paternalistic philosophy, he was always certain he knew what was best for his workers. He was—as were other merchants and industrialists of his day—shocked to think that those whom he paid would shift their allegiance to a union and leaders who had no personal interest in the store's welfare.

Yet he did not forbid his workers to join unions. In 1890, he had been approached by a committee of his wagon drivers. The group informed him that the Knights of Labor was organizing all the horse- and delivery-barn workers into a new union, and many of the men had thought of joining. "You can join," said Field, "but you'll have to remember that you'll be under the union's laws, not ours. Also, a lot of you have been here a

In the violent Teamsters' Strike of 1905, Chicago policemen were assigned to guard delivery wagons. Here is a quartet marching ahead of a police patrol.

long time and get more than the scale pay. If you join, you'll have to get any raises through the union, not through the men you work for."

The men joined, but after a year, dissatisfied with the union's fruitless attempts to win wage boosts for them, returned to Field and told him they were dropping their membership. "Very well," said Field, "there will be no reprisals against anyone."

But now, in the summer of 1905, Field's—and, indeed, the entire city—was thrown into the midst of a savage strike. It began mildly enough when a dozen wagon drivers, all members of the International Teamsters Union, walked out of the barns of Montgomery Ward and Company because the firm had hired nonstriking tailors to thwart garment workers then out on the picket lines. From this beginning the conflict expanded. The union's hard-boiled president, Cornelius "Con" Shea, stormed in from his office in Boston, crying, "I've got a good mind to tie up the whole goddamned city!" He set up headquarters in a Levee brothel, from which he dispatched emissaries to Field and other merchants with word that they would have to deal with him on his terms or be ruined.

The merchants refused to yield. Field was especially adamant, for he had a passionate hatred for what he considered "lawless strikers." Soon other wagon drivers and their helpers had walked out. Eleven big department stores were forced to suspend retail deliveries. To combat this move by Shea, one which soon saw nearly 5,000 men out on strike, an Employers' Teaming Company was formed. Husky strikebreakers were brought into the city in freight cars and placed on the wagons. Mayor Edward F. Dunne, crying out against the "vicious tactics" of Shea and his aides, assigned policemen to each wagon. It was common sight in the sultry summer for policemen, with clubs drawn, to be seen walking in front of a delivery wagon or sitting on the seat beside the driver, while crowds lined the sidewalks hooting, "Scab! Why don't you be a man and git down!"

There were pitched battles in the streets between strikers and nonstrikers. Some strikers dragged the drivers from the seats, and beat them after overturning the wagons and trampling on the packages. Strikebreakers and police invaded union offices and meeting places and pummeled striking drivers and their sympathizers. Even many Chicagoans, not directly concerned in the conflict but sympathetic to unions, threw themselves in front of prancing horses when the scab drivers refused to halt.

In August the strike was finally ended through the efforts of a mediation committee led by Stanley Field. The toll amounted to twenty-five killed, 400 wounded, and a loss of $1,000,000 in wages and $10,000,000 in business. Even those who backed labor's rights deplored the tactics used by Shea. They accused him of squandering union funds at the infamous Everleigh Club and in the House of All Nations in the Levee district. He was indicted on charges of conspiring to injure private business and public trade, but managed to go free in court. The lessons Shea learned then in labor violence, however, were put to use years later when he became an aide of "Big Tim" Murphy, one of the biggest labor racketeers during Chicago's gangland era.

As for Field, he soured on unions and union leaders. Throughout the strike he was sorely troubled. "Don't let the strikers get you down, Grandpa," his grandson, Marshall III, wrote him. He contributed heavily to the Employers' Teaming Company and took the trouble to put down in a letter to Victor Lawson, editor of the *Chicago Daily News*, his views on the conflict. "We have no quarrel with anyone. We only ask to use the streets for all lawful purposes entirely unmolested." For a while after the bitter fight, union leaders who came to shop in the store and were recognized were quietly asked to take their business elsewhere.

IV

A far less violent but no less significant sign of the shifting trends also became evident to Field. This was the slow-but-sure reversal in the relation of his retail store to his expansive whole-sale division.

In the early days wholesale had been supreme. Its profits still continued to surpass those of the retail establishment, even after the construction of the dazzling 1902 store. But a schism had developed because wholesale was buying less and less goods for the Chicago retail store. Actually, the two divisions were traveling in opposite directions from their original starting point. The thousands of towns to which the wholesale branch sent millions of dollars worth of goods each year—from $33,900,-000 in 1900 to $42,800,000 in 1905—were far less sophisticated than the Chicago whose residents demanded the latest styles, the latest fashions, the latest in everything.

Selfridge had been vociferous in his demands that the retail branch be permitted to drop the traditional purchasing system and do all of its buying on its own. Shedd had opposed this idea, insisting always that even when Selfridge went into other markets and bought directly from manufacturers such wares as pottery, Tiffany glass, wallpaper, expensive men's clothing—for which there was little demand among the majority of the firm's wholesale customers—the usual 6 per cent had to be paid to the wholesale division.

The argument went on after Selfridge left. The retail store continued to buy much of its goods from the wholesale house, principally such wares as ready-made clothes, furs, and upholstery. But more and more retail buyers had gone into the markets themselves, roving the international field to buy what they thought would satisfy the tastes of the big city dwellers.

While noting this growing antagonism, Field also sensed the beginnings of another wholesale problem. More manufacturers now sent their representatives directly into those territories

Field's lace department in the early 1900's featured frilly parasol covers, some of which are seen here hanging above the heads of the salespeople.

The lady shopper loved to linger in the yard-goods section, pausing beneath the new electric lights to examine fabrics with a rich, expensive look.

where his salesmen had established themselves. More and more merchants took advantage of manufacturers' offers to come to the cities and factories on buying trips with all their expenses paid. Speed, symbolized by the automobile, replaced the leisurely, personalized pace at which Field's wholesale trade had been carried on. This creeping sickness was scarcely observable then, despite the symptoms revealed in the antidepartment-store agitation a while back. Yet, Field was getting worried. Something was wrong—something would have to be done. But there was time, he felt, to watch and wait for developments.

v

There was less time for this and other problems than Marshall Field thought. The last tragic days of the merchant prince were rapidly approaching.

Since Nannie Field's departure in 1892 for the south of France—where she died a few years later—and the marriages of his son and daughter Ethel, Field had been lonely. He lived with his servants in the Prairie Avenue mansion. His moments of pleasure came when his grandson, Marshall III, visited him or when his good friend, Mrs. Delia Caton, wife of Arthur Caton, a wealthy lawyer and sportsman, invited friends to a party for him. There were some who stared in amazement at these affairs as Mrs. Caton, a lively woman, did a little dance for her guests and then commanded Field to pass the collection plate; he sheepishly did as he was told and seemed to enjoy it.

But such times of pleasure were rare. Field could only nod sadly when his most devoted salesman, Pierre Funck, visiting at his mansion one night when Ethel was away in Europe and Marshall II and his family at an eastern summer resort, remarked, "Marshall, you have no home, no family, no happiness —nothing but money."

Eager to end his long loneliness, he took Mrs. Caton to England in the summer of 1905, a few months after her husband died; and on September 5 they were married in St. Margaret's Church by the Rev. Herbert Hensley, canon of Westminster Abbey. At the wedding breakfast in Claridge's, Ambassador Whitelaw Reid toasted the couple, and Field gave his bride an incredibly valuable set of necklaces, tiaras, rings, and brooches —all studded with diamonds and pearls. Field's new wife was good for the aged merchant. They went to horse shows and to the opera and took young Marshall III to concerts of the Chicago Symphony at Orchestra Hall, hoping that the boy, an unenthusiastic student of the violin, might practice more diligently if he heard good music.

This happy period ended with tragic suddenness. On the afternoon of November 22, a shot rang through the mansion of the merchant's son, Marshall II, down the block from the old man's home. When servants entered his room, they found Field II fatally wounded on the floor, an automatic pistol lying nearby. He was taken to Mercy Hospital, and a quick telephone call was made to his father, then in New York with his bride. In a private train the elder Field rushed back to Chicago in record time, to be met at the station by photographers and their flash-powder explosions. He visited briefly with his son at the hospital, and when he walked out, head bowed, the photographers were at him again. Field trembled and brandished his cane. "Here you, stop! Why do you do this? Aren't you ashamed?"

For five days Marshall Field II lingered on while gossip raced through the city. The merchant's reluctance to discuss the case stimulated wild reports that Field had been shot by a girl from the Everleigh Club, or that he had wanted to end his life because of disagreements with his father or his own poor health. His physician, however, said young Field had told him, upon his arrival, that the shooting was accidental. When the young man died, that was the verdict of the coroner's jury.

VI

The tragedy of his son's death tore the old merchant apart.

For a week after the private funeral he stayed away from the office, and when he did appear his eyes were dull and his features pallid. As he stopped by the desk of the firm's cashier, Henry D. James, beside whom Field II had clerked in his days in the wholesale house, the old man blinked and asked James why he had not come to the funeral.

"We were told the services were private," replied James softly. "We thought we were showing respect by staying away."

Field wept. "It was all terribly mismanaged," he moaned. "Who did they think I'd rather see there, a young man who worked with my son, or a lot of social parasites?"

His mood remained somber, his manner lethargic. Sometimes he roused himself to discuss with Shedd plans for a new building which would link all the units of the store into one magnificent structure. In December he went with his brother-in-law, Henry Dibblee, who handled his important real-estate deals, to visit Leon Mandel, whose lease on the property where Mandel Brothers store stood was running out. Mandel had informed Field that he was thinking of moving to Michigan Avenue.

With a flash of his old enthusiasm for the future of State Street, Field urged Mandel to remain. "This is still the best place for merchants," he insisted. "You stay and I'll let you have a ninety-nine-year lease. Mandel agreed to the deal, and the papers were drawn up.

VII

Soon the world was hearing of Marshall Field's last illness.

It started with an unusual stunt—a golf game with red balls on New Year's Day, 1906. In the snow, Field played eighteen holes with Stanley Field, James Simpson, and Robert Todd Lincoln. By the time the afternoon's sport was finished, Field had developed a sore throat. But this did not stop him from visiting his store and wholesale offices or conferring with Ernest Graham, the architect, on how much would be needed to build the new Field Museum on the lake front or consulting with Stanley Field about financial matters and his estate. "You're the one of the family I've got to rely on," he told his nephew.

He discussed business affairs and the changing times with Stanley. He smiled faintly as he pictured the contemplated splendor of the new addition that would unify the retail store. He reviewed the woes of wholesale. "Wholesale," he told his nephew, "is a dying business. The trend is to retail."

At seventy Marshall Field was a sad-eyed man who possessed great wealth, little happiness. His second wife, Delia, was a sprightly woman who did manage, however, to bring some joy into the aged merchant's last years.

Then, despite a persistent cough, he left with his wife for New York. By the time they reached the Holland House, Field was so ill that he could barely walk to his suite of rooms. Stanley Field, informed of his uncle's condition, summoned Dr. Frank Billings, the noted Chicago physician, and the two hurried to New York. Dr. Billings diagnosed the illness as pneumonia.

On January 16, 1906, the aged merchant's temperature soared to 107 degrees. In a few hours, with his wife at his bedside, Marshall Field was dead. To reporters who soon pressed her for her husband's dying utterance, Mrs. Field offered a stately reply. "Mr. Field's last words," she said quietly, "were for me and not for the world."

VIII

In the hour Field died, a doleful bell resounded through his big store. All the shades were drawn and the aisles darkened and business suspended for the next few days.

On a gray morning four days later the merchant's funeral was held in the city where he had gained his riches and renown. One might have thought the President or a governor had died. All the State Street stores, large and small, were closed. The Board of Trade suspended in the afternoon, while at the noon hour flags all over Chicago flew at half-mast, and the various firms with which Field had been connected shut their doors for the rest of the day. At the funeral service in the First Presbyterian Church, the Rev. Dr. John A. Morison intoned, "Whether as members of this church, which for long years was the spiritual home of Marshall Field, or as citizens of this mighty city of Chicago, with all of us today there is one thought that is uppermost in mind and heart—Marshall Field is dead."

Through sleet-filled streets a cortege of carriages inched along with the hearse bearing the merchant to Graceland Cemetery. Thousands of sad-faced Chicagoans lined the wet curbs, buying from street vendors deep lavender mourning-ribbons or black-circled buttons with Field's picture. At the cemetery the sleet fell more thickly as Field was laid in a grave near those of the son whose recent death he had mourned so bitterly and his first wife with whom he had failed to find lasting happiness. Then thousands of Field employees filed into the Auditorium Theater for a special memorial service to hear sermons and speeches from ministers and public officials extolling Marshall Field as a man who had made his millions through patient industry and intelligent square dealing.

Such sentiments were echoed in the nation's journals. As they drew around to evaluate this merchant among merchants who had left behind a firm that sent goods to thousands of stores from the Allegheny Mountains to the Sierras and a retail store that was an institution of magnificence, quality, and splendor, the editorialists saw, as one, that as Chicago and the nation had grown, so had Marshall Field prospered and grown.

"The chief secret of his business growth was an infallible sympathy with conditions and environments," wrote one. "He saw what Chicago was and would be, what it would want and what it could be made to want," said another. "He was the most encouraging and stimulating illustration of the fact that wealth may be honorably and legitimately acquired without wrong doing or sharp practices," remarked a third. "His conscience had not permitted him to incur and to deserve the contempt or hatred of the public by doing the things which some other millionaires have done," said another. "He was shackled to his business; it was his taste, his judgment, his strong character, sound perception, impetus and inspiration that upheld the whole enterprise," read still another tribute.

Here and there someone questioned the value of amassing a fortune estimated at $120,000,000, yet never achieving genuine and deeply felt happiness. Some criticized Field mildly for not taking a greater interest in the politics of his city and country. And when the details were disclosed of his remarkable, airtight will by which his huge fortune would be conserved for decades with minimum payment of taxes, critics arose whose cries in legislative halls ultimately led to stricter inheritance-tax laws.

On one point all agreed. Marshall Field's enduring monument was his store.

STATE AND WASHINGTON CORNER
DURING CONSTRUCTION PROGRAM, 1906–1907

A FABULOUS BAZAAR

The mourning period ended. The last dirge was sung and the thousands of messages of condolence received and read. On the fifth day after Marshall Field's death, the retail store and the wholesale house opened for business again under a new president, John Graves Shedd.

The trustees' choice was largely unquestioned. Had not Marshall Field himself called Shedd "the greatest merchant in the United States" before a congressional tariff committee a few months before? Of all the closest associates of "The Founder," as Field was now reverently titled, only Shedd, Stanley Field, and James Simpson, Field's personal secretary who had tried his hand at managing the retail store, were still active in the firm. Higinbotham had retired in 1901 with his $2,000,000 in accumulated profits; and the other partners were gone, too, while Joe Field preferred to remain in Europe watching over the import trade. Now the trustees, to back up Shedd, chose Stanley Field, the nephew on whom the aged merchant had transferred the hopes he once held for his own son, as one vice-president and James Simpson, who was said to have absorbed the "Field viewpoint" better than any man, as the other.

Although Shedd was generally hailed as a logical successor, there were gossips who wondered if he would ride off in new directions. Some whispered that he planned to stamp his own name above Field's atop the store's doorways. And others doubted that Shedd or any other mortal could fill the shoes of Marshall Field. But John Shedd was not one of these. He applied to himself the advice he piped to young men seeking the recipe for success: "Believe in yourself! Then you are never timorous!" And he believed mightily in the principles and traditions of The Founder.

Back in 1905, Shedd had constantly pressed Field to tear down the original store at State and Washington streets and build a new one, joining the 1902 store and all other units into one grand establishment. Field had swerved from full approval to full refusal. In July, 1905, while vacationing in Switzerland, Field made a final decision. "If I am willing to go ahead and build," he wrote, "I will cable the word 'Singer' inside 30 days. Meantime if you have any thing more to say in favor of the building, please give it to me. On the other hand if I cable the word 'Singer' and you have any reason for not building you will *not* go ahead." Within a month, he cabled the magic word.

But now, as John Shedd took up his duties, it was clear that trouble lay ahead. A panic, as bad as the worst of the earlier ones, was in the making. New York bankers, desperately shipping in capital from abroad, hiked their interest rates but still found it necessary to call upon the government for gold to save them. Finance tycoons, squandering millions in a battle for control of railroad and steel empires, headed for an inevitable crash. The Field Estate trustees shuddered at the contemplated expansion program. Could it be done without the calm and sure guidance of Marshall Field? Would Field himself have gone ahead in such uncertain times?

Shedd met them head-on. He waved the vital cablegram with the one word—"Singer." He was full of plans, ideas, enthusiasm. He argued that Marshall Field's could withstand any

Always, as long as he was connected with the firm, John Shedd kept a picture of Marshall Field on his office wall—and on his desk two red roses.

panic, any troubles in the future as it had in the past. The vast capital the trustees wanted to conserve was worthless, insisted Shedd, unless it was put to work. The new building must go up, in even greater magnificence than ever, as a fitting memorial to Marshall Field. The trustees were not convinced. Shedd took his cablegram to court and won the legal right to proceed.

No longer the quiet, reserved man, Shedd surged into a fury of activity. He harangued Ernest R. Graham, the architect, and the builders, demanding more and more speed, offering a bonus for quick completion of the job. Told that much-needed steel was not available, Shedd rushed a letter to Elbert H. Gary, chairman of the United States Steel Corporation, reminding him that it was for Gary's old friend, Marshall Field, that the steel had to be acquired. Back came a quick reply: "I remember Mr. Field's conversation about the steel. I will see to it personally."

II

The work moved at a record-setting pace. Down came the old structure. Up went the steel framework.

Night after night Shedd gathered his store executives and the architects in his office, hammering away at the ideas he said would have found favor with Marshall Field. There would be harmony and unity in this store; refinement, gentility, courteous and efficient service, stability, elegance—all the expressions of the Field theme. The fundamental appeal of the entire store would be to patrons of wealth and taste. All others would follow.

But the functional needs of an enormous mart would not be forgotten. Three basements deep, under Chicago's Loop, resting on huge caissons sunk to bedrock, the store would connect directly with the city's new tunnel railroad, the source of incoming stocks from wholesale and the exit for ashes, empty packing cases, and store waste. Here would be placed the boilers and power units to heat the edifice, operate the elevators, pneumatic tubes, conveyor belts, and the ice machines in fur storage.

In the second basement would be a modern and efficient shipping room; no longer would its sweating workers call it the "stink hole." The first basement would be, of course, the great basement salesroom, that pet of Selfridge's; but now, Shedd decreed, it would match in furnishings and appointments the finest retail store in any part of the city.

Across thirty-five acres of selling space in the main store would be distributed more than 150 retail sections, each a unit, yet each placed to complement the whole and keep the public circulating through the vast series of buildings. To this planning task Shedd assigned Simpson and David M. Yates, retail maintenance manager. They made drawings and models, conferred with Stanley Field, met at nightly parleys with Shedd and Graham. Before final decisions were made, all section heads were called in to make suggestions for changes.

There were some hot arguments when Simpson or Yates broached a new idea. Yates startled them all by proposing that dress goods, the very essential of a dry-goods store, be removed from the main floor to the second floor.

"We should put things on the first floor that customers will want to buy the minute their eyes light on them," said Yates. "We should have notions, gifts, things to beautify women and their homes on that floor. The era of piece goods is ending, but women who want them will go to the second floor. They'll go even higher for linens and ready-to-wear clothes."

Shedd paced about nervously as some executives shouted Yates down and others agreed with him. "Merchants all over the country will throw up their hands when they hear about this," he decided. "They'll think we've gone crazy. But we'll do it!"

Yet, when Yates proposed that laces, too, be shifted to the second floor, Shedd angrily squelched him; in laces he had won his first fame with the firm. Laces would receive prominence, and did, in a dazzling department with special lighting tricks and a huge vault at the rear to which clerks carried the most expensive selections—"real laces," Shedd called them fondly—for safekeeping every night.

Seeking a dominant, unifying symbol of the store's splendor, Shedd was pleased when Graham proposed that Louis Comfort Tiffany be engaged to design a costly dome of multicolored Favrile glass for the light well in the new building. Tiffany made countless sketches and drawings and finally decided that such a dome could be created at the sixth-floor level. It would be unique, the biggest glass mosaic in existence, covering 6,000 square feet with some 1,600,000 pieces of iridescent glass. Sunlight by day and a system of powerful electric lights by night would make the dome a sight of unutterable beauty, Tiffany promised. He was commissioned to go ahead at once.

Shedd gave every phase of the designs and construction great personal attention. He planned the curving plate-glass counters that would stretch along the 385-foot main-floor aisle, longest in the world. He selected the lighting fixtures, supervised the final drafts of the layout arrangements, picked the rare Circassian walnut and blue Wilton carpets for the tearooms and restaurant on the seventh floor. And he paid much heed to special elegant rooms he wanted for the display of costly goods to those customers of wealth and taste he proposed to pamper.

Informed by his buyers in Europe that the fashion trends would be toward classicism and period styles, he devised a series of period rooms, calling on his artists and technicians to do meticulous research. They produced sketches for a Louis Quatorze Salon for fine gowns; the Salon des Debutantes; the Elizabethan Room for the display of fine linens; the Deal Room, duplicating the great hall of a London mansion; the American Colonial Room; the French Room, for handmade lingerie; and the Oak Room, where fine antiques would be shown in the atmosphere of a millionaire's drawing room.

III

During much of his first year as president, Shedd's time was taken up with plans for the unifying addition. But he busied himself, too, with the big job of managing the entire company, from the retail counters and the wholesale house to the growing network of factories started a decade earlier.

He was somewhat austere and imperious, but most employees liked him. He frowned on cigars and cigarettes and was a fervent believer in the Temperance movement. Any man who failed to report because of drunkenness was instantly discharged, although Shedd always saw to it that Dr. Leonard J. Munson, head of the new welfare department, was dispatched to see that the drinker's family was not suffering by his misdeeds.

Like Field, he insisted that in the everyday run of business his department heads and executives make their own decisions.

Once, when a section chief approached with a problem, Shedd waved him away. "My dear fellow," he said crisply, "I put you in charge of the department. You are the man to run it and solve its problems."

He insisted, as had Field and Selfridge, that all employees adhere strictly to company principles. Shortly after he became president, he heard a customer complain that a clerk had been discourteous when a piece of merchandise had been returned. Shedd promptly summoned all executives and section chiefs to inform them that Field's policies had changed in no way. To make his point, he handed out notices reading:

"We desire again to emphasize the well known policy of this house in taking back merchandise promptly and pleasantly, issuing cash credits when desired. Especial attention is called to the manner in which such transactions are made. Everyone knows that it is possible to say the right words, and yet say them in such a manner as to offend the customer.

"We insist that the manner be right also—usually a pleasant word and a smile, and an actual indication that we take pleasure in being able to please the customer in the matter, and yet without any sense of doing more than our duty. It is, to say the least, poor taste to suggest that we are doing the magnanimous thing— let us leave that for the customer to discern and appreciate. In short, let us meet the customer in the same spirit of courtesy and interest that we do in making a sale."

None of the flair for the pungent word, none of the lofty tone of Selfridge's prose; but the idea, stemming from the store's earliest days, was the same.

IV

For months before the new addition was to open, Shedd was busy making preparations. He instructed his foreign buyers to seek out rare items for the event. He brought to Chicago

Gustav Van Derbergen, the Belgian sculptor famed for his work at the St. Louis Exposition, to develop the central motif of the opening—the contribution of merchants to civilization. Such a theme, harking back to Greek and Roman classicism, was a shrewdly chosen one since Shedd had learned from his foreign representatives that the coming season's fashion trends would run along classical lines. Van Derbergen worked with Arthur Fraser in fashioning the window displays and contributed his own ideas to the interior decoration of the store.

When the financial crisis ripped through the country in the summer of 1907, Shedd was too engrossed in the forthcoming opening to worry. While other merchants retrenched, Shedd went boldly ahead—as Potter Palmer had in 1857 and as Marshall Field had done in half-a-dozen panics. The West and the South, where the firm's retail and wholesale trade was heaviest, were completely sound, Shedd informed his directors. The troubles in the East, frightening though they were, were really a "synthetic bank panic," he said. Although President Theodore Roosevelt was jolted half out of his wits by the economic straits of the country, John Shedd was not.

He asked for and received from the trustees an appropriation of $100,000 more to spend on the grand opening. Then he summoned his advertising force, headed by Waldo P. Warren, the man who had learned much from Selfridge. Again he lectured them on the traditions of the firm and the meaning of the new store. Theirs would be an exquisite exercise in counterpoint, he reminded them. The institution itself—not merely the merchandise—would set the theme of the opening.

There would be no crass shouting of wares, no bugling of price reductions, no mention of specific lines of goods, no boasting even of superior quality. The country would meet Marshall Field & Company, a personality. It would learn more of Field traditions, Field history, and Field service. The formal opening would be arranged to invite the good friends of the store to a superlative exposition, much as a grand host might formally invite friends to a sumptuous dinner. Refinement and discrimination must be the keynote of their creations. The country's best artists must be commissioned to lend their talents to this lofty institutional campaign.

Veteran advertising men shook their heads. With the panic raging, competition in Chicago was fierce, and the other stores were shouting their heads off in their advertisements with lavish claims and price quotations. Field's, in normal times, bought less space than the others and still refused to advertise in the fat Sunday newspapers. Now Shedd appeared to be adding to this handicap by ordering high-toned advertisements at a time when the most raucous hullabaloo seemed to be needed. It was even rumored that Shedd intended to take price tags off all merchandise during opening week!

But the advertising men had their orders. All through September full-page advertisements appeared. They represented reproductions of original drawings by fine artists, and the text was as dignified: "We announce the formal opening of our completed retail store. The entire public is invited to see the world's greatest store at its best. Marshall Field & Company."

Only once, when one of Harrison Fisher's drawings of "The New American Girl" graced the page, did the copy writers show a flash of exuberance. "The superlative achievements of the world's foremost designers of apparel, fabrics, and accessories for women's fashionable attire are revealed in our Formal Opening Displays. Under the inspiration of this notable occasion the designers have outdone their past efforts in giving exquisite expression to the utmost refinement, individuality and character."

Then all was ready. Shedd conferred with subordinates, received reports from all sections, puttered up and down aisles, and snapped commands here and there. And he even issued this official Order of the Day to give them the final directives:

> The store is nearly completed and within a few days the great building program entered upon three years ago will have been entirely consummated.

> This event is the most important ever known in the history of retailing and we wish to signalize it by a formal opening that will be entirely in accord with its importance.

> There must be no spot in the store open to adverse criticism. Each section manager, each division superintendent will see that all work under his control is done absolutely right. Each stock head and each salesman will see that he does his part.

> This organization has never been called upon for unusual effort without immediate and enthusiastic response. This is the one instance beyond all others where enthusiastic preparation is needed because it will be the most important event in our history.

v

For an hour before eight o'clock on the brisk morning of September 30, 1907, some 8,000 persons—nearly all of them women—line the sidewalks around the new store. They are impatient but in good humor. Small boys scurry through the ever growing throng, thumping into bustled ladies, evading policemen, kicking a tumbling derby blown free by the Chicago wind. From time to time many of the ladies, clad in thick, long skirts and white, tight-collared shirtwaists and close-fitting jackets with balloon sleeves, glance up at the great new clock hanging from one corner of the store. Finally it is 7:59.

Inside the store, in another minute, there is a quiet command: "All right!" The window curtains smoothly retract. The doors

An artist's graphic sketch of the Field store after its completion in 1907.

swing open, and into Marshall Field's newest store pour the first chattering, hurrying hundreds of that week's 300,000 visitors.

Those who cannot yet enter begin an inspection outside of the much-heralded window displays. They pause first before a replica of a Greek amphitheater, set against a background of foliage, with a seat in the foreground, a length of drapery tossed over it, and a broken festoon of roses and a palm branch dropped carelessly beside it.

What does it mean? Many will not know until they later consult the newspapers. "The window depicts the classic Greek period. It honors the drapers. Marshall Field would have approved. He was essentially a draper. There lay the beginnings of his merchandising genius." There were other windows to honor merchandising through the ages, twenty-seven of them. The symbolism was sometimes perplexing, *Dry Goods Magazine* later conceded, but it was highly cultural.

Inside the store, visitors brush past John Shedd and his executives. Shedd is wearing a dark, braid-trimmed business suit, mauve vest, high wing collar, and billowing cravat ornamented with a pearl stickpin; but few stop to notice him. The

crowds are intent on the counters, the decorations, the souve-
nirs—bronze ash trays embossed with a picture of the store,
roses, lithographed posters.

Hundreds rush to gape at the magnificent Tiffany dome. So
great is the throng in the Washington Street stair well, with
people packed there staring up at the flow of blue and gold six
floors above, that Shedd fears for the floor and his precious
decorations. He turns and orders David Yates, "Keep the
crowds moving."

By ten o'clock there are thousands more inside the store,
jamming all floors from the basement to the top-floor workrooms. They stuff themselves into the seventy-six elevators and
crowd the stairways. They follow a steady pattern of traffic—
down the long main aisle past bright showcases of the finest
laces, jewelry, handkerchiefs, embroideries, flashy umbrellas,
neckwear, dress trimmings, perfumes, notions. They head east
across Holden Court to the Wabash Avenue store with its
leather goods, silverware, men's furnishings.

Throughout a wild day they jostle each other past displays
of exquisite imported China, fine American pottery, exotic
gowns and furs, glittering gems, acres of furniture, and sparkling
household wares. They visit the tearooms, prowl the nursery and
ladies' restrooms, pry into the Medical Bureau, invade the
French millinery room and the women's shoe section, a dazzle
of plate glass and polished mahogany cabinets. Some wander
through the picture galleries where exhibits rival the finest at
the Art Institute, then join the throngs to stare at models displaying the newest in Parisian gowns, or peek into the lingerie
room, where are shown imported underthings and sheer French
hose amid palms and flowers framed against walls lined with
pink silk.

There are no price tags on the merchandise, except in the
huge basement salesroom where the clerks eagerly assure visitors

that the merchandise is new, fine, "Field quality," especially purchased to be sold at lower prices.

VI

Most of the visitors did not see it all. The more determined and discriminating ones found the ornate rooms with French names where fine gowns by Worth of Paris were shown, or ventured into shops where custom-made leather goods or jewelry could be ordered. Some visited the Evening Room, designed to show them how gowns would appear under artificial light. A privileged few saw the administrative offices on the

The fabulous Tiffany Dome, which one sees looking upward from the store's first floor, was installed in 1907. It covers 6,000 square feet and is composed of 1,600,000 pieces of iridescent glass. One ecstatic art critic wrote that the dome was "in a class with the nave of St. Peter's in Rome."

ninth floor, looked at the employees' restrooms and lockers on the floor above, or went all the way to the twelfth floor to visit the remodeled fur-storage rooms and the workrooms where 600 women and men were prepared to make alterations on ready-to-wear clothing bought in the store.

The city's newspapers, accustomed to the hoopla of previous openings, used more than mere adjectives to describe Field's. It was, they all agreed, the world's largest store, exceeding John Wanamaker's in Philadelphia by some four acres. It had the biggest single salesroom in the bargain basement and the longest sales aisle. If the Wilton carpeting were rolled out in one strip, it would extend thirty-one and one-fourth miles. There were 76 elevators, 23,000 Grinnell sprinklers. The ice machines for the cold-storage rooms and the restaurants made 100 tons of ice a day. The telephone exchange could handle more than 10,000 calls every day. There were 14 terminal stations for handling sales checks in the store, 446 pneumatic tubes totaling 127,000 feet, and 4,500 carriers for their use. Purchases were rushed to customers' homes by a delivery system using 400 wagons and 700 horses. The value of the building, exclusive of furnishings and fixtures, was estimated at $10,000,000.

The formal opening, newspapers and trade papers agreed, was an enormous triumph. But what pleased Shedd even more, the store was acclaimed an artistic success by no less an authority than Edmund Buckley, world traveler and a professor of fine arts at the University of Chicago. In a purple-prose article in the *Fine Arts Journal* he called the store flatly the finest in the world, whether judged artistically or by any other standards.

Buckley was as pleased with the entire building as he was with the Ionic granite monolith columns which stood fifty feet high at the main entrance on State Street. The display windows "constitute an array unrivaled anywhere upon earth for combined extent, united and detailed beauty of effect." He likened the vista of the main aisle to "the many-pillared hall of the Madura Temple in South India." Nothing, he vowed, matched the noble and restful spaciousness of Field's first floor.

The Tiffany vault was in a class with the nave and transept of St. Peter's in Rome, "yet unique, combining the architectural triumphs of Christendom with the coloration techniques of the Byzantines." And he added, "One must concede that this western metropolis now holds pre-eminence for modern mosaic, at any rate in the western world; while the mosaics in Europe have a content so hopelessly medieval that no modern, possessed with proper *Zeitgeist*, could live with them for a week round."

Pointing to the wealth of artistic objects in the store and commending Field's for its great mullioned windows in the Tudor-style Oak Room, the beauty of color combinations, and its excellent collection of American pottery, Buckley hurled a challenge and defiance to the "art Philistines." They, he raged, would probably disapprove of the spending of over $250,000 on the Tiffany dome.

"Some greedy graspers who want to own everything in sight," he wrote, "can only be chagrined at meeting with an object they can never hope to acquire. They are too besotted with their lucre and luxury to respond disinterestedly to free and independent beauty. . . . . But lovers of beauty may see in this masterly mosaic over a mart of trade where people most do congregate, one step forward in realization of William Morris' prediction, 'Some day we shall win back art, that is to say the pleasures of life, to the people.' "

MARSHALL FIELD & CO

1906

MARSHALL FIELD & COMPANY

JOHN SHEDD
PLEASES THE LADIES

Once and for all, John Shedd had answered those critics who asserted the store would never be the same after the death of Marshall Field. He had succeeded in retaining the merchandising principles symbolized by Field and carrying them through the transition period into the imposing pile of masonry in Chicago's Loop.

Although he was basically a wholesaler and despite the important fact that wholesale had run up twice the gross sales and net profits of the retail store in 1906, Shedd continued to give much of his attention to the State Street establishment. It was here, he knew, that the spirit of Field's could best be exemplified, and he constantly reminded his section heads of that with flurries of notes.

"If the customer says she hasn't received satisfaction," he advised, "we are not going to *challenge* the customer. Why should we say in effect to the customer, 'You lie'? Let us probe our own organization and ascertain *why* the customer had not received the right merchandise that we are 99 per cent certain was in our immense stock."

To the advertising department he wrote, "When we say 'The Customer is always right,' that means far more than the simple duty of not remonstrating or questioning her actions. It means that the customer is right in her desire to be given an honest value and to be treated with every possible consideration. It means that every piece of merchandise must be precisely and exactly what it is represented to be. It means the customer must know from our advertising exactly what it is we have to sell. It means the elimination of empty and meaningless catch phrases in every step of the sales effort. What we write and what we say about our merchandise or our services must be strictly, scrupulously, unfailingly the truth."

These echoes of the statements of Potter Palmer, of Marshall Field, and of Harry Selfridge left no doubt in the minds of the lady shoppers that the store was ready to satisfy her most grandiose demand or slightest whim.

And she responded by coming quickly to rely on the store for more than her needs in dry goods or home furnishings. She solicited advice from the new Personal Service Bureau on preparations for weddings, christenings, and even funerals. She asked Field's to select wardrobes, paintings, antiques. Her menfolk telephoned to Field's or wrote letters from distant towns and remote farms, asking the store to choose gifts, gowns, even wedding rings, for sweethearts and wives. Whatever the transaction, Shedd held uppermost the injunction, "Give the lady what she wants!"

II

It was the perfect creed to follow in this year 1907, for the American woman had truly come into her own.

She enjoyed the franchise rights in only the most limited way; but it was she who, according to Department of Commerce estimates, spent 80 per cent of the consumer dollar, a figure unchanged until men took to buying automobiles in large quantities. It was rare to see many men shoppers in Field's or other department stores, especially in sections where women's

At the Washington Street entrance near State Street fashionable ladies stepped from carriages and electric broughams to be welcomed by uniformed greeters.

wares predominated. The clerks called such men shoppers who tagged along with their wives "molly husbands."

The American woman who had swooped into Field's that opening week was no longer the helpless, sheltered type the early Feminists had abhorred. She enjoyed freedom undreamed of in the days when Potter Palmer had opened his Lake Street store and had shrewdly slanted his sales talks to the women. She had taken up the bicycle craze and golf and roller skating and lawn tennis—and she demanded the outfits for these sports. Grimly, in tight-necked ulsters and goggles, she was learning to drive automobiles. She was healthier, more athletic, taller, stronger, self-assured, and, most important for those who sought her patronage, she had the right, opportunity, and ability to earn her own money.

277

That day when *Godey's Lady's Book* campaigned unsuccessfully to have a "female person" admitted as a student in Harvard Medical School was gone. There were now 7,399 women physicians in the United States, plus 92,000 nurses and midwives. Some 3,000 women had gone into the ministry, and 463 were professors in various colleges. Several of the new trades and crafts were dominated by women workers. The garment industry, revolutionizing the dry-goods trade, employed few men. More than 86,000 women had jobs as "typewriters," operating the new typing machines. Chicago alone had 4,300 "hello girls" at the telephone switchboards. The cotton mills in the East and South gave work to 120,000. Between 1900 and 1910 the employment of women almost doubled, from 4,000,-000 to nearly 8,000,000 engaged in 313 different occupations.

Women's wages unquestionably were low. A Russell Sage Foundation survey showed that 60 per cent averaged less than $7.00 a week in industry, 20 per cent got $8.00 a week, and only 17 per cent received more. The remaining 3 per cent, listed as apprentices, were paid as little as $3.00 a week and often less. But men in comparable trades and industries got only $10 to $12 a week. Many women were forced to work outside the home, said *Everybody's*, to enable their families to subsist.

Whether the working girl supplemented the family income, or supported herself, she helped to increase the buying power of the low-income groups. Living standards rose. More women could satisfy their growing appetites for clothes and finery.

Prices were moderate. For $100, the *Chicago Tribune* reported, a lady could buy a complete and elegant wardrobe in the Chicago department stores: a tailor-made suit, $15; cloak, $15; furs, $12; dress hat, $7.50; knock-about hat, $2.95; sweater, $1.90; black taffeta waist, $2.45; white waist, $1.25; evening dress, $20; silk petticoat, $3.95; white skirt, $1.95; two corsets, $2.00; three pairs of stockings, $1.00; dress shoes, $2.96; everyday shoes, $1.79; two pairs of kid gloves, $1.70; puffs, $1.50; vanity purse, 25 cents; chased gold comb, 25 cents; underthings, $3.20; miscellaneous, $1.40.

The "New American Woman" was the rage of 1907. She was celebrated in song, famous artists idealized her for the popular publications, newspapers devoted entire sections to her interests, her exploits, her escapades. Color pages in the Sunday supplements glamorized not only the leading actresses, such as Lillian Russell and Fritzi Scheff, but shopgirls and factory workers, and especially the new cloak and suit models. When the *Tribune* started a page for working girls, claiming that Chicago had more of them than any other city, the *Chicago Daily News* countered with a special column for the woman worker, launched by Miss Jane Addams, of Hull House. Her subject: "Beware of the Wolves Who Prey on Women!"

The papers were packed with feminine style news, household hints, profiles of society leaders, professional women, girl athletes. "Nellie the Cloak Model," generic for all the fashion models employed at Field's and other stores, was a favorite

Whether the American woman wanted costly imported originals or less expensive furniture made in Grand Rapids. Michigan, Field's store supplied her needs.

subject. The *Daily News* told bachelor girls how to build and equip their own homes, illustrating with photographs of Chicago working girls who accomplished such a feat. The *Chicago Examiner*, asserting that American women were growing taller and stronger than men, foresaw a race of Amazons in the country. But when an eastern newspaper insisted that all western women had big feet, Chicago journalists moved hotly to their defense, staging Cinderella contests to disprove the canard.

Women had more rights, though there were extremists still campaigning for woman's suffrage, elimination of the double moral standard, and the right to deny men the privilege of smoking cigarettes and drinking liquor. But this latter campaign boomeranged. Women, in their new-found freedom, flouted moral precepts too, some of them embracing these twin evils.

The week of Field's formal opening, the Chicago Ministerial Union denounced Chicago society women "who engage in drinking orgies at dances and card parties." Thousands of women, it was said, were reading in the privacy of their bedrooms that shocking novel, *Three Weeks*, by Mrs. Elinor Glyn, the English author.

Even more shocking was the disclosure that opening week that the members of the Colony Club in New York, an exclusive feminine retreat, smoked cigarettes and drank cocktails while they played bridge whist in their handsome new building. Such women as Miss Anne Morgan, daughter of the financier, Miss Ethel Barrymore, the actress, Mrs. John Jacob Astor, and Mrs. Gladys Vanderbilt not only engaged in these nefarious practices, but publicly defended them.

"There are 1,000 women in the club who have the spending of more than 1,000 million dollars," said Bertha Damaris Knobe, who revealed the story. "They are going to do what they please. The day of the Puritan is over!"

Pride of Field's was Carpet Hall, where imported rugs and tapestries, as well as American products, were displayed against an oriental background.

There was a yelp of rage from John Graves Shedd. He detested cigarette smoking even more than he hated drinking. Shedd had directed that the ladies' rooms in Field's should rival the Colony Club in elegance of appointments. He was confident they did. But he did not propose to follow the famous club in other matters. No drop of liquor had ever entered Field's except on the breath of a wayward clerk or section chief—and none, vowed Shedd, ever would. He also informed his executives that no woman would be permitted to smoke in the Field tearooms or restrooms, no matter how many millions they had to spend.

III

The ladies who came to Field's came primarily to buy, and Field's gave them their pick of the latest styles. The trends of the season had been anticipated by Shedd's buyers. Joseph Field had not missed the interest of King Edward VII and his Queen Alexandra in Parisian parties and French pageantry. As the dour influence of the late Queen Victoria wore off, Joe foresaw that London would remember Parisian *chic*, and the period balls Edward was reported to be planning would draw their inspiration from the wild Second Empire days. He had passed on his theory to the buyers, and they had acted accordingly. Now Field's was able to offer not only Paris originals of the new styles, but American modifications that might well please a London court lady or a *Parisienne élégante*.

Edmund Buckley, who had gone into ecstasies over Field's store, said the best-dressed women could be found in Chicago. Naturally, he credited Field's for making possible this distinction. A matron of suburban Lake Forest, driven to the Opera House in her imported Isotta-Fraschini, wore a gown and cloak from Field's that matched in modernity and daring decolletage anything described in the dispatches from a Paris opera opening or a ball in London's Albert Hall.

Women who could not buy Paris originals were content with American duplications, copied months in advance and produced in quantity. Laced snugly in a French corset, wearing an hour-glass gown with low corsage and an elegantly billowing *derrière*, luxuriating in sheer French hosiery which she alone would ever see, wearing dainty French slippers, and topped with an imported French hat that was heavy with flowers or stuffed birds, a woman of the American plains, garbed by Field's, could attend the most fashionable affair in complete confidence.

Field's, too, was well in the van of the motoring craze. Some 60,000 automobiles had been imported from Europe in 1906, and as many more had been built in America. The horseless carriage had arrived. And Field's motoring gear, in itself, made possession of an automobile seem desirable. There were richly embroidered suits, thick fur muffs, Siberian pony-skin coats, cute linen dusters and capes, caps or poke bonnets with veils, gauntlet gloves, and goggles. For the young motorist and sportswoman Field's offered a padded, three-quarter jacket of silk or

In this turreted castle Bertha Honoré Palmer reigned for years as Chicago's social queen. In 1950 it came down to make room for a modern building.

satin, gaily colored in red, green, or blue, and a muffler cap and gloves to match—excellent for automobiling, cycling, skating, or riding when worn with a thick wool skirt, divided or not, warm wool stockings, and cloth-top, high-button shoes.

Women bought also the "peek-a-boo" waist, ultimate in daring and denounced by most of the ministers of the land. This upper garment was heavily embroidered with many perforations through which could be seen a lady's camisole, or, at the neck and arms, actual epidermis. Charles R. Barrett, president of Barrett Business College in Chicago, warned his graduating class of 300 "typewriters" against the evils of this diabolical design, which he placed in a category with gum chewing and wine drinking.

"Gum-chewing stenographers," said Barrett in his 1908 commencement address, "are invariably bold, silly and gossipy

Never go to a wineroom with a man. Do not wear the peek-a-boo waist. It can arouse the baser impulses in a man. It will set you on the path toward danger."

Some women were in a mood for danger that winter. They motored, they frequented winerooms in great numbers, they risked tripping on trailing gowns and asphyxiation from too tight corsets, they chanced pneumonia with their decolletage, they blinded themselves with enormous, droopy hats—and they wore the peek-a-boo blouse.

They also spent more time and more money beautifying themselves, attempting to capture the "classic" look Field's had achieved for its grand opening. The look was never precisely described, but the newspapers were filled with prominent and sometimes pretty women who were said to exemplify it.

"The new styles are quite classic," declared Marian Martineau, the *Tribune's* style expert. "The new hats are classic, the new woman will be classic, and the popular girl will be classic also. Your new face will be classic—study your face and try to make it a classic."

For women unable to accomplish this feat without more detailed instructions, Chicago had more than 200 beauty salons, all specializing in the classic mode. For less than $10, a woman could spend an entire day in such a shop, Miss Martineau reported. A shampoo cost 75 cents; a singe, 50 cents; marcel, 75 cents; scalp treatment, $1.50; face massage, $1.50; body massage, $2.00; electric bath, $2.00; pedicure, 75 cents.

Since the classic look seemed to require more hair than most women possessed, scores of toupee shops flourished, manufacturing switches, rolls, and rats to augment a forward thrusting pompadour, similar to that of the Madame de Pompadour shown in the Field window, or to build up a fetching Psyche knot behind, like those of the Grecian ladies who disported themselves under Field's Tiffany dome. An excellent market in human hair developed, but inexpensive hair rolls, made of marcelled mohair, could be bought for as little as 35 cents.

IV

By the summer of 1908, it was clear that Field's retail store was a tremendous success, so Shedd allowed himself a European vacation. He was ever on the alert for ideas and fashions to pass on to the store.

At the races in Paris, he glimpsed a horrifying new creation, the sheath skirt. It was snug about the hips and clung, slinky and sinuous, to the thighs. It created, as London's *Punch* quipped, "a figure like a seal, reared up on end."

Shedd knew that the skirt as worn by the daring Parisian women would take time to catch on even with the most fashionable of his customers. He directed his buyers to see that any sheath skirts they ordered were "modified to American tastes."

And when the fall openings took place that year, the store featured not this shocking style but its adaptions, called the Directoire gowns—fetching, daring, yet modest enough. These frocks came in black, smoke gray, peacock green, wisteria, electric blue, and Alice blue, to be worn with ruchings, bows, or ostrich stoles and huge, plumed hats. "While extremes characterize the styles this season," a store advertisement noted, "refined modifications predominate in our superb collection."

Shedd was right in his assessment of American taste. Few women west of New York dared to wear the sheath skirt—that year, at least—and a brave one who did wear such a gown down Chicago's Randolph Street precipitated a minor riot with men and boys hooting,

> "Tight at the bottom,
> Tight at the top,
> Looks like a wienie in a butcher shop!"

1914

1917

1914

RISE OF THE MILLS

On his return from Europe, John Shedd found newsmen awaiting him.

"Mr. Shedd," they asked, "what is your secret for success?"

Shedd swept them with an imperious eye. "Luck!" he cried in his thin voice. "I think there are as many men who accidentally succeed as there are who accidentally fail. I am a firm believer in luck."

This was not precisely what the reporters had been expecting from a Horatio Alger kind of hero. They tried again: "What quality in a young man helps him most toward success?"

Shedd drummed nervously on his desk. "Once," he said, "Mr. Field asked me such a question. He wasn't wholly impressed with my reply: 'A well-directed nerve!'"

Shedd glared around the room. "But," he continued, "I still believe I was right! You must have the courage to back up your judgment. Otherwise, there's no point in trying to develop good judgment."

The reporters took it down.

"Think well of yourself," Shedd went on. "Self-respect never injures your standing with your employer. Without it you are likely to fall into timorous habits."

"What about hard work?" someone asked.

"Of course!" Shedd snapped. "Too few young men are really determined to achieve first place. They do not want it enough to do the necessary work or to make the necessary sacrifices. But I don't think life should be all work. One third of the time for work, one third for rest, one third for refreshment and relaxation." Shedd tugged at his mustache and smiled at them. "A man who wants to succeed should learn to play a good game of golf," he declared.

II

John Shedd had shown that he was a man with a well-directed nerve when he forced through the completion of the retail store in the midst of financial panic. But that had been as much a labor of love as a sound business project, for Shedd had done what he believed Marshall Field would have done.

Now, while he continued to watch closely the affairs of the retail store, he turned to a project which Field might never have approved on the scale Shedd contemplated. He proposed a huge expansion of the company's factory system.

Actually Shedd had been instrumental back in 1896 in persuading Field to extend the workroom methods by which the firm was able to offer exclusive products to its customers. Some such wares had long been made in the shops on the top floors of the retail store, and Field's also owned several small plants in Chicago where specialty goods and burlap bags were made.

Irked by the fact that specifications for certain articles were not always met by manufacturers, Shedd had gone to Field with a plan for final processing of goods in their own factories. Field had been hard to convince, but when Shedd showed, by small-scale experiments with yarns and thread, that manufacturing could reduce costs by 10 per cent and also provide the company with exclusive merchandise, he was given a chance to probe further into the possibilities.

In 1902 Shedd had sent his nephew, Harry Shedd, into the South, where a new textile industry was developing, to seek out a likely company to manufacture exclusively for Field's. After surveying the area from Arkansas to the Carolinas, Harry Shedd contracted with Frank Mebane, head of the American Warehousing Company that operated seven mills in Spray, North Carolina, and nearby Draper, for his entire output of cotton blankets, sheeting, and flannel.

But the Southern mills had far to go before they could match the products of the New England factories. Inexperienced workers, inferior machines, and slipshod methods resulted in imperfect goods. In a few years, although Field's had poured nearly $2,000,000 into the project, Mebane was bankrupt.

Mebane's misfortune was John Shedd's gain as he viewed his chances for broadening the manufacturing program. Through

Marshall Field & Company mills at Spray, North Carolina, as they appear today. The Field factory system, developed by John G. Shedd, once supplied goods to a big wholesale division—but was streamlined after the McKinsey regime.

Mebane's receivers Shedd acquired for Field's the ownership of the seven mills and sent his nephew back again, this time as head of the controlling subsidiary, the Carolina Cotton and Woolen Mills Corporation. Harry Shedd quickly replaced obsolete machinery, set up a training program for workers, and bought land for additional mills at nearby Leaksville. In a short time he had trebled production of better-grade goods, and the firm was starting to regain some of its investment.

Another chance for expansion led John Shedd to acquire the famous lace factories in Zion, Illinois, set up by that religious community's founder, John Alexander Dowie. Dowie, who leaped to fame during the World's Fair as a voluble and grim evangelist, had established the factory to make his followers economically self-sufficient. He had imported machinery and workers from Nottingham, England, to make Valenciennes lace. But by 1906, after Dowie died, the factory's efficiency slipped, and strife in the community and inadequate sales methods produced only losses.

Shedd, an expert on laces since his first days with Field's wholesale house, stepped in quickly. He bought the Zion lace plant and commissioned artists at Chicago's Art Institute, the New York Metropolitan Museum of Art, and the Museum de Cluny in Paris to create new designs. By 1914 the Zion plant was turning out 28,000 yards of Valenciennes lace a year, in addition to lace curtains, lace tablecloths, and handkerchiefs in 150 different styles.

Shedd's factory program was spurred by the successes in North Carolina and in Zion. New mills were added. Within two decades after Shedd had embarked in earnest on this plan, the company's total factory investment stood at $20,000,000. Besides the plants at Spray, Draper, and Leaksville, the firm owned two underwear factories at Roanoke, Virginia, and one at Fieldale, Virginia, for table damask, hosiery, and towels.

Arthur Fraser, Field's window display genius, used headless mannequins as late as 1914. The dash of his creations won the hearts of all passers-by.

Another subsidiary, the Marshall Field Mills Corporation, encompassed seventeen other plants: two in Philadelphia for hosiery and rugs; the Zion lace factory; a shirt and pajama plant in Manistee, Michigan; a silk factory at Union City, New Jersey; thread mills at Monticello, Indiana; a linoleum factory in San Francisco; an underwear factory in Manila and one in Swatow, China; and eight Chicago plants making bias tape, neckties, bedding, lamps, toilet preparations, burlap bags, men's wear, and window shades.

Ultimately the changing demands of customers and economic shifts would force a drastic revision of the Field's manufacturing system as well as its wholesale business. Even now there were hazy but unmistakable signs that the firm's wholesale network was heading for trouble, but Shedd was not inclined to worry too much about them. These were prosperous years, soon to become "normalcy years," and for Shedd, as president, there was far more satisfaction than woe.

III

These were years, too, when the man at the head of such an organization was constantly held up to lesser men as a model, his every utterance to be heeded. As with Field, people asked Shedd for advice on everything from the proper display of dresswear to the best methods of raising children. He talked no more about luck as a requisite for success, but of unremitting hard work, strict honesty, clean living, and utter dependability. "There is no better ballast for keeping the mind steady on its keel and saving it from the wreckage of humanity than continuous employment," Shedd told members of the Young Men's Christian Association, to which he gave $200,000.

"There are things to shun," he advised them and others, "like liquor, tobacco, and all bad companions. A little poison will soon permeate the whole system. Keep your minds and conversation free from evil thoughts and evil talk." Many influential men nodded at such counsel and some—Frank Leslie, the magazine publisher, for one—thought, by 1912, that John Shedd ought to be President of the United States: "A man of vision, the proper business man candidate."

Shedd was a benevolent sort of executive. Although he fought attempts of unions to organize any segment of his work force, he also barred child workers from the southern mills, and he built modern towns with good schools and recreational facilities for the factory employees. He gained approval, in 1911, of a plan to sell a limited amount of common stock to Field executives. And by 1917 employees were permitted to buy stock participation certificates which paid a 9 per cent annual return.

He doted on good employees. It was his boast that the firm "made merchants out of salesmen," and to further this idea he set up a Junior Academy in the store for the training of young workers. While he conceded that perhaps Field's clerks received less pay than those in other department stores, he insisted that the prestige of working there was worth the difference.

Shedd never tired of telling the customers about the merits of the store and its accommodations. Throughout his years as president there was a steady outpour of booklets, pamphlets, catalogues—all designed to acquaint the public with the superior facilities and services of the Field organization rather than to advertise specific merchandise. Some publications merely described the store as a showplace, with little mention of the wares. Many were planned for education of customers—"Important Facts about Shoes," "Labor-Saving in the Home," "The Story of Cotton," "How to Buy Silks," "How to Buy Shoes Intelligently," "How to Buy Furs Intelligently." There were guide books to Chicago. *Field Quality News*, published by the wholesale division, circulated to merchants and jobbers, offering them merchandising ideas, display techniques, advertising help, even instruction in bookkeeping.

Most famous of the Field publications was *Fashions of the Hour*, a magazine for retail customers issued free six times a year. Its first copy in October, 1914, edited by René Mansfield of the advertising department, was sixteen pages and featured a story of the Men's Grill in the new Store for Men. But the publication then and later was designed primarily for the ladies, what with discussions of styles and fashions, social and cultural activities in Chicago, and full-length photographs of well-known actresses and society women in gowns that could be purchased at Field's.

Mrs. Clara P. Wilson, who had studied with James McNeill Whistler, was installed as art editor, and she and Miss Mansfield set out to rival national magazines. By the 1920's regular contributors to *Fashions of the Hour* included Christopher Morley,

Frank Swinnerton, William Rose Benét, Carl Van Vechten, Westbrook Pegler, Emily Post, Emily Kimbrough, Peter Arno, and such actors, society women, and scholars as Cornelia Otis Skinner, Robert Montgomery, Mrs. Edith Rockefeller Mc-Cormick, Charles E. Merriam of the University of Chicago, Lynn Fontanne, and the Marchesa Helen Spinola of Italy. One rule remained permanent: no advertising. Such a policy, believed Shedd and those who were most enthusiastic about the magazine—notably Frederick D. Corley, later one of Shedd's successors—would be of more enduring benefit than page after page of advertisements.

Special care was taken during Shedd's regime to stress the idea that the store existed to perform public service to the community. It was the focal point of many charity drives, campaigns, and public endeavors. In World War I, the store staged innumerable benefits for wounded soldiers and was the headquarters for Red Cross and Liberty Loan drives. On one notable day, $1,500,000 of bonds were sold, with Mary Pickford as the "celebrity" saleslady.

Most of these drives were carried on under the direction of Stanley Field as vice-president. He had had previous experience in this field, for in 1906 he had supervised the collection of nearly $1,000,000 in supplies for the homeless in the devastation of the San Francisco earthquake.

In 1913, when floods overran the great Ohio River Valley, Field sent William F. Hypes, the hymn-singing ex-salesman who was then general sales manager, to the stricken area to supervise rescue and medical work. In 1915, when the steamer "Eastland" sank in the Chicago River with the loss of 812 lives, the store served as a relief station, supplying clothes and other necessities to survivors, and employees worked through the night making stretchers to carry the dead on Field trucks to a temporary morgue in the Second Regiment Armory.

A steady drive was carried on to make the store popular with youngsters who some day, of course, would be the shoppers of the future. Every type of attraction was devised to supplement the perennial lure of the toy department and Christmas displays. A movie showing the Field factories at work was loaned free to theaters which exhibited it at special showings to children who were given half-holidays from school to attend.

For several years the store published the handsome *Juvenile World Magazine*, with puzzles and such cartoon characters as Tweenie Twinkle, Bobbie Binks, and Marjorie Moots. In 1921 this publication was abandoned for newspaper advertising directed to children.

Each Saturday there were special parties and playlets for children. Boy Scout leaders were hired to conduct nature studies, but this was soon halted when eager boys carried frogs and snakes into the elevators on their way to the sessions. There

When the "Eastland" overturned in the Chicago River in 1915, with a loss of 812 lives, Field's was opened as a relief station for rescue workers.

were special exhibitions of all sorts—from "exotic fishes" to Indian Days, with Indian princesses and chiefs in full regalia. There were classes in toymaking and hobbies and model-building. "Children will grow up," said Shedd, "and they must grow up with a real love for the store."

IV

Shedd supervised and planned other major improvements.

Construction of the 1907 store had left only one corner of the square block, that at Randolph and Wabash, untenanted by Field's. Here A. S. Trude, Chicago's leading criminal lawyer, had erected a fourteen-story office building on land for which he had paid only $248,000 twenty-five years earlier. There were frequent rumors that some of Field's competitors planned to buy and remodel this building in the midst of the Field domain. As the rumors grew stronger, Shedd took a ninety-nine-year lease on the property for $1,500,000, razed the building, then erected another twelve-story structure to match the remainder of the Field block.

Even as this project was under way, it was clear that growing retail needs would soon require more space. Since it was impossible to add more floors, Field's would be forced to expand outside its own block. At the suggestion of James Simpson, and with the concurrence of the firm's board of directors, Shedd went ahead with the construction of a twenty-one-story building directly across the street, at Washington and Wabash.

Originally this building was planned with six floors for merchandise and the rest for offices. As it neared completion in 1914, the plan was to move china, glassware, upholstery, and similar lines into it. Then, one morning, Shedd was riding in an elevator in the main retail store when a man puffing a big cigar stepped inside. The smoke filled the elevator, and the ladies coughed and glared. So did Shedd. He was so furious that he

These employees, shown in a locker room in 1919, were forbidden to bob their hair by company rule. Later, hair nets were worn and the order forgotten.

gathered Corley, who was then assistant retail manager, David Yates, retail manager, and Simpson together.

"I've made up my mind to get the men out of this store!" he piped. "We'll put all the men's departments in the new building!"

The annex thereupon became the home of Field's famous Store for Men, featuring exclusively male wearing apparel and fashions. On the sixth floor was the Men's Grill, which had all the appointments of a fine club complete with a Favrile glass dome, marble floors, and dark mahogany furniture set around a central fountain, and an assortment of hearty food. The Store for Men prospered, setting the fashion for competitors to establish similar sections so that male shoppers could roam freely and at ease without any salesladies sneering at them as "molly husbands." In time, the Men's Grill disappeared to make room for additional sales space.

Near the close of Shedd's years as active head, the firm acquired another store. For a long time some of the younger

297

executives had been disturbed by trends that showed customers, principally in low-income groups, preferring goods of lower quality at lower prices. "More people want a lot of things *now*," argued one of these, John McKinlay, "and they feel they can buy more things if they pay less attention to quality."

McKinlay was speaking primarily of the wholesale problems which involved tremendous drops in business among country merchants, and he was urging curtailment of some of the firm's wholesale endeavors. But what the others came to call "McKinlay's Law"—that even a store had to change with the times, no matter what its aristocratic origins—had a point in the retail division too.

There could, of course, be no lowering of quality at Field's retail store since its reputation was based on that attribute. But perhaps, suggested the executives, it would be wise to invest

This early 1920's furniture display reflected the lavish tastes of prosperous times. Field's often duplicated costly rooms to provide the proper settings.

idle capital in another store and feature it as a low-price establishment so that any customers drained from Field's itself still would be patronizing the company. So Field's bought the A. M. Rothschild department store on South State Street for $9,000,000, installed Arthur Davis, wholesale head of floor coverings, as manager, renamed it The Davis Store, and stepped into low-price competition.

v

By 1923, Shedd prepared to give up the presidency for the less active post of chairman of the board. Gross sales had soared to $200,000,000 in 1922. Net profits were averaging $8,000,000 a year. Control of the company had been given over to the active management under a contract signed in 1917. By this agreement, Shedd and James Simpson had acquired slightly more than 50 per cent of the common stock and thirty-five other officers and section managers were buying on contract all of the remaining common shares. Shedd, by the terms of the pact, consented to make way for Simpson, a younger man, on January 1, 1923.

So John Shedd in effect retired, to take the title of chairman of the board of directors and to devote some energies to civic works and the $3,000,000 aquarium he was planning for Chicago. Like Stanley Field, who gave up his post of first vice-president but remained a member of the board, Shedd would still have a say in the affairs of the company, but active jobs would be done by younger men. To them he offered brief parting advice. "I would like you to remember," he said, "that this store is only what the people of Chicago, the West and the nation have made it. It was founded to render a public service."

1927

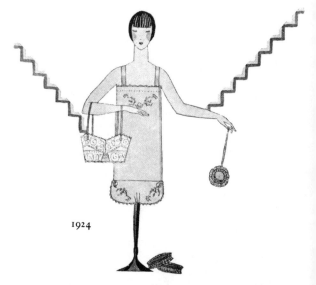

1924

DARK DAYS
FOR WHOLESALE

James Simpson, Marshall Field's office boy and protégé, now took command. He had been impatient for this opportunity, concerned, like Alexander the Great, that no new worlds might be left for him to conquer. Ever since the death of The Founder, he had been Shedd's able assistant in nearly every phase of the business—a liaison man between Shedd and members of the Field family and a high-level public relations man who had concentrated on making the firm's influence solid in the community.

Many of the public-service ideas fostered during Shedd's presidency had come from Simpson. "He thought big," said his friends. Simpson was a Chicago booster in the tradition of Deacon Bross and John Stephen Wright, and few improvement projects got on without him. He helped launch a score of campaigns for charities, for government bonds, and civic betterment. He powered movements for superhighways, lakefront parks, new bridges, public buildings, an opera house, expanded forest preserves, and, of course, better transportation facilities for the hundreds of thousands who came to State Street's shopping district every day. He was a good organizer, shrewd, and impertinent.

That impertinence and cocky confidence had first brought him to the attention of Marshall Field. In 1891, hired as office boy to Cashier John G. Rowe shortly after he arrived in Chicago from Glasgow, Scotland, Simpson, then seventeen, heard that Field was fond of Scotchmen. Acting promptly on this information, he shined his shoes, stuck a pencil behind his ear, and marched boldly into Field's office, demanding a raise.

Startled, Field looked the boy over. "What's your salary?"

"Six dollars a week."

Field fixed his famous stare on Simpson. "When I was your age I got only $5.00 a week."

"Maybe," snapped Simpson, "that's all you were worth, sir."

Field gave Simpson his raise and told Rowe that the young Scotchman with the pencil behind his ear and his sleeves rolled up was a lad to watch.

Within a year Simpson was making $10 a week. But when he heard that an $8.00-a-week boy in Field's office was leaving, he bounded back before Field. "You want this job even if it means a cut in your salary?" asked Field. "Yes, sir," replied Simpson. "I want to work directly for you."

Soon he was head office boy and then Field's personal secretary, second only to the merchant's confidential secretary, A. B. Jones. The old man was genuinely fond of Simpson. Many said that he saw in this eager young man, so full of ideas

His quick tongue and big grin won James Simpson his job as Marshall Field's office boy, and he went on to become president of the firm and a leader in Chicago's business and civic enterprises.

and zest for his job, the kind of person he had hoped his son Marshall II would be. In his will, Field left Simpson $50,000.

II

When Simpson became president, the retail business was still thriving. He was pleased to see that some of his own contributions to the store's development had worked out well.

Most interesting of these was the book department. Back in 1903 Harry Selfridge had sent Homer J. Buckley to New York to absorb ideas for the store. Buckley returned with a proposal to sell books as John Wanamaker was successfully doing in Philadelphia. "Never!" Field had exclaimed. "This is a dry-goods store! Always remember that!" After Field died, Simpson, a heavy reader, took up the idea again.

One of those he consulted was Alfred Harcourt, then a book salesman and later a publisher. Harcourt agreed that a fine book department would add to the prestige and profits of the store. He suggested getting Warren Snyder, the man who had built Wanamaker's section. But Snyder refused to be lured.

Simpson considered others, then hit upon the idea of hiring Marcella Burns, from whom he bought his books at Colonel A. C. McClurg's bookstore. She was a match for Simpson in good-natured impertinence, energy, and drive. She knew books and salesmanship, and she had verve and spirit. Simpson named her chief of the book department in 1914, just as the northeast unit of the retail block was nearing completion.

Marcella could hardly wait for her book section to be finished. Returning one day from a buying trip, she found that the workers were moving too slowly in readying her quarters. She watched impatiently, then cried, "You're loafing! You're a bunch of loafers. You're taking Marshall Field's money, and you ought to get this done a lot faster." The workers quit, and walked out. Carpenters and electricians followed. The news spread through the building, and plumbers, marble finishers, and tile layers quit. Not until the following day was the strike settled, with promises of no more interference from the sharp-tongued Miss Burns.

Her section became one of the most famous book departments in the country. She staged Chicago's first book fair, to which publishers sent leading authors and rare first editions. She originated the idea of autographing parties, but she often grew bored with some of the writing celebrities and invented excuses to escape the festivities.

She was still as tart as ever. She was one company executive who never hesitated to scold other section heads, criticize hallowed store methods, or talk back to management. She railed at the maintenance superintendent if the elevator was slow, objected that linen or dress-goods displays lacked imagination, and often told vice-presidents flatly that they did not know their business. But her department, in Simpson's period, grossed $750,000 in sales annually.

If Marcella Burns seemed to have her way under Simpson's rule, Arthur Fraser was not far behind in his self-willed manners. Fraser had come far from the day when the crowds stood and gawked outside the windows of the 1907 store. Shedd considered him a genius at window trimming and display, and Simpson agreed. Fraser's word was final in window decoration.

The purpose of window displays, insisted Fraser, was to make people think. At first he had been required only to present examples of Field's merchandise against the most authentic backgrounds. If period fashions were to be shown, months of research were allowed to insure complete accuracy of detail. For a splendid set of silver, Field's would spend hundreds of dollars to duplicate the paneled walls of a millionaire's dining room and install furnishings worth thousands to insure the proper atmosphere.

Arthur Fraser, who taught himself the art of window display in Creston, Iowa, won himself and Field's a world-wide reputation with creations such as this.

But Fraser, with his staff of twenty display artists, painters, carpenters, and plaster molders, now refused to be dominated by the firm's merchants. Symbolism and abstract designs to catch the passer-by's eye were uppermost in his mind. Should goods offered for display seem out of harmony with Fraser's unified concepts, he simply ruled them out. The buyer got nowhere by protesting to the executives. If everything in Paris was black and white during a season and the buyer had loaded up on this style, he might discover to his distress that Fraser was displaying a blaze of gold. The color always stayed. Fraser let it be known that he was the world's greatest window artist, and no one dared interfere with him.

Fraser's preoccupation with his meticulously built models of forthcoming windows left him no time to be concerned with the store's interior, except for the main aisle and light wells. This chore was taken over by Mrs. Clara Wilson, who also served as art editor of *Fashions of the Hour*. She helped section

305

chiefs with counter displays and arrangement of goods, called for new color combinations and lighting effects, always with the approval of Fred Corley, then acting as assistant to David Yates, retail general manager.

She ran into trouble in the Grand Salon where women's wear was shown. The room was paneled with mahogany, and Mrs. Wilson objected to the orange-brown hues. She proposed to cover the walls with drapes, to which Yates, normally a calm man, responded with considerable indignation. "You can't cover that with drapes!" Mrs. Wilson was as frank as Marcella Burns would have been in the same situation. "There is a positive worship of mahogany in this place," she said. "It seems to be one of the great articles of faith in the religion of this store." Yates was not amused. "Mrs. Wilson," he replied, "that is *solid* mahogany!"

Mrs. Wilson was sent to the advertising department where her talents were more appreciated. In a survey, she found that household furnishings on the ninth floor were attracting few customers. She proposed to Corley that cooking classes be started. On an experimental basis, she invited several local chefs to prepare meals while she lectured. The plan was so successful that the cooking classes continued for two years, and Mrs. Wilson was given permission to institute other changes in the housewares section.

She went to work willingly. She hoisted drapes and curtains, hauled out Grecian urns which had been standing among the household furnishings since 1907, and rearranged stock. She induced manufacturers of kitchenware to paint the handles of their utensils in colors that would not clash with her decorative scheme. She experimented with "impulse buying"—offering small, attractive articles immediately available to the casual visitor—and "association buying"—grouping articles that were associated in use in one display.

Mrs. Wilson became one of the most sought-after employees early in Simpson's regime. Other section heads began to ask Corley for her services. Soon she and two assistants constituted the interior display department, servicing all of the store except the first-floor main aisle, which remained Fraser's territory. A tiny woman, she climbed ladders and scaffolding at Christmas time to hang decorations on the huge Christmas tree in the Walnut Room.

She revamped the fur department, changing the lights and colors and putting dresses on the steel frames which held the coats. In the women's apparel section she caused a virtual revolution by announcing that she would install there, permanently, one of Fraser's plaster mannequins. No mannequin had ever been used in Field's except in the windows. But Fraser surrendered one to Mrs. Wilson. She dressed it in a fancy gown, then placed it at the end of the sixth-floor aisle where she turned a spotlight on it despite cries of the apparel people that the gown would surely be scorched.

Acceptance of Mrs. Wilson's promotional activities led to a rash of them, many of a cultural nature. There were fashion shows and expositions of furs, laces, gems, and educational toys.

Fraser's classic style charmed Chicago when Field's new store was opened in 1907, as it did in the early 1920's when these mannequins in Parisian gowns were placed against an elaborate background.

The store's display of seventeenth- and eighteenth-century art objects, tapestries, and furniture was considered so fine that Chicago's Art Institute bought several of the interiors intact. Entire houses were set up in the furniture department, complete with lawns, trees, and formal gardens. There were numerous lecture series, such as that on "The Romance of Linens," with James Westfall Thompson, professor of medieval history at the University of Chicago, in charge.

Field newspaper advertising reflected the changes taking place within the store. More artistry was evident in copy and layouts, there was heavy emphasis on the cultural aspects of merchandising, and greater aggressiveness. By 1920 the store had become the biggest newspaper-space buyer in Chicago. Not until 1934, however, did Marshall Field & Company advertise in the Sunday newspapers, a step taken after the famous display windows were finally revealed to the public on Sundays in 1933—a move made at the behest of A Century of Progress officials for the benefit of out-of-town visitors to the Fair.

In 1927 there had been another break with tradition, matching some of the slow changes from ultraconservatism within the store. In a drastic but temporary order, Simpson shut off all institutional advertising, the medium favored by Shedd. But the barring of comparative prices from all copy continued. There was never a "Bargain Sale" at Field's, only "Clearances." The advertising now was concentrated on the job of directly selling merchandise, with fastidious copy and art that won prizes and won business. Retail sales volume continued to mount.

III

The success that attended these changes in the retail store was not accompanied by similar good fortune in wholesale.

The country merchants who had been wholesale's best customers faced disaster. For years the people's buying habits had

This window in the "moderne" mode permitted Fraser to indulge his flair for colorful symbolism. He ignored complaints that "the public doesn't understand."

been changing. Long since, the railroads, which once carried goods from wholesaling centers to the small towns, had been carrying customers to the retail stores of the larger cities. Then the automobile accelerated the trend, sputtering over rural roads with farm families and small-town dwellers to the nearest big town, where department stores or chain stores or specialty shops supplied most of their wants.

At the same time, hard-pressed merchants in many towns and villages were succumbing in ever greater numbers to manufacturers' appeals to "buy direct" at lower prices. Field's was finding it increasingly difficult to serve them as jobbers of goods made by others, or with Field factory products, which, because of the concentration on quality, cost more than the goods of most competitors.

Direct factory buying, the rise of small-city jobbers handling a few lines for a limited trade territory, the appearance of jobbing specialists, particularly in the field of ready-to-wear clothing, the development of huge mail-order houses and mail-order jobbing to country merchants, the arrival of the "drop

Fraser's greatest achievements were his Christmas toy windows. This display, in 1925, fetched thousands of children and grownups to Field's big store.

shipper" who bought from the manufacturer for groups of small merchants and had no warehousing problem, the invention of the chain store—all these plagued the big wholesale houses.

There had been conferences in Shedd's day, and there were more in Simpson's. Several of the executives argued that certain wholesale lines be dropped, but the top men had been trained in wholesale and believed in wholesale. They shuddered at the thought. Robert Bettcher, chief of the linen salesmen, warned that the firm had to recognize that the wants of American consumers were changing. "People are going into apartments and small homes," he said. "They no longer want the big, fine quality damask tablecloth. Quality has become less important than color and variety. The automobile is changing the habits of the people. The small-town merchant is dying."

John McKinlay agreed. "In retail," he noted, "we in our Chicago store can draw enough of those who want quality, who will pay the price for better goods. Our territory and reputation are big. But the smaller merchants can't do it, not even our own wholesale customers here in the city."

Quality goods at comparatively high prices could not be sold in the mass market without losses, he warned. And the losses continued to mount in wholesale.

IV

Simpson thought he knew a way to cut down such losses. At a luncheon for his executives in a private dining room of the Mid-Day Club he put forward a proposal to build in Chicago a massive structure to house not only Field's wholesale and manufacturing divisions, but any competitors who cared to lease space, including manufacturers' agents.

"We've got to bring back wholesale!" Simpson declared. "The business is there if we know how to fight for it. I want to establish in Chicago the greatest wholesale center known. We'll put up the world's biggest building!"

Rapidly he gave them his plans and the proposed dimensions: a building filling two city blocks, rising twenty-four stories on the north bank of the Chicago River at Wells Street, containing 4,000,000 square feet of floor space, 5,500 windows, corridors 650 feet long.

His executives sat entranced by the immensity of the plan and Simpson's audacity. All but one applauded and shared his enthusiasm. When Simpson called for a vote, John McKinlay, now second in command, cried, "No!"

Wholesale simply could not be saved, asserted McKinlay. The firm's old wholesale house was still sufficient, and would continue to be. Field's should not make this advance into the real-estate business, he argued. He warned that building costs were high, and the country was overexpanding. There could be troubles ahead, difficulties wholesale would never survive.

Simpson listened impatiently. "We're going ahead, John," he announced. "Ernest Graham is drafting the plans!"

V

The city throbbed with the news of the gigantic Merchandise Mart on the river as it had in the days when Field and Leiter first announced their plan to move to State Street.

Times were good and it seemed fitting that such a project be sponsored by the biggest store in the Midwest's biggest city. The Mart, said Simpson, as he disclosed the details in March, 1927, would cost $15,000,000. Field's wholesale and manufacturing divisions would occupy half the space, and the rest would be leased to some 2,000 jobbers' representatives and manufacturers' agents. In the Field tradition, this world's biggest building would have the world's biggest restaurant and also the world's largest radiobroadcasting studios. On August 16, 1928, Simpson happily turned the first shovel of earth for the new building that was to rescue wholesale.

That same year, with money plentiful and business excellent about the country, wholesale lost money. A survey completed in 1929 showed that the wholesale division had been losing steadily for a decade. Simpson, watching the progress of his new building, bravely asserted that things would change when the mammoth Merchandise Mart was finished. It would do for wholesale what State Street had done for retail, he believed.

In retail there were profits, bigger than ever as a result of general prosperity and several wise Simpson policies. Over a period of three years, the company had established three new retail stores in the Chicago suburbs—Evanston, Oak Park, and

Charlie Pritzlaff, Field's doorman (*left*), welcomes a customer as a uniformed chauffeur helps him to inaugurate the store's new car-parking service in 1925.

Lake Forest. They were now making money. The Davis Store purchase, sparked by Simpson, earned at a rate of $400,000 a year. And in 1929 he acquired the best Field property outside Chicago, the Frederick & Nelson department store in Seattle, Washington, a fine retail house that for years had paid Field's the sincerest compliment of imitation.

The purchase came about through the visit to Chicago of D. E. Frederick, son of a Georgia plantation owner, who founded the store in 1890 with Nels Nelson, recently arrived from Sweden. The two men bought out Jim Meecham's plumbing and stove shop on Front Street (now First Avenue), swiftly expanded it into a general store as the Alaskan gold rush made Seattle a boom town. By 1901, Frederick & Nelson was the leading department store of the Northwest.

In 1907, Nels Nelson died at sea, and Frederick carried on alone, retaining the partnership name. Nearly a decade later,

313

Frederick decided, as Marshall Field and Levi Leiter had done in Chicago, that a new retail area needed to be established. He acquired land on Pine Street, between Fifth and Sixth avenues, and on it erected the finest five-and-one-half-story department store building on the Pacific coast. "Frederick's Folly," some called it.

But more than 25,000 shoppers crowded into the new store on its opening day, September 3, 1918. They discovered, as they thronged through the wide aisles, the same sort of goods, facilities, and services that had made Marshall Field's in Chicago famous. And Frederick re-emphasized to his clerks that service was the basic policy of his business. "Only as an institution serves the community in which it is placed can an institution prosper," he told the newspaper reporters. The formula worked for Frederick as it had for Marshall Field. By 1929, the sales volume averaged $12,000,000 a year.

Frederick, then almost seventy, was ready for retirement. He wanted to sell his store, but only to a buyer who would continue his policies. That meant, so far as Frederick was concerned, Marshall Field & Company in Chicago. He traveled to Chicago, went directly to Simpson's office in Marshall Field's, found Simpson away. So he wrote on the flap of an envelope, "I will sell my business to Marshall Field & Company and to them only."

Simpson, discovering the note, promptly decided to buy. He knew Frederick & Nelson to be one of the finest retail stores, and the second largest, on the West Coast. Simpson sent John McKinlay, David Yates, general manager of the Chicago store, and Frederick Corley, merchandise manager, to Seattle to make the purchase. They soon discovered that Frederick, despite his admiration for Marshall Field & Company, had his own ideas on terms for the proposed sale. The negotiations almost collapsed before they were completed in July, 1929.

Field's acquired the store fixtures, stock, and accounts receivable; Frederick retained the building and land, leasing it for ninety-nine years.

In Chicago, Simpson was jubilant. He regarded the purchase as the best expansion move in the company's history, a view still held by Field officials. The 2,000 employees of the Seattle store were disturbed, however. But they were assured by Frederick and by representatives of Marshall Field & Company that no changes would be made. The new owners had been invited to continue a policy like their own, not to revise it. William H. St. Clair, a Frederick & Nelson veteran, became president of the new store. Only one man, Thomas Lewis, was sent out from the Chicago store. He became the treasurer at Seattle.

VI

President James Simpson was now ready to retire. He had finished his expansion program. Under his guidance Marshall Field & Company had become a public corporation, offering its common stock in the open market for the first time. The Merchandise Mart was nearing completion, though at a cost of $28,000,000 rather than the $15,000,000 initially contemplated.

Simpson prepared for a trip abroad, which would include a tiger hunt in India. He still believed that his great Mart would shortly solve the remaining Field problem—wholesale. But the dangers of which John McKinlay had warned were at hand. The boom was over. The stock market experienced its bleakest days. Factories were closing, farm prices had collapsed, and the country was heading into the deepest and darkest of depressions. Few investors cared to acquire Field stock, listed at $50 a share. The storm was about to break. And it was John McKinlay who became the new president.

1933

McKINSEY'S PURGE

John McKinlay was truly a member of the "old crowd." He had started with the store in 1888 as a cash boy for $2.25 a week and had gone up through the ranks to become treasurer, vice-president, and now president. He had lived through years of prosperity and years of panic, but now, as the tall, handsome McKinlay settled himself in the president's chair, he was in the midst of one of the worst depressions of all.

The scene was a dismal one. In 1931, true enough, the reliable retail store earned $1,685,000, but wholesale and manufacturing sections not only gobbled up this profit, but added other losses for a grand, depressing total of $5,000,000. In 1932, for the first time since its incorporation three decades earlier, the company paid no dividends. In the same year the total net loss was $8,000,000, with even retail showing a drop of $900,000 under a break-even mark. Tenants were slow coming into the Merchandise Mart, and the firm's wholesale division rattled around in the gigantic building.

In the retail store, McKinlay insisted on a spruced-up appearance, depression or no depression. Realizing that the firm's greatest strength now lay here, he concentrated on improvements even while grappling with the wholesale problem. "We are like a ship," he told gloomy employees at one meeting, "and we are temporarily floundering. But this store and this company will escape disaster and reach shore safely."

He replaced antiquated fixtures with modern ones, re-arranged some of the retail sections, installed new lighting equipment. There were those, however, who felt he was going too far when he called upon engineers of the Westinghouse Company to design escalators for Marshall Field's.

Such rattling conveyances were considered then to be beneath the dignity of a first-class store. But they did get people about, and McKinlay felt they could be handsome and noiseless if prevailing construction methods were changed. Westinghouse executives, eager to get the contract, agreed to do the job at cost. McKinlay rejected several proposed designs, demanding "something revolutionary." As a result, the engineers finally achieved the modern, streamlined, aluminum-faced escalators with rubber treads. They would be efficient, smooth, quiet. McKinlay, satisfied at last, signed the $600,000 contract.

It was a daring move, one of several, in a time when most businessmen were struggling merely to "hold the line." McKinlay's aggressive methods worked out well in retail. But wholesale and manufacturing continued to slip, and slip disastrously.

II

Simpson, who always had been sure that the firm would outstrip its wholesale troubles—especially with the aid of the Merchandise Mart—had acquired new and graver problems than those besetting Field's. Summoned home from his Indian tiger hunt by Chicago bankers to take charge of Samuel Insull's collapsed utility empire, Simpson was fighting to save what he could from that wreckage. He continued to participate in the board meetings of Marshall Field & Company and to hold his sizable investment of $3,300,000 in Field stocks, but it was McKinlay who directly battled the growing losses.

Early in 1933, with the tired old pattern of retail profits and wholesale and manufacturing deficits prevailing, McKinlay mapped out with William Burt, head of the wholesale division, a plan for streamlining operations of the jobbing business. But wholesale had lost too much and too long and too heavily to be saved in the midst of national economic disaster.

To help him, McKinlay summoned Harry Shedd, veteran chief of the manufacturing division. At first Shedd pleaded, "I'm fifty-seven and I don't want the job." But when McKinlay outlined the desperate situation, Shedd consented.

A quick survey convinced Shedd of the horrible truth that major surgery was necessary in the organization his uncle had so frequently called "the heart of Marshall Field & Company."

"Some departments must be killed," he told McKinlay bluntly. "They are gone and gone forever, and they can't come back. The old-time country merchant who used to sustain wholesale has dried up, or he's buying cheaper goods. Another thing—if wholesale paid its fair rent for space in the Mart, the figures would look worse than they do."

George Young, wholesale's sales manager, agreed. "Merchants are buying direct from manufacturers," he said. "In a price competition that's going on and has been going on for a long time, they don't want the quality goods we make for our own retail stores. We can't supply both markets. We've been living off ourselves too long."

McKinlay, although he had warned of these very consequences, could not bring himself to shatter this solid Field tradition—wholesale. "What do you advise?" he asked Shedd.

"Liquidate all the departments that don't show a chance of coming back," Shedd answered. "Remember we have done it before on a smaller scale. When the automobile came in we quit handling derby hats because men didn't want to wear them any more. They were always denting them getting into

319

the closed cars. Let's find out how many departments we can lose, then sell them or close them up and take the losses. It's the only way."

Reluctantly McKinlay agreed. Starting with the men's wear section, Shedd began a quiet liquidation program, selling merchandise for what he could get. It was a gentle process, causing no great stir and upsetting no hoary precedent. Shedd, however, was hesitant about taking the lead in the final act he suspected would come soon. "I might have killed all the wholesale departments," he said years later. "I don't know. All I did then, though, was go after those departments that showed the biggest losses."

Despite the best efforts of McKinlay and his staff, wholesale lost $1,288,259 in 1934, almost wiping out the $1,895,968 combined profit of the retail stores. And it appeared that in 1935 the wholesale losses would be at least $2,000,000 and that the firm's real-estate division was certain to be in the red even before payments on an $18,000,000 loan which financed the building of the Merchandise Mart.

Early in 1935 Simpson called on Marshall Field III, a fellow board member, to discuss the situation of the company, which had paid no dividends on its common stock since 1931.

"Look here," Field told Simpson. "Why don't we get an expert on corporate management in to look the company over?"

Field had such an expert in mind. He was James O. McKinsey, once a professor of accounting and marketing at the University of Chicago, now head of a firm that ministered to ailing corporations. McKinsey had surveyed several important companies on whose boards Field III served.

An hour after Simpson and Field presented the idea to the other directors, it was approved, although some grumbled mildly about the intrusion of an outsider. A telephone call was put through to McKinsey, who was in Cleveland making a survey. He was asked to hurry to Chicago.

Field's built the Merchandise Mart, then the world's biggest building, to serve as a wholesale center, later sold it. In the foreground is a 620-foot converted ore carrier, one of the largest vessels ever to go through the Chicago River.

III

For three months McKinsey and his best workers surveyed the multimillion-dollar Field enterprises. By June, 1935, he was ready to tell the directors what ailed the business. But first he asked for a meeting with McKinlay and his staff of executives.

This was no meek, bespectacled professor who confronted the company heads. McKinsey was a robust six-footer, slightly stooped and balding, but loaded with self-assurance and facts. Speaking brusquely, he conceded that Field's was a splendid institution, with a sound financial structure and well-managed retail divisions. But wholesale, said McKinsey, would have to be reorganized. Most of the textile manufacturing, converting, and importing operations could be retained, with modifications, but domestic jobbing would have to go.

There were young executives at the meeting, among them Hughston McBain, assistant to President McKinlay, assigned to aid McKinsey in his studies. He agreed with the report and even believed it did not go far enough.

But McKinlay and the older executives, schooled in the tradition that Field's was first and finest among the country's jobbers, were shocked. They objected strongly to any quick liquidation program. If jobbing had to go, it must go slowly, as painlessly as possible, and with minimum public notice.

Grimly, McKinsey listened to the objections. Gathering up his papers, he glanced about confidently. "Gentlemen," he said, "I think you will accept my proposals."

Between June and October, 1935, it became clear to the directors that McKinlay would not carry out the McKinsey plan unless he was forced to do so. On October 9 they elected McKinsey chairman of the company, the position vacant since Simpson's resignation in 1932, and designated him the chief executive officer. It was an unprecedented step. For the first time in the history of the company the president was required to take orders from the board chairman. For the first time an outsider had been brought in for a top executive job.

From McKinlay down, the 17,000 employees of the firm expressed surprise and shock. McKinlay offered his resignation, but was urged to stay. Harry Shedd first learned of the change from his office boy, who dashed in, yelling, "Mr. Shedd, we got a new boss. It's McKinsey!" When he hurried to McKinlay's office, Shedd found the president cheerless, saying, "We'll wait and see, Harry, we'll just wait and see."

They saw soon enough. "The way I started," McKinsey reflected later, "is not the way you'd plan to be popular."

McKinsey asked Harry Shedd to help him lop off the jobbing sections of wholesale as rapidly as possible. "I want you to do it," the chairman said. "I need your experience."

Shedd objected to any fast, ruthless action. Again he pleaded for the gradual liquidation he and McKinlay had begun.

But McKinsey was full of fire. Jobbing would be dropped with a great boom and holler. There would be bargain sales like none ever seen before. "It'll be good advertising for Field's!" McKinsey insisted. "We'll attract customers and good will."

Shedd could not bring himself to do it. This was not the "Field way." Within a month, McKinsey demanded and got his resignation.

IV

McKinsey, encountering hostility from most of the old-line executives, turned to younger members of the staff who believed as he did that jobbing had to go, and go fast. He picked McKinlay's young assistant, Hughston McBain, as general manager of wholesale to speed up the liquidation program, allowing him to choose a Field man, Grant Mears, as his sales manager. But, at the same time, he forced in an outsider, James P. Margeson, Jr., of the Phoenix Hosiery Company, one of McKinsey's clients, as assistant general manager. Margeson was at once made a vice-president of the company.

McBain was not pleased with the division of duties. McKinsey asked him to concentrate on the unpleasant and unpopular task of killing off the jobbing sections—and with them scores of jobs for veteran company employees—while Margeson would streamline and build up the new manufacturing division. It was clear, however, that both tasks had to be accomplished if Marshall Field & Company was to survive.

Within six months wholesale had virtually vanished. All that remained were a few sections consolidated with the manufacturing division to supply the retail store and sell only what the firm made or imported to other large retailers, chain stores, mail-order houses, and jobbers. Such items as neckwear, notions, toys, and furniture—old standbys of the earlier wholesale days—were wiped out.

And so were the jobs of nearly 800 wholesale workers, to be followed soon by 400 more in manufacturing and retail. The even flow of the years was broken now, and long afterward there were many who spoke of "McKinsey's purge" with a moan and a shudder.

The veteran executives warred with McKinsey. They knew his actions were overdue and needed, but they resented his method, his superior manner, his lack of feeling for merchandising and Field traditions, and his restrictions on buyer heads of sections. McKinsey sometimes irritated the men by lecturing to them as he would to a class of students. His attempts at analyzing mercantile methods sometimes made him sound naive. Once, discussing with several buyers the problem of when to buy silk, he pontificated, "If we believe silk is low we ought to buy, and if it is high we ought to sell." The buyers, unable to believe that their chairman meant this obvious conclusion as other than a witticism, laughed appreciatively. But McKinsey, his face flushed, stalked out of the room.

McKinsey continued to bring in his own men from the outside: Percy Wilson, Chicago real-estate dealer, to take charge of the real-estate division; Horace Wetmore as treasurer; and Horace Vaile as comptroller. But it was his attempt to introduce cheaper grades of merchandise into the State Street store that brought down the united wrath of the Field staff.

On one occasion, McKinsey had a chance to buy a New England mill specializing in a low-priced grade of hosiery. He conferred with his executives and, to a man, there was disapproval. But McKinsey ignored their advice. He sent a representative to start negotiations. When Stanley Field was informed of the move, he summoned a meeting of the board of directors.

"Who besides you is in favor of this purchase?" he asked.

Field's offered "masculinish" tailored costumes for the ladies in the spring of 1936. Skirts were long and tubular, waists moderate, shoulders extended and padded to give a lean, athletic appearance.

McKinsey could mention no one.

"Then, by heaven," Field said firmly, "I won't agree to going into it!" Field's voice was a powerful one on the board. The plan was dropped.

But John McKinlay had had enough. He was finding it harder to work with the new chairman. In June, 1936, McKinlay quit, shortly to become chairman of the National Tea Company. Into his place went Frederick D. Corley, conservative-minded vice-president in charge of retail merchandising. He was "one of the family," rather than an outsider, having started as a stock boy in 1900 in the millinery section for $4.00 a week. But like McKinlay, he had to report to McKinsey.

McBain also prepared to submit his resignation. After liquidating the jobbing operations, he had turned to manufacturing problems, hiring Joseph Platt, a noted stylist, to redesign many of the Field products and consolidating these products under a single "Fieldcrest" trade name. It was Margeson, however, to whom McKinsey turned for advice. When McKinsey began placing huge orders for raw materials for the manufacturing division, orders in excess of probable needs, McBain had enough. He was dissuaded from quitting, however, by an offer of the post of general merchandise manager of the retail store. Since McKinsey was not concerning himself with retail at the time, McBain accepted in July, 1936.

V

McKinsey's manufacturing woes increased. Even Simpson, once his most powerful backer, grew cool. He appreciated what McKinsey had done, but the quick, magnificent strokes which had put the company slightly in the black in 1935 were losing vigor. Although his decision to sell The Davis Store, which had been earning profits, to Maurice and Nathan Goldblatt for less than the $9,000,000 purchase price was approved, McKinsey's stock declined. Margeson, by McKinsey's order, was not paying bills when due, and, for the first time, the credit rating of Marshall Field & Company slipped.

This alarmed Simpson, who also was nettled by the lack of adequate figures for the directors' meetings. Not even McKinsey's announcement in the spring of 1937 that there had been a profit of nearly $3,000,000 on sales of the retail store totaling $104,000,000 could forestall the inevitable showdown.

It came when Simpson learned that McKinsey had made unusually heavy purchases of raw materials early in 1937. At a board meeting, Simpson demanded the figures.

"By God!" he roared, "you've got them somewhere!"

When McKinsey fetched what he could find, Simpson paled. Silk, bought at $2.00 a pound, had dropped to $1.58. Wool had tumbled from $1.05 to 81 cents, cotton from 14.5 to 8.5 cents a pound. The 1937 recession had caught McKinsey with big inventories, especially of cotton. He expected a small cotton crop, and it turned out to be large.

By September, McKinsey showed signs that he believed his regime at Field's was nearing the end. On his appointment as chairman of the board he had been given, in addition to his $65,000-a-year salary, the option of buying Field stock at $10 a share. The stock had risen from $14 to $20.50, but instead of buying he chose to exercise another clause in his contract providing he could take the difference between the market and the option price in cash—$313,929. He elected to take the cash.

Early in November, in a private interview with Simpson and Marshall Field III, McKinsey was informed that unless he changed his management tactics drastically, his resignation would be demanded at the end of the year. Two weeks later, McKinsey was critically ill of pneumonia at Woodlawn Hospital. To his friend Margeson, who called at his bedside, he observed, "Jim, never in my whole life before did I know how much more difficult it is to make business decisions myself than merely advising others what to do in their businesses, without having to take the final responsibility myself." The following day he was dead.

Corley, as president, now became the chief executive officer. Margeson resigned as head of manufacturing after Hughston McBain reluctantly accepted the task of reviving that division.

"Plans of the present management call for material changes from the program and organization conceived by Mr. McKinsey," President Corley announced.

1936

THE ROAD BACK

Not since Marshall Field and Levi Leiter surveyed the ruins of the Great Fire had the company seemed so near to disaster. Wholesale was gone. Manufacturing tottered. Retail slipped on the skids of the recession. Employee morale sagged.

Possessing full executive powers now, Corley turned to the task of reconstruction. While he launched a "Sales Means Jobs" campaign in the retail stores, McBain started cutting away the wreckage in the manufacturing division. With Luther Hodges, one of the organization's veterans, he streamlined operations. He disposed of unprofitable lines of goods, eliminated all wholesale converting and importing activities, and reduced the number of mills from twenty-two to ten. He pushed production in the remaining plants.

Resolving a dilemma that had plagued Field's for years, McBain settled down to making four lines of goods, destined not only for the Field retail stores but for middle-price outlets wherever they could be found. Buyers would get Field quality, but without trimmings, thereby permitting a moderate price.

By the end of 1938, McBain produced a net mill profit of nearly $140,000, a much happier result than the mill losses of $5,600,000 in 1937. Corley's retail division earned $3,940,000, as compared with $5,000,000 in 1937. And the over-all company profit from all enterprises was now about $3,500,000—a mighty leap from the previous year's net loss of $1,600,000.

Corley and McBain received plaudits. With a nod to the president, *Business Week* assessed the gains as a result of Corley's general policies. Of McBain it stated, "Fans of the present Field management consider its greatest achievement is the revamping of the manufacturing division under Vice President McBain, who has liquidated an assortment of lines from cotton dress goods to Wilton rugs." *Time* cited McBain as "a man to watch."

In this critical period, James Simpson aided Corley with the company's intricate financial problems. After months of negotiation Field's, in May, 1939, bought the land occupied by the State Street store and the Men's Store annex for $15,000,000 from the Field Estate. Simpson represented the firm, Marshall Field III the estate, to which the annual rental of $950,000 was being paid. The purchase, said Corley, would be financed through the sale of $15,000,000 of the company's bonds to the Metropolitan Life Insurance Company, and it would relieve the firm of paying some $80,000,000 in rent over the next eighty-five years. Just before his death on the following November 25 Simpson also completed a plan for eliminating all back dividends on preferred stocks. For the first time in eight years payment of dividends on common stock was resumed.

Simpson's death severed one of the last close links between The Founder and company management. Many of the other top executives, who had been personally trained by Marshall Field, had quit during McKinsey's rule. Now Stanley Field, custodian of Field traditions, became chairman of the executive committee. McBain, boosted to the top vice-presidency, was soon put in charge of all retail stores. Later two new vice-presidents were named: one was James Lindley Palmer—no kin of Potter Palmer—formerly assistant to Corley, to be general operating manager of retail; and the other was Wilbur C. Munnecke,

Stanley Field, a nephew of Marshall Field I, clerked in his uncle's firm, eventually became a top official. Marshall Field, the founder's grandson, is still a member of the board, in addition, the head of Field Enterprises, Inc.

only thirty-four, who had succeeded McBain as head of the manufacturing division.

Field's now had a driving force unmatched since the first days of the business. Things began to happen in the retail store.

II

For all his brusque ways, James McKinsey had performed a major service by blasting away unprofitable operations and the stodginess that can come 'to a firm or individual too immersed in past glories. McBain wanted no part of profitless efforts or mossy myths, such as the legend of wholesale's invincibility. Unlike McKinsey, however, he regarded certain traditions developed during nearly ninety years as important props, to be strengthened and used with care, but without fustiness or excessive reverence for the past.

Whether assigned to the very elaborate "torch wagons" (*left*) of the early 1900's or the sleek "electrics" (*below*) in pre-World War I days, Field's delivery men always were advised: "Be On Time. Be Correct. Deliver Neat Parcels." The drivers worked ten hours a day in those early days.

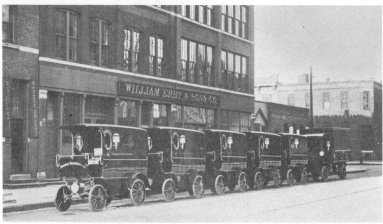

A modern Field's delivery truck. The store is especially proud of the fact that its drivers have a 10,000,000-mile no-accident record. One man, Charles Kraft, has driven more than 400,000 miles in the last twenty-three years without mishap.

It was not in wholesale, McBain realized, that Marshall Field had found real greatness as a merchant, but in the retail store. Here was enshrined the spirit of the luminaries of the house. Here Field's insight, capacity for profit-yielding services, and the ability to grant the public's desires in every way found dramatic expression.

Through the years and in different times, The Founder's Yankee ideas about quality merchandise and fair dealing had rolled up massive revenues in wholesale, but it was in the retail store that they reached the people directly and brought them back again and again. It was in this personality of a store that they best survived. And now it was in the store that the profits lay. What seemed essential was a reassertion of those basic principles that had made the store unique: close relationship with customers, elegance, adroit catering to the feminine shopper, courtesy, consideration, quality in wares, and service.

With the approval of Corley and Stanley Field, a retail improvement program was launched that, within the next decade, cost $16,500,000. Outside talent was hired to advise on color, modern design and decor, new products, styles, services, window trimmings, displays, advertising, and public relations. Out went drab tones, gloomy wainscoting, dim corridors and corners, obsolete equipment, and outmoded styles. The changes, McBain made clear, had to be up-to-date without losing the traditional conservative charm of the store; Field's, with all the innovations, had to remain the store with "tone," the store of refinement, taste, and quality.

The rules of deportment would be no less severe than in the days of Marshall Field, but the rewards, McBain promised, would be greater. The tone would remain on the exquisite levels set by Shedd, the service would match that fostered by Selfridge. Public relations and community service would find inspiration in the accomplishments of Stanley Field and Simpson.

333

The realistic attitudes toward business would stem from John McKinlay. The best of the past would be combined with the ideas of the future, but stodginess of any kind was out—along with the red mahogany furniture and the Grecian urns.

III

One of McBain's first discoveries was that styles at Field's no longer enhanced the store's reputation for first things first. When World War II broke out in Europe, French imports were shut off. The company had failed to turn to American designers, who were finding their outlets in specialty shops of which John McKinlay had warned years earlier. Field's prestige in the fashion world, which had been slipping in the depression years, fell to new lows.

With Corley, McBain discussed the problem. A methodical survey made in 1933 by Palmer when he was a professor of marketing at the University of Chicago had shown that women preferred increasingly to buy their gowns and dresses in the comparative privacy of small dress salons then sprouting by the hundreds all over the country. This report had come during the depression, and Field's had done nothing to halt the trend.

But now McBain was ready to face facts. Field's needed its own specialty shops, catering to women from head to toe, right in the store. The time was good for such an idea although some Field executives frowned on the expense involved. The outbreak of World War II had generated prosperity in America. The nervous nation, geared for defense and eventual all-out war, was earning and spending at a prodigious rate, able to afford and demand the very best, if most expensive, in merchandise. Chicago, undisputed capital of mid-America, thrived on war orders and the lush business provided by a revived agriculture.

McBain envisioned a shop within the store that would epitomize to the ultimate degree the Field idea of elegance. The

Here a craftsman is refurbishing a splendid silver set. Field's many behind-the-scenes service shops range from dress alteration to oil-painting restoration.

entire public would, of course, not habitually patronize such a shop, but John Shedd's theories that other customers would follow the path laid by wealthy customers still seemed valid. Such an exclusive shop would cater, insisted McBain, to "a new aristocracy of taste, supplanting an aristocracy of wealth," and Field's would be once again the home of feminine elegance.

The result was the 28 Shop, designed by Joseph Platt, who had created the Hollywood sets for *Gone with the Wind* before he joined Field's manufacturing division. He was told simply that the new shop must outmatch anything of its kind—even the most fashionable establishments of Paris. Platt worked on plans while other officials signed up leading dress designers to show their best creations; among these were Hattie Carnegie, Nettie Rosenstein, Adrian, Pauline Trigere, Norman Norell, Omar Kiam, and Jo Copeland. Meanwhile, the entire south Wabash wing of the sixth floor was cleared; old dressmaker dummies, clumsy furniture, counters, walls disappeared.

Platt devised a shop of twenty-eight individual rooms encircling a central salon. The store's publication, *Fashions of the Hour*, sighed that Hollywood itself might be proud of his creation. Entrance was through an oval beige foyer. Its pink-

335

beige, hand-rubbed oak walls, carved with horizontal pleated bands, formed the background for a Louis Quinze gilt table and a Regency chair covered with gold-studded turquoise material. Beyond was the main rotunda, a circle broken by alcoves with hand-woven beige and turquoise draperies. The rug, too, was beige, loomed and dyed in the Field mills.

Dressing rooms were individually decorated. One was in rose and pale green, another in black and peach with lacy curtains; a third in apricot and rose, the walls lined with tufted banquettes. Another, for the showing of casual clothes, was finished in *café-au-lait* pigskin. There were mirrored rooms, rooms with frosted glass, a bamboo-paneled room, and seven rooms with sliding panels to form a salon for fashion shows.

This area of bedazzlement got its name from the address of its private elevator entrance at 28 East Washington Street. "It is our hope that it will become the fashion center of mid-America, where the most discriminating women will find their hearts' desire in fashion and service," said *Fashions of the Hour* in prose reminiscent of Selfridge's praise of the 1902 store and Shedd's in 1907. "The shop itself is its own statement—the expression of Marshall Field's credo of taste and clothes."

IV

The formal opening of the 28 Shop, the evening of September 30, 1941, matched in splendor the great Field openings of prior years; but the guest list was limited to some 500 of the Midwest's elite, who received the engraved invitations of Mr. and Mrs. Hughston McBain and the Field directors. Following parties at the Saddle and Cycle, Casino, and Racquet clubs, they converged in their limousines on 28 East Washington Street, where searchlights swept the skies, police on motorcycles kept traffic moving, and thousands of spectators lined the sidewalks to witness the pageantry.

Of all Field's 400 departments, the 28 Shop is undoubtedly the most renowned. Here are shown the spacious salon, lush in blue and beige, and one of the ultra-plush fitting rooms. There are exactly twenty-eight such rooms, two of a kind. One pair is in bamboo, one in tufted pink, another's ceilings are lined with imported lace.

Stately models prepare in this dressing room for Field's fashion shows, which are held several times each week in the seventh floor tearooms. Dresses range from the latest in resort styles to French and British imports.

Field functionaries in green and gold uniforms met the guests, and in the resplendent foyer a butler announced them. Dowagers exclaimed over the new American creations displayed while their husbands gaped at the flood of color and luxury. They tasted the champagne—the only time in the store's history when such a beverage had been allowed. Mrs. Howard Linn, one of Chicago's leading women of fashion, made the very first purchase, a plaid blanket coat. There was music, gayety, a fashion show, and a radio broadcast.

Although only a tiny fraction of Chicago was present, the rest of the public was not denied an intimate glimpse of the scene. For, shortly after the first guests arrived, Howard Vincent O'Brien, *Chicago Daily News* columnist and the city's most beloved essayist, happened to be strolling up Wabash Avenue, returning from a meeting of his camera club. Startled by the lights and turmoil outside Field's, he investigated. His press card, he discovered, was worthless on this particular night but, in time, a Field official recognized him.

O'Brien, it turned out, had been invited to the affair, but had forgotten about it. He was promptly piloted into the private elevator and to the pinky-beige foyer, where among the splendid gowns and evening clothes his wrinkled business suit seemed even more remarkable than the Louis Quinze gilt chair. He told his readers all about it in his next day's column.

"It was like a Hollywood première," he wrote. "A stream of high hats poured from a succession of limousines while the flash bulbs winked merrily. The store itself was brilliantly lighted and a group of tall men in dinner coats stood around the entrance scrutinizing the credentials of all who passed. . . .

"They led me into a large round room. It was brightly lighted and filled with dowagers in diamond tiaras and butlers ferrying champagne. Alec Templeton was playing the piano; models, in the peculiar lope of their craft, glided in and out, and photographers snapped pictures of such an aggregation of wealth, beauty, fashion as these old eyes have seldom rested upon. I wasn't in evening clothes. I cringed under resentful stares."

v

Not only did O'Brien's readers learn of the amazing shop, but so did those who scanned the society columns and such magazines as *Town and Country, Vogue, Harper's Bazaar, The Architectural Forum,* and even *Atlantida,* the Latin American fashion magazine. The publicity of opening night alone, *Fortune* magazine later estimated, was worth a good deal more than the $300,000 investment.

The new retail executives were pleased. They frankly considered the 28 Shop their most sensational achievement, and sales figures quickly proved them right. In its first year sales reached $500,000 as women bought frocks for as little as $30, or an exclusive creation for as much as $600. Three years after the 28 Shop opened, annual sales averaged over $1,000,000.

The success of the 28 Shop stimulated other fashion innovations. In the new Tip-to-Toe Shop, experts not only outfitted a lady for as little as $600, but could do it from photographs and measurements if she cared to order by mail. In the new Brides' Room—"where the whole trousseau can be assembled, from furs to a blue wedding garter"—and the Shoe Salon, designed by Platt with mirror-lined walls and silver-oak paneling, the ladies discovered a new, ultramodern Marshall Field's.

They came, were thrilled, and continued to come and buy, if not in the 28 Shop itself, then in another part of the store. The number of shoppers rose in 1943 to as many as 100,000 a day—250,000 a day during the Christmas shopping season. Once more Field's was on its way to retail glory.

FURNITURE REPAIRING

MONOGRAMMING

A NEW TEAM:
McBAIN AND PALMER

On February 2, 1943, Hughston McBain, then only forty, moved up to the presidency of the firm when Corley resigned his $75,000-a-year job. There was no official explanation for Corley's action, not even in the directors' minutes, but two years earlier he had indicated his weariness with business life and his wish to spend more time in leisure. The developments did not surprise the editors of *Women's Wear Daily*, close followers of the nation's retail business. "McBain's election was expected," they wrote. "He has been looked upon as the next president of Field's for the past five years. The question has been, when would Frederick Corley retire?"

The public now learned more about the new president. He had once hoped for a career in journalism, serving as night city editor of the student newspaper while attending the University of Michigan. One summer he worked for the advertising department of the *Chicago Tribune*, but his uncle, Lowell Bassford, an executive in Field's wholesale division, persuaded him to come to Field's.

McBain longed to be a buyer, especially in the foreign department, and so informed his uncle. But Bassford, in true company style, replied, "I can't promise you that. I can get you started where your performance can be observed, but

Crowds of female shoppers, either in the latest fashion or, as here, in the 1945 "short-skirt look," are always to be found around the cosmetic counters.

from that minute you'll be on your own." McBain became a retail bill adjuster in 1922, then took a cut in prestige but a lift in experience to become office boy and secretary to John Shedd.

By this time Shedd had shifted most of his duties to James Simpson, so he had much free time to lecture McBain, who he thought showed promise or, at least, an ability to listen hard. Sometimes McBain stood at attention for three hours by Shedd's desk while the aged merchant enunciated the firm's principles.

"What I was getting was a great course of lectures on business from a pioneer and a master," McBain told reporters who came to interview him. "Slowly I caught hold of the principles he laid down—always keep an adequate assortment of goods; always keep service up to perfection; never get into debt; nothing pays off like integrity; the only way to run a business is to delegate authority; always give department heads and buyers extraordinary leeway, letting them succeed or fail on their own decisions as to everything but the broadest fundamentals."

McBain still longed to travel for the firm when he was with Shedd, but he went only a few yards—to the real-estate and tax division in 1927. Five years later he was head of Simpson's big Merchandise Mart. Then came his onerous duties in whole-sale under McKinsey, culminating in his decision to resign; his assignment to retail, his later effective reorganization of manu-facturing, followed by a return to retail as general manager of the division and first vice-president of the company.

James L. Palmer now advanced with McBain, becoming first vice-president and second in command. Unlike McBain, he had no grounding in humble jobs with the organization. He had come directly from the campus of the University of Chicago in 1937 to put to practical use his classroom theories in market-ing. Palmer did not lack business experience, however. A Maine boy who graduated from Brown University in 1919, he worked for two years with the Cincinnati Screw Company before be-coming professor of marketing at Chicago. While teaching, he acted as business consultant for Sears-Roebuck, Armour, the Crane Company, the *Chicago Daily News*, Kroger, and oth-ers. After he completed a series of market surveys for Field's, Corley made him his full-time staff consultant.

McBain, dynamic and full of enthusiasm, and the reticent, cigar-smoking Palmer agreed they would work as a team—each keeping the other fully informed of his activities. McBain took responsibility for the retail and manufacturing divisions, assign-ing to Palmer supervision over the comptroller, treasurer, and secretary of the company. Palmer, because of his determination in paring down operating costs, was soon referred to at Field's as "a man with ice water in his veins." His strict methods, cutting through waste and delay, would eventually eliminate the long-term debt which totaled $25,000,000 on January 1, 1943.

II

The McBain-Palmer team worked well.

President McBain, turning to plans for modernizing the store and expanding its services, re-emphasized the employee's place in the scheme of things. "Our over-all objectives," he said, "must represent ethical and social goals to which our people can subscribe and in which they take pride. Each individual must believe his job has meaning and significance, from top brass down to the front line worker. We must see that our people really have opportunity, that there are rewards for ability and merit. We must assure every employee the freedom and dignity of a member of society, to believe what he believes, to say what he thinks and help protect him against refusal of that privilege from any one."

Again the employees, in undertones of the past, heard of their responsibilities. "Remember," McBain told them, "the customer is always right! Keep in mind it is more important to please a customer than to make a sale. Never exaggerate. Honor promises. Insist upon good taste. Never forget the customer is a customer of the store, not any section alone. Render distinctive service." While reciting principles, McBain and Palmer acted to lift employee morale.

Heads of sections again became supreme, as they had been under Marshall Field. "Each section manager will decide what to buy, how much to buy, what colors to buy, from whom to buy and what price to pay," McBain said. "Contrary to the practices of 90 per cent of the big stores in America, no countersignature is required to the section manager's order. He or she is boss."

Palmer devised a pension plan, to be paid for by the company. Coupled with social security, it provided benefits as high as 60 per cent of an employee's earnings, plus annuity opportunities in which workers shared costs. More liberal vacations with pay, group and hospital insurance, training programs conducted by Northwestern University faculty, were new to the company program. They were added to such continuing policies as nonprofit restaurants for workers, 20 per cent dis-

In the Brides' Room, the entire trousseau is carefully planned and the prospective bride may obtain information on weddings, honeymoon retreats, and, if she wishes, how to care for a home. Friends planning to buy gifts learn the bride's preferences from Field's Wedding Bureau, and thus buy with confidence.

counts, and recreational activities, including the well-known Marshall Field choral society. The rate of promotions was increased so that by 1948 there were nearly 2,000 advancements in the retail force of 10,000. McBain noted that among the 500 executives in the total working force of 20,000, 92 per cent had come up from jobs as stock men, office boys, clerks, or salesmen.

In all these moves McBain and Palmer were unanimously backed by the Field board of directors, led by Stanley Field, a director since 1906, who was made chairman of the executive committee. Other board members, in addition to McBain and Palmer, were Marshall Field III; John P. Wilson, general counselor of the company; Charles Y. Freeman, Simpson's successor as head of Insull utilities; A. B. Dick, Jr., president of the firm bearing his name; Henry Isham, head of the Clearing Industrial District, Inc.; and James Simpson, Jr., son of the former president of the company.

III

The years of World War II created the major problem of obtaining goods since there was an almost complete shutoff of imports. Under McBain's program the factory division was supplying only 5 per cent of its output to the Field retail stores —most of this to the State Street Budget Floor, once known as the basement salesroom. Because of the war emergency the company now restricted its factory sales to jobbers, wholesalers, and its regular customers among selected retail outlets.

Field factories turned out large amounts of war goods: silk bags for gunpowder, parachute cloth, camouflage netting, wool blankets, cotton duck, sheets and towels, mosquito netting, woolen Army overcoats, uniforms for Army and Navy officers, hosiery for Wacs. Temporarily the firm gave up advertising its primary products—Fieldcrest sheets and pillowcases, Fieldbilt garments and household items, La France full-fashioned hosiery, and "Zionets" lace curtains.

Selling in the war years was no problem if the goods could be obtained and processed. The factory system, through its New York offices, disposed of all it could make—about 42.5 per cent to independent retail stores, 16.8 to independent distributors, 12.7 to jobbers, and 28 per cent to chain stores and mail-order houses. Most of the merchandise appeared under Field labels, but some carried private brands of the jobber or distributor who handled the merchandise.

Field's fashion shows have been top Chicago social events for years and frequently are staged as charity benefits, attracting foremost designers as well as blue-book society. This creation by Balenciaga, an evening gown with taffeta wrap, thrilled ladies witnessing its preview at the fashionable Blackstone Hotel.

IV

By the end of 1944, after nearly two years of the McBain-Palmer regime, Field's was on a smooth course. In that year the firm earned $20,000,000 before taxes—twice the net of Macy's although the New York store had bigger revenues. The fixed debt had been cut from $32,000,000 in 1930 to $21,300,000, an item McBain and Palmer hoped to remove entirely by selling the Merchandise Mart.

The Field face-lifting had been most successful. Along with a new appearance came new ideas in promotion and sale. There were wartime exhibits, benefits, drives for bonds, and campaigns for blood for fighting men. Field officials were loaned out to government agencies. Field advertising had received a beauty treatment, based on the findings in that 1933 survey by Palmer that women buyers seemed to prefer the more readable, eye-catching advertisements of the closest competitor, Carson, Pirie, Scott & Company. Foreign buying, which brought to the woman shopper the most exotic delights, had to be shut down during the war, not to be resumed again until 1950 when Field's buyers again set up shop in Paris, London, Switzerland, Italy, Germany, Hongkong, and Tokyo.

Despite wartime difficulties Field's diligent efforts to please the ladies continued. Style shows, cooking schools, displays of gems, rare tapestries, miniature rooms, furs, and dolls lured in the feminine customer. She was pampered as in the days of Marshall Field and Potter Palmer. Response was excellent. And this "New Woman" was quite different from the Feminist of 1852. Now she worked at 19,000,000 gainful jobs, controlled 80 per cent of the family budget, owned 70 per cent of the nation's wealth. She could afford to buy, and she did.

As excellent evidence that the town's women of fashion shop at Field's, the store's "Women of Chicago" advertising displays presented sketches of society women wearing Paris creations designed especially for Field's.

To keep women aware of the latest in fashions and attractions of the store, *Pace*, a newspaper within a newspaper devised by Harold J. Nutting, the retail general manager, appeared in Chicago newspapers. It combined all the slickest features of news reporting, magazine writing, and fashion descriptions. Soon Field's was again winning prizes for the excellence of its advertising copy.

At Frederick & Nelson in Seattle, things were going well. As President St. Clair, in ill health, prepared for retirement, youthful men were brought in to aid him: William S. Street, general manager of the Boston store in Milwaukee, became assistant general manager, and Hector Escobosa, who had gained his merchandising experience in San Francisco, was named as general merchandise manager. Later Street, at the insistence of McBain, would serve as general manager of Field's Chicago store until 1946 when he returned to Seattle to resume his duties as president. While these changes were in progress and Charles C. Bunker, Field's veteran merchandiser, went to Seattle to assist the rising young executives, Frederick & Nelson net sales approached $25,000,000 a year, as compared with a low of $6,000,000 in 1932.

McBain took action to eliminate the last inherited headache, the Merchandise Mart. Although the gigantic building finally brought in some $3,500,000 annually in rents, it still was losing money and its operations put the company deeply into the real-estate business. With wholesale jobbing gone and the manufacturing offices in New York, the Merchandise Mart was a side show, so far as McBain was concerned; he wanted to concentrate on the "main tent"—the retail stores. After extended negotiations the Mart was sold to a combine headed by Joseph P. Kennedy, former ambassador to Great Britain. The sale was at a loss, but coupled with permitted tax deductions enabled the company to retire its $18,750,000 bonded debt.

349

THE TOY SECTION

"NOTHING IS IMPOSSIBLE FOR FIELD'S!"

Chicagoans strolling on State Street one spring morning in 1948 blinked in amazement and took a sharp second look. There, from the broad sidewalk fronting the block-long Marshall Field & Company store, grew six splendid Moline elms, at least twenty-five feet high, calmly rustling their leaves at their reflections in the store windows. They had not been there the day before.

Even the most hardened Chicago Loop dweller knows, of course, that trees do not grow from sidewalks, especially when there is a tunnel for subway trains underneath. This, clearly, was either a mirage, or the work of Marshall Field's. Dozens of excited citizens hastened into the store to demand an explanation from Mrs. Elizabeth Skinner, who presides over the Personal Service staff near the State-Washington entrance.

They learned that the elms were quite genuine, and that Field's expected them to grow in State Street for many years. When the subway was being built, Field's employed workers to construct under the sidewalks six concrete pits, large enough to contain the roots of a full-grown tree. Arrangements were made with the Davey Tree Company to select six sturdy Moline elms for planting in the pits. Special pit covers, ringing the trunks but allowing room for growth, were constructed. Field's was informed by the tree experts that the elms could live for forty-five years in the concrete boxes, and grow to full height, if properly watered and artificially fed.

Chicago has been in love with the State Street elm trees ever since. When a bird roosts in one, a dozen persons will hurry into the store to report the phenomenon. Scores write letters advising the store on the care of elms; a few protest that the trees should be given their "freedom." Thousands became bird watchers when Field's announced wren houses would be placed in the trees, but careful scrutiny has failed to disclose any wrens.

When a schoolboy wrote Field's, wanting to know how it was possible to grow trees through concrete from the roof of a subway, the store used full-page advertisements to publish his letter and the explanation. They were, said *Women's Wear Daily*, some of the finest institutional ads in recent years. A year later, boxes of growing flowers over each of the State Street entrances further enhanced the pastoral scene. They were added on direct orders from McBain, who had seen such boxes in London. Neither tree-bird inquiries nor questions on the care of flowers disturbed Mrs. Elizabeth Skinner. As chief of the Personal Service desk, she has become accustomed to such oddities. Thousands of persons come her way with all sorts of strange inquiries and requests, many of them in no way related to Marshall Field's. Whatever the boon sought, Mrs. Skinner tries to provide it. Her job is to give service.

Back in 1890, the store relied on Eddie Anderson, general factotum, to give personal service to customers and visitors. In 1893, Eddie acquired a staff of interpreters, needed to speak the languages of foreign visitors expected for the World's Fair. Many of the distinguished guests Eddie himself escorted about the store, aiding them with shopping problems.

Soon Chicagoans, too, were demanding this service. The ladies of the first families began telephoning Eddie to ask him to shop for them. They wanted quick delivery of a gift, or a black hat, veil, and gloves to be sent in advance of a funeral. La Salle Street brokers wanted presents for their wives. In time Eddie became a department, and a profitable one. He demanded and got assistance. Mrs. Skinner was the first to join him. Eddie gave her only broadest instructions. "Nothing," he said, "is impossible for Marshall Field's."

Mostly Mrs. Skinner answered questions about section locations, store hours, price and quality of goods, railroad and bus schedules, and similar information. She sent customers to floorwalkers for service, or summoned interpreters. Then personal shoppers were added, to escort visitors and advise them, and twice-a-day guided tours were arranged.

Mrs. Skinner commandeered a fleet of baby buggies, to be placed at the disposal of mothers with infants. She started a lost-and-found service, recovering children, parcels, missing pets, even adults from out of town who had become lost in the city. One man, unwilling to meet his ex-wife, or to trust the mails, started leaving his alimony payments at the Personal Service desk where his former spouse appeared regularly to collect them. An Evanston woman expanded the service by bringing in an umbrella and a pair of rubbers a South Side friend had forgotten. The friend, she explained, could pick them up more conveniently at Field's.

A customer, losing an important package on a streetcar, went not to the trolley company, but to Field's, who got it back for him. A man from Denver wanted Personal Service to find his friend who had moved to Chicago. He didn't have the address, of course, but Mrs. Skinner learned the friend had been in the drug business. She called Chicago drug houses until he was found. Three out-of-town schoolteachers ordered embroidered napkins from a shop near Field's, but couldn't recall its name or location. By deduction, Mrs. Skinner solved their problem.

353

When a lady came weeping to the store, to report she had put a friend and her baby on a New York train, but forgot to include the baby's diapers and bottle, Field's telephoned a South Bend department store, got the needed equipment delivered as the train made a two-minute South Bend stop. Mrs. Skinner was only temporarily shaken by the telephone call from Winnipeg, Canada, requesting a Willkie campaign button by the next noon. The campaign was two years past, but the caller had wagered he could find such a button within twenty-four hours. He won. Field's found two, air mailed them to Winnipeg in time, gaining another life-long Canadian friend.

II

Field's Personal Service activities are not limited to Mrs. Skinner's department. A few years back, a ruddy, wind-burned Westerner in a ten-gallon hat stomped into the jewelry department to announce to a startled girl clerk that he wished to purchase a silver rooster, about four feet high. The clerk learned he actually had seen such a rooster in the foyer of the Waldorf-Astoria in New York. He wanted a duplicate for his ranch.

The department buyer was summoned. He placed a telephone call to Field's New York office, which called the Waldorf. There was such a rooster, all right, made in Japan. The customer, so informed, still wanted his bird. Field's photographed the Waldorf original, sent pictures and specifications to the Tokyo office, and a few months later delivered the silver rooster to a farm in Wyoming. The clerk got her commission on the $1,500 sale.

One of the successors to Eddie Anderson was suave, salmon-faced Arthur "Sandy" Atkinson, a majestic Field functionary who still returns to greet distinguished guests on special occasions. Sandy, discovering the public was constantly leaving messages for friends at the Personal Service desk, started the

In the many years that Field's has thrived in Chicago, famous visitors have joined the regular shoppers in roaming through the aisles and buying at the counters. Here is Queen Marie of Romania in the luggage section when she stopped off for a tour of the store during her visit to Chicago and other American cities in the 1920's.

Field guest books, which now contain one of the finest collections of important autographs in existence at this time.

Atkinson has personally escorted many· famous visitors through the store, among them President William Howard Taft, Winston Churchill, Eleanor Roosevelt, Queen Marie of Romania, Jack Dempsey, Martha, Crown Princess of Norway, Al Jolson. Few movie stars pass through Chicago without stopping at Field's. Among Sandy's favorites are Joan Crawford, Claudette Colbert, Greta Garbo, Lucille Ball, Lena Horne, Bette Davis, and Shirley Temple. Sandy also escorted Sally Rand and Gypsy Rose Lee, who, he insists, showed inordinate interest in clothes. One visitor who proceeded without Sandy's aid was Al Capone, the Chicago hoodlum, who once bought ten silk shirts from Fred Stokes in the Men's Store at $35 each.

The demand for Personal Service led to the creation of special units to handle telephone calls and orders by mail. An Australian visitor, for example, phoned Field's from his hotel to order a wardrobe for his wife; limit, $600. A Personal Service shopper requested her measurements, a photograph—which was sent over by messenger—and a brief description of her social life. And the next day, when the Australian had finished his business in Chicago and was ready to leave, a complete wardrobe for his wife was on its way. A note from Australia weeks later informed Field's that the lady was pleased. They had a new mail-order customer who has been buying ever since.

Thousands of others outside Chicago purchase by mail through Personal Service. Field's has charge-account customers in every state and almost every foreign country free to trade with America. One regular buyer is the household of Emperor Haile Selassie, ruler of Ethiopia.

A few years ago, as a political campaign was under way in a southwestern state, the wife of a candidate for governor wrote Field's asking aid. Her husband, she confided, was likely to be elected. "Do you provide wardrobes of various types, suitable for the wife of a governor?" she inquired. "Never having filled the position, I am not sure what kind would be proper."

Back from Personal Service went suggestions. When the returns were in, showing the lady's husband elected, Field's dispatched a $2,000 wardrobe to her by air express. In gratitude for the service, she invited a representative of the store to be her guest at the inaugural.

Many of the 40,000 telephone calls Field's averages daily merely seek information. One customer sent a nickel, asking that it be given to the newsboy on the corner. The customer had taken a paper but had no change to pay for it. Most queries, whether by mail or telephone, are answered by special booklets, published by the store for free distribution. Now and then a caller wants information on the hours, policies, or prices of a rival establishment.

III

Since Field officials know that the store is most directly represented to the public by clerks, elevator operators, and delivery men, special training is provided for employees in these categories. No huckstering is permitted. Workers must be careful of their dress, deportment, and diction. When bobbed hair was becoming popular in 1920, store officials barred the style for clerks. One resigned in a huff. Several others who had trimmed their hair put on nets, as requested. Soon not even Field's could withstand the trend, and the order was forgotten. Now the rulebook merely prescribes neatness for clerks' dress. Courtesy and gentility are emphasized, and the workers best exhibiting such qualities are cited in *The Field Glass*, house organ of the Chicago stores, and *Between Ourselves*, the publication of Frederick & Nelson in Seattle.

Field visitors, on their way to the various departments, rarely fail to take a second look at the elevator girls. Four of these comely young women have won motion-picture contracts, among them Mary Leta Lambour, better known as Dorothy Lamour. In 1947, Field's began sending the elevator girls to a charm school, to be trained in poise, diction, and general on-the-job glamour.

Field delivery men have their own glamour. Trim, polite, cheerful, they are praised in a big proportion of the letters written to the store lauding workers for tact and courtesy. A staff of 470 delivery men, using 314 trucks and 52 passenger cars, make about 25,000 deliveries a day. Goods bought in the State Street store are hauled by night to the main garage and sorting house on Polk Street where they are rough-sorted on conveyor belts for the outlying delivery stations. The smallest purchase is delivered free, though Field's earnest campaign to get customers to carry small parcels has shown impressive results. Drivers are schooled in courtesy, cited for good deeds reported by customers, and honored for safe driving records. It is the store's boast that in 1950 Field delivery men drove the equivalent of 367 times around the world without an accident.

IV

Marshall Field & Company gives more attention than do many businesses to the creation of long-range good will. At the same time, the ultimate objective is to get people into the store and to make of them contented, continuing buyers. Since price competition is taboo and customer-luring activities must be conducted in a rather fastidious manner, planners of the store's promotions have been required to develop ingenuity.

Field's, of course, like other stores, can have children's parties, style shows, hobby displays, art exhibits, lectures, cooking schools, demonstrations. It does all these things. But it is incumbent upon Field's to be unique, or at least first. Some of the "firsts" date back many years. But each year adds to the list, especially in the modern period.

Back in 1924, a wedding secretary service was created to advise brides-to-be. This has become the Wedding Bureau. Here the prospective bride can leave a gift-preference list for the guidance of relatives and friends and get counsel on her silver and crystal patterns, the size of the reception, color scheme of attendants' gowns, the wedding-breakfast menu, places to honeymoon, and her trousseau. The Bureau will suggest a caterer for the wedding reception, has a fat file of weather reports on honeymoon spots, and can, if asked, provide help on home planning and cooking instruction.

Seasonal promotions, such as the Gift Court, where all sorts of novelties and rarities are gathered in one place for the convenience of the customer, have become year-round attractions. In the Men's Store there is the Stag Line, the only place in the store barred to women. Here males get advice on gifts for wives, sweethearts, and female kin.

Some of the promotional novelties have grown up to become big business. During the war McBain became interested

The Cloud Room Restaurant at Midway Airport is maintained by Field's to accommodate air travelers. It is, also, one of Chicago's favorite dining spots.

in frozen foods. Some day, he decided, housewives would order entire meals precooked and frozen. Field's should pioneer, he felt. In 1947, he set up in the Evanston store a frozen food section as a pilot operation. Trained workers once a week telephoned selected housewives—those who had deepfreeze units or had decided to buy one from Field's—offering an entire week's meals, each a selected, carefully balanced menu, to be delivered in Field trucks.

The service has been so successful the company has considered plans to develop extensive facilities for the supply of frozen and precooked foods. More customers want the prepared meals than can be supplied. Women with small children, women who work outside the home, and women who cannot obtain servants are on the waiting list should the service be extended. Currently it is not advertised and is limited to the district served by the Evanston store.

Another food venture, The Pantry, established to lure the epicure, now does a lively business with a general clientele. In this shop customers can obtain fine, rare, and exotic foods—

from Field's own Thousand Island dressing, a best seller, to Chinese water chestnuts and bamboo shoots, Mexican fried worms, rattlesnake meat, Strasbourg *pâté de foie gras*, French rooster in red wine, eighteen varieties of imported honey, wild boar meat, French roasted chestnuts in brandy, guinea hen, partridge, squab, and squid in its natural ink.

The candy section, started experimentally in 1914, quickly crowded out other departments near the third-floor waiting room. Now Field's has one of the biggest, most modern candy kitchens in the country, supplying the section with twenty-seven varieties of chocolates, twenty different bulk items. The restaurants, modestly started as a teatime service, attract as many as 25,000 persons a day, who consume some 150 dozens of eggs, 300 pounds of butter, 500 chickens.

v

The best known Field restaurant, next to the Walnut Room, is not in the store at all, but at Midway Airport, miles from the Loop. It grew out of the success of the store's restaurants, Field's reputation, and a little-known but profitable activity, the Contract Bureau.

In the 1880's Field's was frequently called upon to equip the mansions of rich families, and later to provide a similar service for offices and hotels. By 1903, the Hotel Supply Bureau had developed, and later Field's was in all phases of supply and interior decoration on a contract basis. When the Stevens Hotel, the world's biggest, opened in Chicago in 1927, with 3,000 rooms and costing $27,000,000, Field's had the furnishings contract, aided by Carson, Pirie, Scott & Company, which provided the carpeting.

Later, the Contract Bureau equipped the big Chicago Theater, a motion-picture palace on State Street, and loomed the biggest oval rug ever made—thirty-five by fifty-five feet—for the Palm Court of the Hotel Roanoke, Roanoke, Virginia. In December, 1947, Field's signed the largest hotel-supply contract ever written, agreeing to procure all linens, bedding, carpets, furniture, china, silverware, draperies, upholsteries, soap, and kitchen equipment for the vast Hilton hotel chain, which has hostelries in the United States, Bermuda, and Latin America. To insure the opening on time of the new Caribe Hilton, in San Juan, Puerto Rico, Field's flew there 600 beds, 304 chests of drawers, 352 vanities, 700 chairs, 50 sofas, 2,000 dozen glasses, and 326 air-conditioning cabinets in ten cargo airplanes.

After Chicago had endless trouble and complaints about the restaurant concessionnaires in the municipally-owned Midway Airport, Field representatives approached Public Works Commissioner Oscar Hewitt and offered to take over. Visitors from everywhere got their first impression of Chicago at Midway, world's busiest airport, and Hughston McBain wanted it to be a good one.

Besides, a fine restaurant at the airport, he decided, would also remind air travelers of Marshall Field & Company. Hewitt eagerly accepted the Field proposal. Experts of the firm's restaurants and Contract Bureau went to work. The Cloud Room, costing $600,000, opened with typical showmanship March 19, 1948. Airlines flew in flowers, souvenirs, and delicacies from over the world: leis from Hawaii, orchids from Mexico, lobster from Africa, potatoes from Bermuda, mushrooms from Oregon, strawberries from California, and a shillelagh from Ireland.

VI

Some Field promotional activities are so specialized as to be comparatively unknown to the general public, yet they bring into the store a cosmopolitan group of buyers. In the Men's Store, always advertised as an independent store rather than a

The elephant shown here is Judy, stamping her autograph in a children's book. A special three-story ramp had to be built to get her out of Field's.

department, Field's began the sale of airplanes in 1945. On the sportsman's floor famous ski champions advise on gear and techniques in the Swiss Chalet, and ex-professional football players, champion swimmers, boxers, and great hunters aid the shopper. Prince Abdul Illah, of Bagdad, made quickly for this section to buy equipment for his string of polo ponies—wool coolers, embroidered in gold with his crest, and bridles, bits, and saddles.

Texas millionaires order hand-tooled, silver-inlaid saddles from the Saddle and Harness Shop. Hunters come to Field's to equip themselves for a week end of duck hunting, or an African safari. To the Gun Shop, where Henry Vogt directs Field's own gunsmiths, come police officers and FBI men for advice on weapons. The shop rebores, reblues, heat treats, engraves, mounts telescopic sights, and often produces custom-built weapons for men from all parts of the world.

Perhaps the most consistently successful of the Field departmental promotions are those of the book section, which rocketed sales from $235,000 annually in 1915 to an all-time high of $1,500,000 in 1951. Authors welcomed the invitation of Rose Oller Harbaugh, the manager and buyer, to appear at the Field autographing parties.

Through the years Mrs. Harbaugh presented such writers as Somerset Maugham, G. K. Chesterton, Aldous Huxley, Theodore Dreiser, Willa Cather, and Carl Sandburg. Ladies fought for the opportunity to buy his books when Richard Halliburton appeared, loaded up on poetry when Edgar Lee Masters was the honored guest. And some were shocked from time to time, as when Chesterton, in the midst of a soliloquy, paused to stare appreciatively at the legs of a comely salesgirl, then forgot to resume; or Huxley, asked, "What is the most important thing in life, Mr. Huxley?" snapped a one-word reply, "Sex!"

Book promotions are not always on an exalted literary level. Dogs perform in the bookstore to advertise dog books, Indians stalk about to tout volumes on the red man, six clowns from Ringling's once appeared to add zest to the sale of a circus book. And, on one memorable occasion, Mrs. Harbaugh presented to her public a live elephant. She was Judy, and she had been trained to autograph with a rubber stamp a children's book published by Chicago's Rand McNally, in which an elephant, who happened to have been named Eddie, was the hero.

Judy, brought to the third-floor book section by freight elevator, liked it so well she refused to leave. After the awed crowds had departed, the place was in turmoil as the beguiled Judy, munching a wisp of hay, wandered about, knocking over displays, then returned from time to time to gaze fondly at Eddie's picture on the book jackets.

Not until after hours of cajoling, while guards stood by with 30-30 rifles ready, did Judy agree to leave the store by way of a special ramp Field's carpenters hastily built for her from the third floor down to the street level. The store's advertising and promotion department did not let this opportunity go unused. Before Judy was back in her barn, Chicago's morning newspapers were printing Field advertisements, telling the public all about Judy and how much she liked Marshall Field's store.

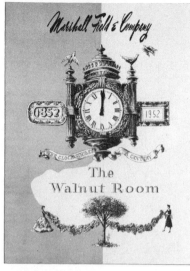

ANNIVERSARY MENU

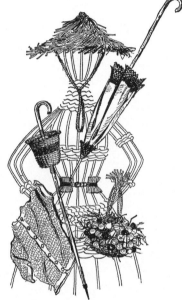

DISPLAY FIGURE
WOMEN'S ACCESSORIES SECTION

PREPARING FOR
A NEW CENTURY

Every Chicago child, most women, and many men regard a visit to Marshall Field's at Christmas time a required and delightful part of the holiday festivities. They are joined by multitudes from over America—250,000 daily at the peak of the season. Of whatever faith, race, or nationality, they share with one another the thrills of a journey to a glittering fairyland, a glimpse of the world's most gorgeous Christmas tree, a brilliant pageantry which Field's takes an entire year to create.

When November snows fly in Chicago, Field's display windows and first floor are a dazzling land of make-believe rivaled only by the toy center on the fourth floor. Over the main aisles —wreathed with holly, mistletoe, ribbon, and tinsel—silver reindeer and gauzy white angels hover above a panorama of twinkling Christmas stars, colored lights, white Christmas trees, festoons of flowers and pine boughs, silvery streamers, and, of course, hundreds upon hundreds of wide-eyed moppets. Down the thirteen-story light wells, astride a sled packed with toys, glides a plump Santa Claus and his eight scurrying reindeer, bound for the chocolate and gingerbread rooftops below, the land of fifty-foot peppermint sticks, soft opalescent lights, candy-cane lanes, and magnificent poinsettias—a land that is actually Marshall Field's glove section.

In the surrounding windows mechanical toys perform, or take part in pageantry telling the story of the most wonderful time of the year to earnest youngsters and their nostalgic elders. Above, on the fourth floor, is the wonderland of toys in a forest of fir, guarded by grinning plaster creatures contrived months before. Still higher, in the Walnut Room on the seventh floor, is the majestic Marshall Field Christmas tree, the world's biggest tree indoors. Elsewhere, every section is ablaze with color and displays of the newest and finest in holiday goods.

Some 4,000 extra workers stand ready to aid the veterans in handling the holiday rush. They have been schooled in Field lore and shown a training film in which the god Jupiter, lecturing on courtesy, strums a harp to emphasize the word. As sweet Christmas music soothes shoppers in the store, there is a gentle interjection now and then—the softly plucked notes of a harp, reminding the employees to be ladies and gentlemen.

Field's began preparing all this in February of the winter before, for then the planning is started. The secret theme is selected for next Christmas, the window displays and interior decorations are put on the drafting board, and the buyers scatter to Europe, Asia, and the toy marts of America to seek out novelties. By July a dozen craftsmen are at work creating the 1,500 king-size ornaments for the big tree, window models have been built, and the plaster figures for the windows and for toyland are being molded.

In late autumn, a member of the Field staff heads for Lake Superior country to select the Christmas tree with the aid of professional timber cruisers. A symmetrical balsam fir, seventy feet tall is required. Carefully, the top forty-eight feet are lopped and lowered by block and tackle to prevent damage to branches, which are bound tight to the trunk for their protection. A bulldozer breaks a patch through the forest, and the tree is hauled by sled to the railroad where a flatcar is waiting.

In the Christmas season, Field's attracts thousands who come to see the famous forty-eight-foot Yule tree in the Walnut Room. They also visit Uncle Mistletoe, a popular sprite invented by the store to help Santa Claus.

The tree arrives in Chicago as near to Saturday night as possible. When the last customer has left the store, workers get into action. Chicago streets are blocked off to permit a huge trailer truck to carry the tree to the store. The revolving doors at the State and Randolph entrance are removed. The tree, its base packed in peat moss, slides neatly through the opening, is hoisted seven floors through the light well, then moved to the Walnut Room where the fish pond has been drained and block and tackle are ready to erect it.

Within three hours, the best time to date, the forest giant is upright in the fish pond, thrusting up almost four stories. Eighteen trimmers, some suspended in boatswain's chairs, cut the wires holding the branches and begin their work of applying the prepared decorations, while below a supervisor with a master chart calls directions. Other workmen install an elaborate fire extinguisher system, intertwined with trunk and branches, which will spray a chemical through the tree should a blaze break out.

By Monday morning 1,500 handmade ornaments have been placed. Thousands of yards of cranberry strings—made of artificial cranberries big as golf balls—have been hung. Plastic angels, snowballs, icicles, and fairyland figures dangle from the branches. The first of three firemen who will guard the tree in shifts, twenty-four hours a day, takes his place. Musicians and carolers in eighteenth-century costumes tune up. The spotlights go on. The great tree is ready.

Below, in the toy section and on the main floor, nearly 100 other specialists from maintenance and display sections have been laboring to prepare for the Yule visitors. They have been busy erecting the huge candy canes, decking pillars with holly and fir branches, putting scores of Christmas trees in place, suspending reindeer and cherubs by invisible wires, hoisting huge chandelier finials—ribbon-bound clumps of foliage—assembling animal groups, toy groups, and a throne room for Santa Claus.

On the eighth floor still other workers put together the famous Cloud Cottage for Uncle Mistletoe.

Uncle Mistletoe, a comparative newcomer to Christmas legend, dwells exclusively at Field's. The brain-child of Vice-President Lawrence Sizer, Field's director of public relations, and John Moss, successor to Arthur Fraser as chief of the display division, Uncle Mistletoe was created for the windows in 1948 after some other stores copied the famed "Night Before Christmas" window pageant initiated by Sizer two years before. A black-browed, winged sprite, wearing a cape and top hat, Uncle Mistletoe was modeled after a Pickwickian character in Dickens but looks more like a benign and smiling John L. Lewis.

After his first appearance in Field's windows, Uncle Mistletoe's popularity threatened to rival that of Santa Claus. As an assistant to the Christmas saint, Uncle Mistletoe works the year around, urging children to be good. For him, Sizer and Moss created a wife, Aunt Holly, and a residence, the Cloud Cottage. Thousands of youngsters visit Uncle Mistletoe, telephone him, send him letters, watch him on television, sing the two songs published in his honor, join his Happiness clubs.

A Field competitor, hearing that Santa Claus had been sabotaged, came over to see for himself. Outside the store he found barricades before the display windows to keep the crowds from shattering them. Led by Field's officials to the Cloud Cottage, where hundreds of children clamored for audience with the beetle-browed sprite, while Santa Claus gloomed almost alone a few floors below, the visitor whacked a fist into his palm.

"By Heaven!" he exclaimed in awe and envy, "you fellows have stolen Christmas!"

II

As Marshall Field & Company headed toward its second century, Hughston McBain became chairman of the board. His first act was to recommend James Palmer for the presidency, not only in appreciation for the services of his teammate, but

In Field's Gun Shop gunsmiths can repair, convert, or remodel all kinds of weapons. On sale is everything from an ordinary shotgun to a costly rifle.

because Palmer had turned down the job of president of Montgomery Ward and Company to remain with Field's.

The two men could look back over an impressive decade. The manufacturing division had been revamped, the retail stores refurbished; both were earning profits. Sales in 1951, an all-time high for Marshall Field & Company, totaled a whopping $225,-000,000, earning a net of $5,000,000, or $2.23 a common share, after deduction of $9,100,000 for payment of one tax or another —city, county, state, federal, income, and social security. Employee relations and public relations were excellent. Some 15,000 persons owned Marshall Field & Company stock, with no one individual possessing more than 6 per cent.

The strides in Chicago were matched by those in Seattle. In June, 1949, the directors of Marshall Field & Company went west for their first meeting outside Chicago in the company's history. They toured the five-story Frederick & Nelson store on Pine Street—once called "Frederick's Folly"—inspected the new escalators and furnishings installed after World War II, visited the new Frederick & Nelson shopping center opened in suburban Bellevue in 1946. Then, after a formal meeting in the grillroom of the downtown store, they announced a decision to spend $6,250,000 to add five floors to the building D. E. Frederick had erected at a cost of $1,250,000 back in 1918.

Construction began the following spring. As it proceeded, further improvements were incorporated to bring the final cost to $9,000,000. While business continued on the lower floors, walls and foundations were strengthened, new display windows were added, a shop similar to the 28 Shop in Chicago was constructed, a medical center and cafeteria for employees were built.

Floor space was increased by the addition of 250,000 square feet of space on the upper floors. As the work neared completion in time for the centennial festivities of the parent company in 1952, Field executives happily concluded that Frederick & Nelson had become the biggest store in the Northwest, one of the finest in the country. Seattle newspapers agreed.

Frederick & Nelson, with its new store building rivaling Field's on State Street, had become a mercantile giant, possessing a subsidiary suburban store, four warehouse and service buildings. To a Frederick & Nelson style show came thirty-six of the nation's top designers. The store had a training program for workers and a chorus known through the Pacific Northwest, was a center for many civic and charitable activities, sent its own buyers into the world markets, won prizes for civic and mercantile promotions.

McBain, glowing, told newsmen on one of his frequent visits: "Our business in Seattle has more than justified this expansion. We have faith in the ultimate prosperity of the nation in general, and particularly the Pacific Northwest. We're proud to have a part in creating for this area one of the world's finest stores."

While the Seattle construction was under way, Field's spent $4,200,000 on its retail stores in the Chicago region in 1950, and expended another million on the Fieldcrest Mills, under the supervision of Milton C. Mumford, who had chalked up a 36 per cent increase in business in his first year on the new job.

Mumford is typical of the young executives being developed by McBain and Palmer under a theory that modern business must discharge its civic responsibilities by active participation in them. Back from the Navy at the end of World War II, having been, at thirty, one of the youngest men ever to attain the rank of commander, Mumford was ready to resume his former duties at Field's. Instead, McBain launched him on a series of community projects, from the vexing Loop parking problem to heading a slum-clearance commission. In his two years on loan to the public, Mumford got various projects successfully under way. He then returned to Field's, was made a vice-president, and took charge of the manufacturing division. Others, almost as youthful, are being groomed for top executive positions in a similar way, with McBain himself setting an example as director of the Children's Memorial Hospital and the Chicago Natural History Museum.

As the centennial year approached, it was greeted with the boldest announcement of plans for retail expansion since the completion of the State Street store in 1907. In the town of Skokie, sixteen miles northwest of Chicago's Loop, the company will construct a retail sales center at a cost of more than $25,000,000. It will be another State Street, transferred to a prairie near Chicago's fastest-growing suburban area. "It will be something like constructing the entire shopping district of Indianapolis in one whack," commented *Magazine of Building* when the giant project was announced.

Plans for the development were devised after careful surveys by John McKinlay, Jr., son of the former Field president and vice-president of the company. His surveys showed the nature of Chicago's continuing change. While the city itself had grown only 7 per cent in a decade, the suburbs had spurted by 30 per cent; in the specific area selected, the gain had been nearly 100 per cent. To serve this vast suburbia, Field's will erect buildings not only for its own store, but at least two other competing department stores, eighty-five specialty shops, and a community auditorium. There will be adjacent parking space for 7,300 automobiles. As in the days when Marshall Field lured competitors to State Street, the present company expects to attract them to the new Skokie shopping center.

Four of the country's top architectural firms were invited to draw plans for this spectacular development. "This is a design problem so big," observed *Magazine of Building,* "that almost every normal study procedure must be projected into the unknown." Since it was to eclipse anything done or planned else-

As the new century for Field's begins, the store continues to "give the lady what she wants," either in an original Dior creation or less expensive adaptions.

where in the category of outlying shopping centers, the architects turned to the study of State Street itself. Four models and four sets of designs have been provided, from which Field executives will make final selections. Whatever their decision may be, the new center will be a compact "State Street," easily accessible to automobiles, a "State Street" with trees, grass, and flowers. The ultramodern buildings will stretch along a rectangular mall, reached by depressed drives for busses and trucks. They will house the same sort of stores and shops found on State Street since Field executives believe that a major shopping center must offer everything the customer might hope to find in the city.

373

Field's own store will occupy 350,000 or more square feet of space. An additional 1,000,000 square feet will be available to competitors, and probably will be taken by firms already competing with Field's in State Street. The annual sales volume of the combined stores in the center is expected to total well above $100,000,000.

Chairman McBain made clear that the new shopping center will not mean the end of State Street. "Marshall Field's has grown up on State Street and the whole metropolitan area of Chicago," he said. "It continues to have faith and confidence in State Street as one of the greatest shopping centers in the world. Just as it enlarged our ability to serve our rapidly growing suburbs by opening the Oak Park, Lake Forest, and Evanston stores more than twenty years ago, it hopes to further enlarge its capacity to serve Chicagoland with this newest development."

While the architects worked on designs for the Skokie project, Field's formed a wholly-owned subsidiary, Chicago Suburban Centers, Inc., headed by McKinlay, to construct this and other such developments. Then it turned to a search for an appropriate name for the Skokie enterprise. Employees were invited to contribute their suggestions. Some 1,200 proposals were received, culled, and rejected, mostly because they duplicated existing commercial names.

At a dinner McBain spoke of his plans and remaining difficulty to Mrs. Stanley Field, wife of the chairman of the executive committee. "We've got everything but a name," mourned McBain.

"Why don't you call it 'Old Orchard'?" asked Mrs. Field.

McBain beamed. "That's it! Perfect! Why didn't we think of it!" Old Orchard, he reflected, was a revered name in the Skokie area, perpetuated until recently as the designation for the major airport northwest of Chicago. "You seem to be a student of Chicago history," McBain added.

Hughston McBain, chairman of the board, and President James L. Palmer (*left*) study model of $25,000,000 Old Orchard Shopping Center to be built in Skokie.

"Not necessarily," replied Mrs. Field. "You see, when Stanley came courting me in Baltimore years ago, my father somehow couldn't remember the name Field. He called him Mr. Orchard and, in the family, that name stuck. In recent years, it's become Old Orchard. Please don't tell Stanley . . . . !"

A few days later, "Old Orchard" was formally adopted as the name of the new shopping center. Construction is expected to start in Field's centennial year.

III

Field's has been emulated in Chicago and elsewhere by competitors and imitators who find similar success in the Yankee policies of its founders. But Field uniqueness persists, to the delight of many proud Chicagoans. It is not incredible that, on the day of Pearl Harbor, a North Side dowager exclaimed, as has been reported: "Nothing is left any more, except, thank God, Marshall Field's."

Field's remains the fastidious woman's club, bearing the patina of time and an aura of worldliness. Yet it is corn-fed as Iowa pigs, earthy as a Kansas farmer. It is, though some of the clerks and officials sometimes forget, the neighborly store of personal service. Whether a customer buys carpet tacks or an airplane, a can opener or a mink coat, she is entitled at Field's to a personal interest few other businesses could afford or would care to provide. The discriminating woman can usually find what she wants at Field's. The male can buy with confidence, since if his wife doesn't like what he gets, the personnel must be pleased to accept its return.

In 1946, a lady walked into Field's shoe department carrying a pair of button shoes purchased in 1908. They were like new.

"Shortly after I bought them I broke my ankle," she explained. "I put them away and forgot them. Now I've found them again, and the sales slip, too."

She got her refund, $2.97.

In suburban Oak Park, a prosperous, fifty-year customer of Field's came to the end of his days. His widow found boxes of underwear and shirts in his effects, goods bought from Field's over a twenty-year period but never taken from their wrappings. The sales slips were wrapped with them. She called the store. The items were out of style, she conceded, but could they be returned?

"Bring them in for a full refund," she was instructed.

Frequently, almost daily, a few still try to cheat the store, returning goods which have been used, or purchased elsewhere.

One woman returned a fur coat, in good condition, yet obviously not new. She had lost her sales slip. The adjusting people checked.

"Madam," she was informed, "we're sorry, but this coat was bought seven years ago and clearly has been worn."

The woman paled. "Heavens!" she exclaimed, turning sharply to leave, "how time flies!"

Field officials, however, continue to believe that the customer is right and usually find she is. A Texas woman ordered a china service plate, costing $12, to be sent as a wedding gift to a friend. She was dismayed when she got the bride's thank-you note mentioning not one, but a dozen plates. It was shortly followed by Field's bill—$144.

The Texas customer protested, insisting she had ordered but one plate. Investigation disclosed that a shipping clerk had made a mistake. Field's sent an apology and told the lady to forget about paying for the eleven extra plates.

Such capacity for pleasing women is no longer unusual, as it seemed in the days when young Potter Palmer tended his counters or a white-gloved Marshall Field bowed over a dowager's hand. Storekeepers everywhere have discovered that the century past was Woman's Century, in which all the goals of the most ardent Feminists were achieved or surpassed. Since 1940, even the fustiest statisticians in the federal Department of Commerce have come to designate the modern department store as "a store catering chiefly to women." Most merchants have learned that it is sound and profitable policy to give the lady what she wants.

There are other stores as venerable as Marshall Field's, or older—the City of Paris in San Francisco, Scruggs, Vandervoort & Barney in St. Louis, Wanamaker's in Philadelphia, Jordan Marsh in Boston, Lord and Taylor in New York, Harrod's in London, the Ville de Paris and the Bon Marché in Paris. Yet no other store is more internationally famous, has bigger profits or better prospects than Field's in America's heartland. And none has quite pleased so many ladies so well for so many years.

INDEX

379

PRINTED IN U.S.A.